John Newton's Theology of Suffering *and* Its Application to Pastoral Care

John Newton's Theology of Suffering *and* Its Application to Pastoral Care

Keith Palmer

WIPF & STOCK · Eugene, Oregon

JOHN NEWTON'S THEOLOGY OF SUFFERING AND ITS APPLICATION TO PASTORAL CARE

Copyright © 2025 Keith Palmer. All rights reserved. Except for brief quotations in critical publications or reviews, no part of this book may be reproduced in any manner without prior written permission from the publisher. Write: Permissions, Wipf and Stock Publishers, 199 W. 8th Ave., Suite 3, Eugene, OR 97401.

Wipf & Stock
An Imprint of Wipf and Stock Publishers
199 W. 8th Ave., Suite 3
Eugene, OR 97401

www.wipfandstock.com

PAPERBACK ISBN: 979-8-3852-3936-8
HARDCOVER ISBN: 979-8-3852-3937-5
EBOOK ISBN: 979-8-3852-3938-2

VERSION NUMBER 05/21/25

Unless otherwise indicated, Scripture quotations taken from the (NASB®) New American Standard Bible®, Copyright © 1960, 1971, 1977, 1995, 2020 by The Lockman Foundation. Used by permission. All rights reserved. lockman.org.

Scripture quotations marked "KJV" from The Authorized (King James) Version. Rights in the Authorized Version in the United Kingdom are vested in the Crown. Reproduced by permission of the Crown's patentee, Cambridge University Press

To Greg Warren
for introducing me to Newton,
and for being a true "Newtonian" friend
who always points to Christ's sufficiency

חאֲמֶ קבָד בֵהֹא שִׁיֵו

Proverbs 18:24b

For Alan, Aimee, and Aric
Your dad loves you very much
May you always lean on Christ

Mr. Newton expresses my prayer for you:

I trust you find the name and grace of Jesus more and more precious to you: His promises more sweet, and your hope in them more abiding; your sense of your own weakness and unworthiness daily increasing; your persuasion of His all-sufficiency to guide, support, and comfort you, more confirmed.

—John Newton

Contents

Acknowledgments | ix

Introduction | 1
    Research Question | 2
    Thesis Statement | 2
    Definition of Terms | 3
    Biblical Counseling and the Need for Historical Models | 5
    Research Interest | 7
    Chapter Summaries | 7

1 Newton's Life and Influences | 10
    The Life of John Newton | 10
    The Shaping of Newton's Life and Theology: Experiences | 19
    The Shaping of Newton's Life and Theology: People | 25
    The Shaping of Newton's Life and Theology: Authors and Books | 31
    Conclusion | 41

2 Newton's Theology of Suffering | 43
    God's Sovereign Goodness: The Character of God
        and the Interpretation of Suffering | 44
    The Work of Christ: How Jesus Helps
        Believers Who Are Suffering | 48
    Suffering Redeemed: How God Works to Benefit
        Believers Through Suffering | 55

A Divine Perspective: How Christians Should
   Interpret Their Suffering | 65
  Satan and Temptation in the Context of Trials | 74
  Conclusion | 79

3 Newton's Pastoral Care | 81
  Overview of John Newton's Pastoral Care Ministry | 81
  Pastoral Care Is Applied Theology | 85
  Five Pathways of Effective Ministry in Pastoral Care | 86
  Expectations in Pastoral Care | 93
  Understanding People in Pastoral Care | 97
  The Value of Personal Affliction in Pastoral Care | 101
  Personal Dynamics in Pastoral Care | 106
  Keeping Christ Central in Pastoral Care | 113
  Conclusion | 117

4 Case Studies in Newton's Pastoral Care | 118
  Mrs. Mary Catlett Newton | 119
  Mr. William Cowper | 141
  Conclusion | 164

5 Conclusion | 166
  Summary of the Study | 166
  Contribution of the Study | 167
  Suggestions for Further Research | 168
  Conclusion of the Study | 169

*Appendix: Scripture Verses Often Cited by Newton in
   His Theology of Suffering* | 171
Bibliography | 173

Acknowledgments

THIS PROJECT COULD NOT have been completed without the help, encouragement, and assistance of many people. Drs. Dale Johnson and Stephen Yuille supported me in this work and challenged me to strengthen it in countless ways. Dr. Mike Massey convinced me to pursue the PhD degree and has been a blessing every step of the way. Dr. Rick Holland first directed me to Midwestern and has been a faithful encourager and friend.

My church family at Grace Bible Church has prayed for me, encouraged me, and supported the work from the beginning. I am especially grateful for my elders: Terry Enns, David Brown, Don Dittrich, Lee Slaughter, and Greg Warren, who granted me sabbatical time to finish the dissertation, bearing much of the ministry load in my absence. Greg Warren spent many lunches with me conversing about Newton. Lacey Looper, our administrative assistant, worked joyfully on many of the administrative dynamics. Nancy Dixon, our church secretary, provided encouragement and administrative help. I cannot adequately express my gratitude to Renée and Elsbeth Ryniec who transcribed dozens of Newton's letters from photographs. I remain overwhelmed by your kindness. Irene Reed did valuable work on the Newton letter database. I am grateful to Ike and Trisha Thomas who provided their condo for me to use during my writing sabbatical. My parents-in-law, Rich and Carla Boyd, have encouraged me along the way and graciously offered their home as a quiet study location.

This project also allowed me to meet several new friends who assisted in the work. I am greatly indebted to Marylynn Rouse of the John Newton Project. Her knowledge, support, encouragement, and friendship made this work possible. Dr. Grant Gordon supplied many resources on Newton. Todd Murray provided encouragement and friendship. I am grateful to

Acknowledgments

Mrs. Elizabeth Knight for taking time to meet with me in Olney. Kate Bostock of the Cowper and Newton Museum in Olney and Sally Mason of the Buckinghamshire Archive provided valuable research assistance. Adrienne Rusinko of the Princeton University Special Archives and Polly Cancro of the Morgan Library and Museum aided in locating unpublished material. I am especially grateful for Alasdair, Rhoda, Will, Ethan, Jude, and Cole MacPherson for their friendship, hospitality, and support during my stay in the United Kingdom.

The most significant sacrifices for this work were made by my family. I am thankful to Alan, Aimee, and Aric, who were patient with me when writing produced occasional moments of "Zombie Dad" and always encouraged me with their love and support. My best friend and wife, Lisa, was the greatest support as she encouraged, prayed, and sacrificed time together so I could write. "Many daughters have done nobly, but you excel them all!" (Prov 31:29).

Finally, I am grateful to my Lord and Savior, Jesus Christ. He has used this study of Newton to draw me closer to Him. "Now to the King eternal, immortal, invisible, the only God, be honor and glory forever and ever. Amen" (1 Tim 1:17).

Introduction

JOHN NEWTON, AN EIGHTEENTH-CENTURY converted slave-ship captain, is most famous for his authorship of the hymn "Amazing Grace." According to Newton's biographer, Jonathan Aitken, it is the "most sung, most recorded, and most loved hymn in the world."[1] He penned or coauthored hundreds of hymns throughout his life, which had a massive impact on the hymnody of the English-speaking world.[2] Yet, just as valuable, though far less known, was Newton's significant contribution in the area of pastoral care and counseling.

During his forty-three years as a pastor, Newton wrote over one thousand letters of personal, pastoral counsel.[3] J. I. Packer states that Newton was "perhaps the greatest pastoral letter-writer of all time."[4] Due to the significant number of letters he wrote and the widespread impact they had on both the pastoral community and the laity, he was considered in his day to be the "leading evangelical commentator on religious subjects in Britain."[5] Despite these conclusions, Newton's pastoral care and counseling are relatively unknown to the modern world and have been largely neglected in pastoral care and counseling literature. Thus, the letters of Newton are a vast, untapped resource in the field of biblical counseling.

---

1. Aitken, *John Newton*, 224.

2. Aitken, *John Newton*, 224–37. For a closer look at the hymnology of John Newton, see Hindmarsh, *English Evangelical Tradition*, 257–88.

3. Reinke, *Newton*, 15.

4. Packer, as quoted in Murray, *Beyond Amazing Grace*, 7.

5. Aitken, *John Newton*, 244.

John Newton's Theology of Suffering and Its Application to Pastoral Care

Newton often found himself ministering to those who were suffering. As such, trials became a "frequent and favourite" topic of his ministry.[6] He writes:

> I have often preached to others of the benefit of affliction; but my own path for many years has been so smooth, and my trials, though I have not been without trials, comparatively so light and few, that I have seemed to myself to speak by rote upon a subject of which I had not a proper feeling. Yet the many exercises of my poor afflicted people, and the sympathy the Lord has given me with them in their troubles, has made this a frequent and favourite topic of my ministry among them. The advantages of afflictions, when the Lord is pleased to employ them for the good of his people, are many and great.[7]

It was Newton's perspective on suffering and trials, particularly the "advantages of afflictions," that significantly influenced and shaped his pastoral care to hurting people.

Research Question

This work will examine the relationship between Newton's view on suffering and his pastoral ministry to suffering people. Along the way, the following questions will be addressed: Why was this topic, "the benefit of affliction," a favorite subject for Newton in his care for others? How did Newton's theology of suffering influence his perspective and practice of pastoral care? In what ways was the manner of his pastoral counseling guided by the view of suffering that he derived from the Bible? As these research questions are considered, this author hopes to demonstrate the validity of the following thesis.

Thesis Statement

John Newton's theology of suffering formed an essential structure which served to shape, inform, and direct his model of pastoral care and counseling. Several points will be established to validate this thesis. First, Newton's theology of suffering is developed, demonstrating primarily from his letters

---

6. Richard Cecil, one of Newton's biographers, noted that over his whole lifetime, "His house was an asylum for the perplexed or afflicted." *Memoirs of the Rev. John Newton*, in Newton, *Works* (1985), 1:95.

7. Newton, *Works* (1985), 2:22.

Introduction

what he believed about the nature and purpose of suffering. As part of this development, several influences are traced that shaped his theology of suffering, including various experiences from his life. Second, a connection is established, demonstrating that Newton's theology of suffering shaped, informed, and directed his pastoral care. This point is substantiated through a study of his letters to various individuals who were suffering. Third, the link between his theology of suffering and his pastoral care is verified in more detail by looking at two specific examples where Newton ministered to suffering people: his wife, Polly, and his close friend, the poet William Cowper.

This thesis is highly relevant to the field of pastoral care and counseling in three specific ways. First, it makes a historical contribution. No substantial work has been written regarding Newton's pastoral care and counseling. Second, this thesis makes a theological contribution. Newton's life and ministry demonstrate that theology drives pastoral care, and thus careful, biblical theology must inform any counseling that aims to be biblical in nature. Finally, this work makes a pastoral contribution. Newton's counsel to people struggling with various afflictions, informed by his theology of suffering, provides a refreshing, biblical model for the care of hurting people today.

Definition of Terms

Pastoral Care and Pastoral Counseling

Unless distinguished in the immediate context, these two terms will be used synonymously to reference the pastor's role to care for and counsel people, understood from the perspective of the classic tradition.[8] Thomas Oden notes that pastoral care is "that branch of Christian theology that deals with the care of persons by pastors."[9] Similarly, Andrew Purves defines pastoral care as "lived out doctrine at the points of connection between the Gospel

---

8. "Classic tradition" refers to pastoral care and counseling before the discipline shifted to a more therapeutic model in the nineteenth century. Writers such as E. Brooks Holifield, Thomas Oden, and Andrew Purves address pastoral care and counseling from this perspective. See Holifield, *Pastoral Care*; Oden, *Care of Souls*; Purves, *Pastoral Theology*. For documentation of the historical shift toward a more psychotherapeutic approach, see Holifield. For insight regarding this transition particularly in the Southern Baptist Convention, see Johnson, *Professionalization of Pastoral Care*.

9. Oden, *Classical Pastoral Care*, 5.

and the lives of people."[10] When a distinction is intended, pastoral counseling will be defined as "counseling practiced by God's people in the context of His church and under the authority of Scripture."[11]

Biblical Counseling

Biblical counseling is a form of pastoral counseling that stresses the sufficiency and authority of Christ and the Scriptures for the care of souls.[12] Though the term is a relatively new expression, biblical counseling aligns with pastoral counseling represented in the classic tradition, particularly the model espoused by the Puritans.[13]

Theology of Suffering

This term refers to a system of biblical doctrines that attempts to explain how Christians ought to understand and respond to suffering.[14] Theology of suffering is used synonymously with the phrase "doctrine of affliction."

---

10. Purves, *Pastoral Theology*, 4. Elsewhere, he writes: "Pastoral work is concerned always with the gospel of God's redemption in and through Jesus Christ, no matter the problem that someone presents. Pastoral work by definition connects the gospel story—the truths and realities of God's saving economy—with the actual lives and situations of people. Biblical and theological perspectives guide all pastoral work, and these perspectives, properly rooted in the gospel of salvation, are discovered to be inherently pastoral" (2–3).

11. Babler et al., *Counseling by the Book*, xiv.

12. See Babler et al., *Counseling by the Book*, 57–72; Scott and Lambert, *Counseling the Hard Cases*, 1–24. The sufficiency and authority of Christ and Scripture are largely the distinguishing marks of biblical counseling as compared with other Christian counseling approaches. For example, See Scott, "Biblical Counseling Approach," 158. Viewed from a more comprehensive angle, David Powlison describes the biblical counseling approach as built upon seven foundations: (1) God is the center of counseling; (2) commitment to God has epistemological consequences; (3) sin, in all its dimensions; (4) the gospel of Jesus Christ is the answer; (5) the change process counseling must aim at is progressive sanctification; (6) the situational difficulties people face are not the random cause of problems in living; and (7) counseling is fundamentally a pastoral activity and must be church-based; Powlison, "Biblical Counseling," 56–59.

13. Biblical counseling aligns with Purves's definition of "pastoral work" stated above (Purves, *Pastoral Theology*, 2–3). For insight regarding the counseling approach of the Puritans as reflective of modern biblical counseling, see Sarles, "English Puritans," 21–43; Deckard, *Helpful Truth*.

14. Brian Cosby's work *Suffering and Sovereignty* represents a theology of suffering gleaned from the writings of John Flavel. He writes, "As a systematic theology seeks to

Introduction

Biblical Counseling and the Need for Historical Models

Historically, soul care has been the discipline of Christian pastors who recognized that the Scriptures require faithful ministers to care for and counsel believers from the Bible as a function of their shepherding role (1 Pet 5:1–3; Col 1:28–29; Acts 20:20).[15] However, the modern psychological movement of the nineteenth century produced a massive shift in soul care in two main areas. First, the main content of soul care changed from the Bible to modern psychology. As one example, E. Brooks Holifield notes that historically, the four main Christian traditions "envisioned the cure of souls primarily as a remedy for sin."[16] In other words, "soul care" was fundamentally understood as the task of clergy who would diagnose and provide remedies for people as understood from the Bible. Second, the soul care clinician changed from the Christian minister to the professional counselor. This shift largely moved counseling away from the church into professional arenas.[17] As a result, soul care that is both historic and biblical was largely lost until the latter half of the twentieth century when the modern biblical counseling movement began.[18] This historic shift brought about by modern psychology means that much of the present-day pastoral counseling literature is more influenced by psychology than the Bible. As such, Christians today must look to the past to find biblical models of soul care. Two works in the area of pastoral care and counseling have been produced along these lines. In *Care of Souls in the Classic Tradition*, Thomas Oden uses the example of Gregory the Great as a historic model for soul care. Andrew Purves, in his work *Pastoral Theology in the Classic Tradition*,

---

identify theological themes from Scripture and organize them in a helpful way, so also this study has sought to identify those themes related to human suffering and divine sovereignty and organize them in such a way as to organically build a theology of suffering from Flavel's writings" (11). Though the scope and purpose of this work is different, it uses the term "theology of suffering" in a similar way.

15. For a biblical argument of this point, see Adams, *Competent to Counsel*, 65–66, and Purves, *Pastoral Theology*. For historical evidence of this reality, see Oden, *Care of Souls*, and Kemp, *Physicians of the Soul*.

16. Holifield, *Pastoral Care*, 17.

17. For the history of the change, see esp. chapter 14 of Kemp's *Physicians of the Soul*, though Holifield, Oden, and Purves all document this shift.

18. In 1970, Jay Adams published his book *Competent to Counsel*, which began a rediscovery of the care of souls from a biblical standpoint. For the history of the biblical counseling movement, see Powlison, *Biblical Counseling Movement*.

surveys five key pastoral counseling texts from pre-nineteenth-century church history.[19]

More recently, Timothy Keller has noted that the English Puritans of the seventeenth century offer a refreshingly biblical model of soul care. In fact, Keller argues that they were the "first Protestant school of Biblical Counseling."[20] The Puritans followed a biblical model of soul care in part because they were not influenced by secular psychology as so many Christian counselors are today. Keller writes:

> Many Christian counselors [today] tend to mirror secular approaches that either focus their treatment largely on the feelings (such as the client-centered approach of Rogers), on the actions (such as the behaviorist approach of Skinner and his kin), or on the "thinking" (such as the rational-emotive therapies of Ellis and Beck). But the Puritans do not fit into any of these modern categories.[21]

In their counseling, the Puritans do not fall into these categories because they lived and ministered before the dawn of the modern psychological movement. The Puritans built their counseling system upon a commitment to the functional authority of the Scriptures, the centrality of sinful heart worship in understanding human problems, and belief in the gospel of Jesus as the "essential spiritual remedy."[22]

Though Newton lived after the Puritans, he was greatly influenced by them through their writings. He was particularly interested in Puritan authors who wrote in the area of soul care. For example, Hindmarsh notes that Newton read the Puritan soul care expert Richard Baxter because he was "a superb pastor and a man of deep spirituality."[23] On one occasion, Newton's friend William Wilberforce wrote him to inquire about book recommendations for the spiritual life. In Newton's response letter, he lists four authors, all of whom were Puritans who wrote in the arena of soul care: John Bunyan, Richard Baxter, Joseph Alleine, and John Flavel.[24]

---

19. Purves, *Pastoral Theology*, 5.

20. Keller, "Puritan Resources," 11. For a closer look at some Puritan authors who wrote in the areas of soul care, see Deckard, *Helpful Truth*.

21. Keller, "Puritan Resources," 11.

22. Keller, "Puritan Resources," 11.

23. Hindmarsh, *English Evangelical Tradition*, 81.

24. Newton, "Letter to William Wilberforce."

Introduction

Like the Puritans, John Newton is a key candidate for study to understand historic, biblically informed pastoral care and counseling. However, very little has been written on Newton as a pastoral counselor. With over one thousand letters of pastoral counsel available to study, John Newton remains a largely untapped resource for study concerning biblical, pastoral counseling. A significant investigation into his theology and biblical counseling practice would be exceedingly valuable for the modern biblical counseling movement.

Research Interest

Like many Christians, I was casually familiar with John Newton as the author of the hymn "Amazing Grace." But I was unaware that Newton was also a pastor and utterly ignorant of his pastoral counseling ministry of letter-writing. On March 9, 2007, Pastor Mark Dever delivered a sermon on Christian faithfulness and suffering from Dan 1–6 at the Shepherds' Conference. In the message, Dever concluded with a quote from one of Newton's pastoral letters written to his friend, the Rev. John Ryland. Moved by the message and particularly by the Newton quote, a friend of mine who attended the conference began investigating the ministry of Newton and eventually purchased a copy of Josiah Bull's *Letters of John Newton*. He was so helped and encouraged by the contents of Newton's letters that he began sharing the letters with me and the other elders at my church.

As my involvement in pastoral care and counseling increased, Newton's letters became a source of encouragement and direction in counseling. As I read more, Newton's "frequent and favourite" topic of suffering was a striking and compelling theme throughout his letters. It became clear that Newton was a valuable source for pastoral counseling wisdom. It surprised me to learn later that Newton was largely unknown in biblical counseling literature. I hope that this work will bring exposure and attention to John Newton's letters as a wealth of insight and help for the field of pastoral care and biblical counseling.

Chapter Summaries

Chapter 1 will explore the historical background of John Newton, including his upbringing by a Christian mother, his sinful lifestyle in his young adult years at sea, his conversion to Christianity, and his work as a minister in the church of England. It will also discuss events and experiences that helped to shape his theology and his pastoral care model. First, influential relationships with certain individuals will be presented, such as George Whitefield and Alexander Clunie. Second, the impact of critical authors will be explored, such as Isaac Watts, John Owen, and John Bunyan. Finally, books that were vital to Newton's development will be identified, such as *Some Remarkable Passages in the Life of Colonel James Gardiner* by Philip Doddridge and *The Life of God in the Soul of Man* by Henry Scougal. The chapter will demonstrate how these influences developed Newton's theology of affliction and his pastoral care practice.

Chapter 2 will unfold Newton's theology of suffering, demonstrating what he believed about the nature and purposes of trials in the Christian life. Five key components will be identified that form the basic structure of Newton's understanding of affliction. First, his view of the sovereignty of God and the attributes of God will be addressed in regard to suffering. Second, Newton's Christology will be unfolded, connecting his viewpoint of Christ to the topic of trials. Third, the redemption of suffering for good purposes will be explained. Fourth, his unique perspectives on affliction will be discussed. Finally, Newton's understanding of temptation and Satan will be revealed as they relate to a believer's suffering. The chapter will show how these vital doctrines form a central structure that undergirds his pastoral care model.

Chapter 3 will develop the associations between Newton's theology of suffering and his practice of pastoral counseling. First, an overview of Newton's pastoral care will be presented. Second, connections will be made between Newton's five doctrinal distinctives of suffering and his methodology in pastoral care. Third, a link will be developed between Newton's beliefs and his expectations in counseling. Fourth, Newton's practice of studying people will be shown to emerge from his convictions about afflictions. Fifth, his viewpoint that personal suffering is valuable to the minister and essential for his effectiveness in care will be revealed. Sixth, Newton's personal dynamics in counseling will be linked to his doctrinal viewpoints of suffering. Finally, the connection will be made between the centrality of Christ in his pastoral care and his theology of suffering. These associations will show the crucial link between Newton's theology of trials and his approach to ministerial care.

Chapter 4 will present two case studies that explore Newton's pastoral care to two different individuals. First, Newton's relationship with his wife,

Introduction

Polly, will be developed. The study of this relationship will show that he was consistent in his application of his theology of suffering with his spouse and closest friend through more than three decades of Polly's chronic health issues. Second, Newton's friendship with William Cowper will be explored. This case study will demonstrate the consistency of Newton's doctrine of trials in a long-standing and complex case of pastoral care. These two examples will affirm Newton's viewpoint on affliction and validate the link between his theology and his ministerial care methodology.

Chapter 5 will offer an overview of the project, provide reflection on the work, present suggestions for future study, and draw several conclusions.

1

Newton's Life and Influences

BOTH SCRIPTURE AND LIFE experience influenced John Newton's theology and pastoral philosophy. This chapter argues that critical life events, particular persons, and key books shaped Newton's theology of suffering and contributed to the development of his perspective on pastoral care.[1] Newton's life story provides the best context for understanding how these experiences influenced his doctrine and pastoral practice.

The Life of John Newton

Formative Years and Early Career (1725–48)

John Newton was born on July 24, 1725, in London. His father, John, was a well-respected captain of merchant ships, but he was not overly religious and spent most of Newton's childhood years at sea. His mother Elizabeth was very involved in her Christian faith and was Newton's first spiritual influence. She was a member at Old Grave Lane Independent Meeting House, a "Dissenting" congregation led by Dr. David Jennings.[2] Elizabeth hoped

---

1. This chapter will focus on Newton's life experiences, key people, and particular authors and books that shaped his theology. Chapter 3 will highlight key scriptural texts that influenced his doctrinal convictions. Appendix A contains a chart of Newton's favorite biblical passages that undergird his theology of suffering.

2. Newton recounts the influence of his mother and other early-life experiences in

that her son would one day enter the ministry, and he showed early signs of giftedness to this end through his incredible memory and ability to learn Latin at six years of age.[3] However, she tragically died on July 11, 1732, just a few days before Newton's seventh birthday, cutting off her hopes of seeing her son grow up to be a minister.

Newton's father quickly remarried, and as other children came into the family, young Newton faded into the background. His father sent him to boarding school in 1733, where he struggled under the leadership of a stern headmaster but later excelled academically in his final months following a change of administration. After two years at the school, his father elected to remove him and take him onboard his merchant ship. Newton made several voyages with his father until 1742. During this season of his life, he notes that his "temper and conduct were exceedingly various."[4] He had fallen away from much of his religious upbringing but occasionally experienced moments of conviction that produced temporary new efforts at religion. After one such experience, Newton became like a Pharisee, stating, "I did everything that might be expected from a person entirely ignorant of God's righteousness, and desirous to establish his own."[5]

In December 1742, when Newton was seventeen years old, his father procured for him a lucrative job offer in Jamaica. However, a few days before he was to depart on this new venture, he visited the home of a family relative, Elizabeth Catlett, his late mother's cousin. A young girl of thirteen years, Polly Catlett, greeted Newton at the door. Newton would later write of this encounter: "Almost at the first sight of this girl . . . I was impressed with an affection for her, which never abated."[6] Moved by this new relationship, he intentionally stalled long enough to miss the ship's departure, thereby forfeiting the job of a lifetime. His father was furious but later softened and made one last effort to procure a sailing career for him. This time, the senior Newton was successful. Newton sailed with a family friend to Venice. The exposure to "common sailors" moved him away from his religious convictions, leading him to "make large strides toward a total apostasy

---

Letter II of his spiritual autobiography, *An Authentic Narrative*, 1:10, and also in Cecil's *Memoirs*, found in *Works* (2015), 1:xxi. Later in life, Newton reached out to his boyhood pastor, David Jennings, for spiritual advice. See Aitken, *John Newton*, 120. The influence of Elizabeth Newton will be explored later in this chapter.

3. Newton, *Narrative*, in *Works* (2015), 1:11.
4. Newton, *Narrative*, in *Works* (2015), 1:12.
5. Newton, *Narrative*, in *Works* (2015), 1:13.
6. Newton, *Narrative*, in *Works* (2015), 1:16; cf. Aitken, *John Newton*, 36–37.

from God."[7] After his voyage, some sailors press-ganged Newton into joining the Royal Navy since the war with France was imminent and sailors were needed. While in the Navy, Newton's religious morals continued to decline while his desire to be with Polly increased. He delayed his return to ship during a one-day leave to prolong his visit with Polly, which resulted in disciplinary measures. Later, he attempted a total desertion from the Navy since the prospect of being away from Polly long-term was out of the question for him. Newton was caught, publicly flogged, and degraded among his peers. Knowing that he would now certainly lack the opportunity to see Polly for a long duration, he slumped into such bitter despair that he even contemplated suicide as he sailed away from the English coast.[8]

Newton was transferred to a merchant ship in an "exchange" a few weeks later. Instead of being grateful for this newfound freedom and the opportunities it would bring, he spiraled even more into depravity: "I was exceedingly vile. . . . I not only sinned with a high hand myself but made it my study to tempt and seduce others upon every occasion."[9] When the captain suddenly died, Newton concluded that his situation would worsen as the new captain disliked him and threatened to transfer him back to the Navy. Determined to stay in private life and motivated by a new friendship with a slave trader who told of the fortune that could be made in that business, Newton became an employee in the trade on the Plantain Islands just off the coast of Guinea.

Newton's "golden dreams" quickly soured when he became the slave of his employer's mistress through an odd turn of events. Imprisoned, starved, abused, ridiculed, and exposed to the elements, Newton spent much of the next two years in misery. He would later write that these events "quite broke my constitution and my spirits. . . . I lost all resolution and almost all reflection."[10]

---

7. Newton, *Narrative*, in *Works* (2015), 1:18.

8. "My breast was filled with the most excruciating passions, eager desire, bitter rage, and black despair. . . . I was tempted to throw myself into the sea. According to the wicked system I had adopted, this would put a period to all my sorrows once more." Newton, *Narrative*, in *Works* (2015), 1:24.

9. Newton, *Narrative*, in *Works* (2015), 1:28–29.

10. Newton, *Narrative*, in *Works* (2015), 1:34–35.

Conversion, Conclusion of Seafaring, and Call to Ministry (1748–64)

As time passed, Newton changed employers, which granted both freedom and better living arrangements. He had also smuggled out a few letters, requesting help from his father. This effort succeeded; a ship from Liverpool rescued him in 1747. Yet his immoral and depraved conduct reemerged under these improved circumstances. Newton wrote, "My whole life, when awake, was a course of most horrid impiety and profaneness, I know not that I have ever since met so daring a blasphemer: not content with common oaths and imprecations, I daily invented new ones."[11] But it was on this trip home to England that the Lord began to work in Newton's heart.

It took many months for the ship to reach Liverpool. Newton read through the few books on board to pass the time, including *The Imitation of Christ* by Thomas à Kempis. Though usually indifferent to what he was reading, he noted on March 9, 1748, "What if these things should be true?" He quickly extinguished the thought and retired for the night. Later, he was suddenly awakened by a violent storm.

The ship was sinking due to a hole in the bow. Newton and his companions spent several hours bailing water, but they could not keep up. He continued "pumping in the storm with no hope or expectation of surviving a quarter of an hour."[12] Facing imminent death, Newton commented to the captain: "If this [last effort to save the boat] will not do, the Lord have mercy on us."[13] In his words, "this . . . was the first desire I had breathed for mercy for the space of many years."[14] These were the first signs of a divine work in Newton's heart.

The ship avoided sinking because it was hauling large quantities of beeswax and camwood, which kept the damaged vessel buoyant. However, it would take hours of bailing and plugging holes before survival seemed possible. Later that evening, as the ship was finally free of water, Newton wrote, "I thought I saw the hand of God displayed in our favour: I began to pray."[15] Over the next four weeks, the crew struggled to survive with an inadequate food supply. Eventually, they were able to navigate the ailing ship back to land. During these weeks, Newton employed his leisure

---

11. Newton, *Narrative*, in *Works* (2015), 1:41.
12. Aitken, *John Newton*, 76.
13. Newton, *Narrative*, in *Works* (2015), 1:45.
14. Newton, *Narrative*, in *Works* (2015), 1:45.
15. Newton, *Narrative*, in *Works* (2015), 1:47.

time "reading and meditating on the Scripture, and praying to the Lord for mercy and instruction."[16] The ship arrived in Ireland on April 8, 1748.

Upon arrival, Newton wrote, "To all appearance, I was a new man."[17] Though he immediately stopped swearing and started reading Scripture and praying regularly, he still lacked true saving faith. He later accepted a job on a slave ship and began working along the African coast. He quickly regressed to his immoral ways, writing, "I was almost as bad as before."[18] Shortly after, he contracted a severe fever, which brought him to seek mercy from the Lord. It was through this experience that Newton was likely converted. He wrote, "I was enabled to hope and believe in a crucified Saviour. . . . From that time, I trust, I have been delivered from the power and dominion of sin."[19]

During this voyage to Africa, Newton grew in his faith. When he returned to London, he made plans to visit Polly in Kent. Though a few obstacles remained, Newton secured her hand in marriage, and they were married in February of 1750. While Newton's father had given his consent to the union, he died in a swimming accident shortly after the wedding and before Newton could reconcile with him over his past failures.[20] To add to this sorrow, Newton began to realize that his new bride was only a "nominal" Christian.[21] Though happy in each other, Newton felt a tension between his growing faith and her cultural Christianity.[22] While he desired

---

16. Newton, *Narrative*, in *Works* (2015), 1:48.
17. Newton, *Narrative*, in *Works* (2015), 1:53.
18. Newton, *Narrative*, in *Works* (2015), 1:58.
19. Newton, *Narrative*, in *Works* (2015), 1:59.
20. "His father had come to believe that the *Greyhound* had been lost at sea; so Captain Newton must have been overjoyed to learn that his eldest son was safe and sound. He immediately began making plans for John to sail with him on his next voyage. . . . Unfortunately, the plan to be accompanied by his son was frustrated by extended delays over the repairs to the *Greyhound*. As a result of the extra work that had to be carried out on the ship in Ireland, John Newton Junior arrived back in England a few days after John Newton Senior had sailed for Canada. This narrowly missed opportunity for a reunion between father and son was to prove a great sadness, for although they corresponded affectionately over the next two years, the premature death of the Captain in a swimming accident in Hudson's Bay in 1750 meant that the two John Newtons were destined never to meet again." Aitken, *John Newton*, 86–87.
21. It is difficult to determine the exact timing of Polly's conversion. For more detail on this event, see chapter 4.
22. Aitken, *John Newton*, 105.

to remain home to be with Polly, financial pressures led him to accept a job offer to captain a slave ship.

Over the next four years, Newton captained two different slave ships. He enjoyed plenty of leisure time in which he immersed himself in the Scriptures, prayer, meditation, and the study of some Christian books that shaped and sharpened his theology.[23] He writes, "I never knew sweeter or more frequent hours of divine communion than in my two last voyages to Guinea."[24] Not only was Newton growing in fellowship with God, but he also began to apply his faith in ministry to others. He held worship services aboard the ship and even adapted the Anglican prayer book so that his sailors could understand it. Newton later wrote to his childhood pastor Dr. David Jennings, "There are few moments of my life affording me a more real pleasure than when I am thus attempting the part of the minister."[25]

While Newton's spiritual life was growing and his newfound love for ministry increasing, an event occurred in November 1754 that changed the course of his life. Following his return from his third trip to Africa and just days before he was to sail again, he experienced a seizure. While he mostly recovered, it left him with pain and dizziness, which rendered him unfit to sail. He resigned his command and ended his seafaring career.

Newton's seizure led to two significant problems in his life.[26] First, his medical state and forfeiture of his captain position sent Polly into an inexplicable illness that "no physicians could define, or medicines remove."[27] Over the next several months, she declined to the point that Newton believed her death was imminent.[28] As her health deteriorated, Newton faced a second challenge: unemployment. After nine months of struggle, a friend offered Newton the position of surveyor of tides in Liverpool. The job provided financial stability and gave Newton the freedom to spend many hours in study. Though the job forced him to leave Polly at the height of her illness to move to Liverpool, it put Newton in a context that steered him toward the ministry.

---

23. The books that had the most impact in Newton's life will be explored in a later section of this book.
24. Newton, *Narrative*, in *Works* (2015), 1:68.
25. As quoted in Aitken, *John Newton*, 120.
26. Newton calls these "two trials." *Narrative*, *Works* (2015), 1:78.
27. Newton, *Narrative*, in *Works* (2015), 1:76.
28. "I had daily more reason to fear that the hour of separation was at hand." Newton, *Narrative*, in *Works* (2015), 1:78.

Shortly after Newton's move, Polly recovered, and they were reunited. Life in Liverpool allowed Newton to hear many gospel preachers, establish Christian friendships, and spend significant hours each week in biblical study. Over the next three years, he taught himself Greek and Hebrew, gave up reading the classics to focus solely on the study of spiritual books (chiefly, the Bible), befriended George Whitefield, and listened to several preachers from both the Anglican and Dissenting churches.

Following his conversion, he was struck by Gal 1:23–24: "But they had heard only, That he which persecuted us in times past now preacheth the faith which once he destroyed. And they glorified God in me" (KJV). Viewing himself as the "chief of sinners" who was dramatically preserved by God and saved through the riches of divine grace in Christ, Newton began to wonder if the Lord "might call me into this service [of ministry]."[29] At this time in his life at Liverpool, some of Newton's friends encouraged him to consider pastoral ministry. About eight months later, he set aside a season of life for daily prayer, study, and self-evaluation in view of entering religious service.[30] As a result of these exercises, on August 4, 1758, which was Newton's thirty-third birthday, he concluded that God would have him enter the ministry. He wrote out five resolutions to guide his efforts moving forward.[31] Initially, Newton believed he lacked the appropriate academic qualifications to be ordained in the Church of England, and many of the most influential figures in his life were Dissenting ministers. However, a conversation with Rev. Henry Crooke changed his mind and gave him hope that ordination in the established church might be possible.[32]

Newton's initiation into pastoral ministry was difficult. His first effort at preaching was a disaster; his mind froze just a few minutes into his sermon, and he lacked any notes to aid him. Through the encouragement of friends and additional opportunities, Newton improved his preaching

---

29. Newton, *Narrative*, in *Works* (2015), 1:81.

30. Newton documented this journey in a detailed journal that has been transcribed by Marylynn Rouse and published by the John Newton Project under the title *Ministry on My Mind*.

31. Newton resolved to spend the whole of his conversation and reading in spiritual and scriptural topics; to pray for a reverent frame of spirit; to pray for a spirit of moderation in all things; to faithfully declare the truths of the gospel plainly and honestly whenever given the opportunity; and to primarily focus on three branches of doctrine: Jesus Christ crucified, love as the "life and soul" of the gospel, and the practice of gospel holiness. Newton, *Ministry on My Mind*, 20–23.

32. Newton, *Narrative*, in *Works* (2015), 1:81; Aitken, *John Newton*, 146–47.

skills. His ordination process took seven years due to multiple delays and rejections. However, through the influence of two acquaintances, the Earl of Dartmouth and his friend Thomas Haweis, Newton was finally ordained on April 29, 1764. He became the new curate at St. Peter and St. Paul's Church in Olney.

Pastoral Ministry in Olney and London (1764–1807)

Newton spent the next forty-three years in pastoral ministry in two parishes: St. Peter and St. Paul's Church in Olney and St. Mary Woolnoth Church in London. Shortly after arriving in Olney, he published his autobiography, *An Authentic Narrative*.[33] Immediately, the book became a popular bestseller and enjoyed wide circulation throughout Europe.[34] The book's influence led many people to visit Olney to hear Newton preach.

Newton pursued a diverse ministry that would set the course for the rest of his life. He preached twice on Sunday and held an informal lecture on Sunday nights. He held midweek prayer meetings, created a ministry for youth, and established a service for children to learn hymns and hear Bible stories. Newton would visit individual families in his church in the afternoons to converse with them. He also gave spiritual counsel each week through meetings in his study, and later through a growing writing ministry. Under his leadership, church membership grew from two hundred to over six hundred, which necessitated building a gallery.[35]

During his time in Olney, Newton met the poet William Cowper. They established a close, lifelong friendship. They ministered together and wrote many hymns, which they published in 1779 as the *Olney Hymns*. Newton wrote his best-known hymn, "Amazing Grace," in December 1772 to accompany his New Year's Day sermon based on 1 Chr 17:16–17.[36]

---

33. The full title is *An Authentic Narrative of Some Remarkable and Interesting Particulars in the Life of John Newton, Communicated in a Series of Letters, to the Rev. T. Haweis, Rector of Aldwinckle, Northamptonshire, and by Him, at the Request of Friends, Now Made Public*. It is published in the first volume of his *Works* (2015).

34. In the first six months, it would go through five editions. It was translated into at least five languages in Europe. See Aitken, *John Newton*, 185.

35. Aitken, *John Newton*, 191.

36. "Amazing Grace" was originally titled "Faith's Review and Expectation," hymn number 41 in the *Olney Hymns*. For more background on the hymn, see Aitken, *John Newton*, 223–29.

As Newton's popularity as a pastor grew, people from all over England wrote to him seeking his counsel on various spiritual subjects. His pastoral letters were so well received that he had some of them published in the *Gospel Magazine* (1771) under the name *Omicron*.[37] The popularity of Newton's letters led to the publication of *Cardiphonia; Or the Utterance of Heart: In the Course of Real Correspondence* (1781/1783). Throughout his life, Newton penned over one thousand pastoral letters to dozens of individuals.[38] Though he would later publish a book on church history and another on the African slave trade, his letters show him at his best as a minister who pastored people amid life's many difficulties. Newton's biographer Jonathan Aitken claims that he was the "leading evangelical commentator on religious subjects in Britain."[39]

As Newton grew in popularity, he received regular preaching requests and traveled extensively throughout England. With more public exposure, he also received inquiries regarding other ministry roles. In 1779, he accepted one of these invitations and became the rector of St. Mary Woolnoth Church in London.

During his ministry in London, his influence continued to grow. In 1783, Newton formed an evangelical discussion group attended by local pastors and significant laypersons in the evangelical movement. It came to be known as the Eclectic Society and expanded evangelical influence in England through various pursuits, including the establishment of a missionary society.[40] Newton's mentorship of a young member of Parliament, William Wilberforce, played a significant role in the abolition of the slave trade in 1807.[41]

In London, Newton was at the pinnacle of his ministry due to the vast influence he had through sermons, writings, and a pastoral training school. But as the end of the century approached, his ministry began to slow down. Polly died of cancer in December 1790, an experience Newton called his "great trial." Newton's aging body began to limit his travel as well. He preached his final sermon in October 1806 and died just over a year later in December 1807. His friend, William Jay, recorded some of his

37. Aitken, *John Newton*, 241.
38. Reinke, *Newton*,15.
39. Aitken, *John Newton*, 244.
40. Aitken, *John Newton*, 292.
41. Newton also published a work, *Thoughts Upon the African Slave Trade*, and appeared before a committee of Parliament to personally testify to the horrors of slavery.

last words. They are a fitting testimony to Newton's life and ministry: "My memory is nearly gone, but I remember two things: That I am a great sinner and that Christ is a great Savior."[42]

Newton made a unique and lasting contribution to the evangelical movement. Grant Gordon states that he was "the prominent link between the first generation [of evangelicals] (e.g., Wesley, Whitfield) and the second (e.g., Wilberforce)."[43] Church historian A. Skevington Wood states, "For twenty-eight years [in London], Newton delivered the evangelical message from this strategic pulpit and did perhaps more than any other to commend the cause."[44] More specifically, Newton excelled in pastoral care to suffering people, establishing himself as the pastoral counselor par excellence of the eighteenth century.

Looking back on his life, particular experiences, people, and books developed Newton's theology and ministerial life. This next section explores these influences.

The Shaping of Newton's Life and Theology: Experiences

John Newton was a Calvinist Anglican minister, raised by a mother who attended a Dissenting congregation and influenced by the Methodism of eighteenth-century England. He was born shortly before the dawn of the Evangelical Revival.[45] During his life, he was influenced by the movement and became a key contributor to it. One of his most outstanding contributions was his theology of suffering, which enabled him to provide effective pastoral care to many hurting people. Newton's doctrine of afflictions and trials will be explored in chapter 2 of this work.

He built his view of suffering upon five central doctrines: the character of God (particularly God's sovereignty over suffering), the doctrine of Christ (particularly how Christ ministers to people in suffering), redemption (particularly how the work of Christ redeems suffering), perspective (how believers should understand and interpret suffering in light of Christian faith), and temptation (how Satan uses suffering to gain an advantage

---

42. As quoted in Aitken, *John Newton*, 347.
43. Gordon, "John Newton," 27.
44. Wood, *Inextinguishable Blaze*, 205.
45. Leading historians such as Bebbington state that the evangelical movement in Britain began in the 1730s when Newton was a child. See Bebbington, *Evangelicalism in Modern Britain*.

John Newton's Theology of Suffering and Its Application to Pastoral Care

over believers). This section explores the influences that contributed to these doctrinal positions, including his own experiences of suffering and trial.[46]

Newton acknowledges that he came to much of his theology through his own musings and life experience. In his autobiography, he writes, "It pleased the Lord, for some time, that I should learn no more than what he enabled me to collect from my own experience and reflection."[47] Newton's first significant experience was his godly mother's premature death just a few days before his seventh birthday. Elizabeth Newton was a devout believer who taught her son Scripture and brought him to church. Newton wrote, "She made it the chief business and pleasure of her life to instruct me, to bring me up in the nurture and admonition of the Lord."[48] His mother taught him to read and filled his mind with Scripture and biblical doctrine. At an early age, Newton could recite the questions and answers in the *Westminster Shorter Catechism*, including the proofs, and the children's catechisms and book of hymns for children produced by Isaac Watts.[49] Newton remarks, "She stored my memory, which was then very retentive, with many valuable pieces, chapters, and portions of Scripture, catechisms, hymns, and poems."[50] These books, coupled with the shepherding efforts of Dr. Jennings, anchored the young Newton in Reformed theology as understood from the Dissenting perspective.[51] As an adult, when God began to awaken Newton's heart, it is not surprising that he started to interpret the events of his life as expressions of divine providence and that he eventually turned to his childhood pastor for guidance.[52]

---

46. This section will particularly develop Newton's theology of suffering and pastoral care. For a more general discussion of Newton's overall theological development, see Hindmarsh, *English Evangelical Tradition*.

47. Newton, *Narrative*, in *Works* (2015), 1:62.

48. Cecil, *Memoirs*, in *Works* (1985), 1:xxi.

49. Cecil, *Memoirs*, in *Works* (1985). Isaac Watts (1674–748) wrote several unique catechisms for children and adapted the Westminster Shorter Catechism for children. His first original catechism is intended for children up to seven years old, the second for children seven to twelve years old, and the third is a general work written to help children avoid the "sins and follies of childhood and youth." Watts is also credited with producing *Divine and Moral Songs for Children*, the first hymnal specifically for children.

50. Newton, *Narrative*, in *Works* (2015), 1:10.

51. Hindmarsh states that these early experiences, though minimally influential in Newton's younger years, were very significant following his conversion. Hindmarsh, *English Evangelical Tradition*, 52.

52. Aitken, *John Newton*, 120.

Newton's Life and Influences

Newton was influenced not only through the life and ministry of his godly mother but also through her tragic death. Looking back on this event as an adult, Newton wrote, "The Lord's designs were far beyond the views of an earthly parent: he was pleased to reserve me for an unusual proof of his patience, providence, and grace; and therefore overruled the purpose of my friends, by depriving me of this excellent parent when I was something under seven years old."[53] This sorrowful event, likely his earliest experience of suffering, brought together many of the critical elements that would form his theology of suffering, such as God's providence, grace, and wisdom that often directs Him to "overrule" the plans of people to produce a greater good.

Divine providence continued to be a theme of Newton's early years. His perception that God's gracious providence had spared his life on many occasions stirred the first motions of divine grace in his heart. In his autobiography, Newton catalogs over a dozen occasions that occurred before his conversion when God's sovereign hand seemed to preserve him from certain death.[54] For example, Newton was thrown from a horse, landing within a few inches of a row of stakes upon a hedgerow that would have killed him.[55] On another occasion, he missed the sailing of a boat that later sunk, killing several people, including an "intimate companion."[56] He was almost washed overboard in a storm; he was prevented at the last moment from jumping overboard while drunk; and he nearly shot himself on a hunting trip.[57] Events like these often motivated Newton to renew his religious efforts to pray and read Scripture, but he always regressed to his old ways, becoming "worse than before."[58]

Later in life, Newton realized that divine providence had not merely preserved his life but also acted to restrain his wickedness. Events of

---

53. Newton, *Narrative*, in *Works* (2015), 1:11.

54. Hindmarsh, *English Evangelical Tradition*, 59.

55. Newton, *Narrative*, in *Works* (2015), 1:12.

56. Newton, *Narrative*, in *Works* (2015), 1:13. A similar event occurred later in life during his seafaring career. The captain had picked Newton to lead an expedition but suddenly developed a strong notion that he should not let Newton go on the trip. The captain informed Newton that he would not be going on the boat, and Newton then learned later that the boat had sunk, killing Newton's replacement. Aitken, *John Newton*, 95–96.

57. Aitken, *John Newton*, 71, 75, 86. Aitken notes two other incidents while Newton was onboard the *Greyhound* where Newton could have died were it not for divine providence, which brought a change of circumstances (85–86).

58. Newton, *Narrative*, in *Works* (2015), 1:12.

suffering or difficulty were divine rescue missions meant to humble him and restrain his depravity. For example, Newton was press-ganged to enter naval service but later deserted, leading to a public flogging and degradation in front of his fellow sailors. A short time later, he was exchanged out of the Navy into private life on board a merchant ship, which led to his involvement in the slave trade. In an odd turn of events, Newton became a slave of his employer's mistress. He was put in chains, starved, mocked, exposed to the elements, physically and verbally abused, and came close to death several times.[59] But Newton later perceived that these abuses were expressions of God's restraining grace for his good. Hindmarsh explains, "It was, therefore, a mercy that he was banished to a region where his wickedness was restrained by relative isolation and tempered by suffering."[60] God's providence not only preserves, but it also restrains. This point became a theme of Newton's counsel to many suffering people throughout his ministry. Later in life, he penned, "My poor story would soon be much worse, did not he support, restrain, and watch over me every minute."[61]

Newton's life experiences led him to embrace the doctrine of God's providence, which preserves and restrains. Later events helped him discover that God redeems suffering for good. During his life, he made three journeys aboard slave ships. His involvement in the slave trade became a source of lifelong shame for him. William Wilberforce stated that he had "never spent one half hour of [Newton's] company without hearing some allusion to it."[62] Yet, God later redeemed Newton's involvement in the slave trade by using him as a chief instrument to abolish it through his mentorship of Wilberforce.[63] Newton furthered his effort to abolish slavery by publishing a book, *Thoughts Upon the African Slave Trade*, and personally testifying of its horrors to a committee of Parliament. Newton eventually applied this redemptive view of suffering to many of his most difficult challenges, including the seizure that ended his sailing career, his struggle to be ordained, Polly's ongoing illness, and his young niece's death.

---

59. Aitken, *John Newton*, 57–61.

60. Hindmarsh, *English Evangelical Tradition*, 18.

61. Newton, *Works* (1985), 1:626.

62. As quoted in Aitken, *John Newton*, 319. Newton wrote, "I hope it will always be a subject of humiliating reflection to me that I was once an active instrument in a business at which my heart now shudders" (*Thoughts Upon the African Slave Trade*, as quoted in Aitken, *John Newton*, 319).

63. Aitken, *John Newton*, 309–28.

In May 1754, Newton returned from his second voyage as a slave ship captain of the *African*. Just a few days before his departure for a third journey, which was to begin in November, he experienced a mysterious seizure that left him with ongoing pain and dizziness.[64] Doctors determined he was unfit to sail, and he resigned command of his ship, ending his career. In yet another example of divine providence, Newton later interpreted this event as answered prayer: "I had often petitioned in my prayer that the Lord in his own time would be pleased to fix me in a more humane calling and place me where I might be freed from those long separations from home that very often were hard to bear."[65] The Lord had redeemed another experience of suffering to produce spiritual good in his life.

A few years later, following a six-week process of self-examination, Newton concluded that God would have him enter full-time ministry.[66] But his first effort at ordination was denied by the archbishop because of Newton's association with the Methodists.[67] Over the next six years, Newton was rejected three times by various bishops and archbishops.[68] He entertained other options, such as joining the Presbyterians or the Independents. Amid these rejections, he was able to see God's redemptive hand working for his good. He wrote, "It is sufficient that he knows how to dispose of me, and that he both can and will do what is best. To him I commend myself: I trust that his will and my true interest are inseparable."[69] Though the bishop of Lincoln eventually ordained Newton in April 1764, his interpretation of the rejections and delays of the previous six years demonstrates his redemptive view of suffering, which would be a key theme of his letters throughout his ministry.

The most severe affliction suffered by Newton was the chronic, debilitating illness of his dear wife, Polly. He called this experience "my great trial."[70] Her condition first manifested itself shortly after Newton's seizure. Over the next thirty-six years, she suffered on and off, experiencing seasons

---

64. Cecil, *Life of John Newton*, 71.

65. Newton, *Works* (2015), 1:75.

66. Newton documents his journey in a notebook which has been published as *Ministry on My Mind*.

67. The stated grounds for the rejection was Newton's lack of a formal degree from Oxford or Cambridge, but since this "rule" was often not practiced, many believe he was denied ordination because of his involvement with the "enthusiasm" of the evangelical movement. See Aitken, *John Newton*, 153–54.

68. Aitken, *John Newton*, 157–77.

69. Cecil, *Memoirs*, in *Works* (1985), 1:50–51.

70. Reinke, *Newton*, 203.

of significant pain that kept her bedridden but occasionally enjoying times of good health. Though Polly was Newton's unquestioned "best friend," his closest companion outside of his marriage was William Cowper. While Polly suffered from an inexplicable physical ailment that resulted in spiritual struggles, Cowper struggled with chronic depression, resulting in multiple suicide attempts and a stay at a mental asylum.[71] Following Cowper's move to Olney, where he and Newton became neighbors, Cowper attempted suicide again following a particularly dark time of nightmares and hallucinations. Newton intervened and cared for his friend daily for the next several weeks. At Cowper's request, he eventually had Cowper move in with him so that he could better minister to his friend.

Both of these experiences of chronic suffering, experienced by two of Newton's closest friends, forced him to "work out" his view of suffering. Newton wrote, "Things appear quite otherwise, when felt experimentally, to what they do, when only read in a book."[72] His "experimental" theology of suffering becomes apparent when studying his advice to his wife and Cowper.[73] Writing to a friend regarding Polly's illness, Newton again highlights God's redemption of suffering: "Therefore, let us not fear: whatever sufferings may be yet appointed for us, they shall work together for our good."[74] Likewise, writing to Cowper following a season of his depression, he encouraged his friend: "He often thwarts our wishes for our good; but if we are not mistaken, if any measure we have in view would, upon the whole, promote our comfort or his glory, He will surely bring it to pass in answer to prayer, how improbable soever it may appear."[75]

Though the Newtons had no biological children, they adopted two nieces, Betsy and Eliza. Young Eliza arrived at the Newton's home at twelve years of age, suffering from mild tuberculosis. Her father and two older siblings had already died of the disease. Her mother was in the final stages of life, which prompted Eliza's adoption. The Newtons accepted her and raised her as their own. Sadly, Eliza died two years later at the age of fourteen. Newton was so moved by his love for Eliza and her faith in the Lord that he wrote

---

71. Aitken, *John Newton*, 206.

72. Newton, *Letters*, 152.

73. Chapter 4 will develop this point in detail. His letters to Polly and Cowper demonstrate consistency between his stated doctrinal viewpoints and his actual advice to them.

74. Newton, *Works* (1985), 6:63.

75. Newton, *Letters*, 153.

a short testimony about her life and death.[76] Greatly affected by how God used her illness to her spiritual benefit, he appealed to his young readers:

> Oh! my dear young friends, had you seen with what dignity of spirit she filled up the last scene of her life, you must have been affected by it! Let not the liveliness of your spirits, and the gaiety of the prospect around you, prevent you from considering, that to you likewise days will certainly come, (unless you are suddenly snatched out of life,) when you will say and feel, that the world, and all in it, can afford you no pleasure. But there is a Saviour, and a mighty One, always near, always gracious to those who seek him. May you, like her, be enabled to choose him, as the Guide of your youth, and the Lord of your hearts. Then, like her, you will find support and comfort under affliction, wisdom to direct your conduct, a good hope in death, and by death a happy translation to everlasting life.[77]

As Newton's hymn so famously states, "Through many dangers, toils, and snares, I have already come." Newton's words were truly autobiographical. God worked out Newton's doctrine of suffering through the many near-death experiences, disappointments, tragedies, and experiences of great affliction. Newton's friend and biographer, Richard Cecil, stated it this way: "We cannot wonder that Mr. N. latterly retained a strong impression of a Particular Providence, superintending and conducting the steps of man; since he was so often reminded of it in his own history."[78]

The Shaping of Newton's Life and Theology: People

Life experiences initially shaped Newton's theology of suffering; later, it was further molded through the influence of friends and associates. Early in Newton's spiritual awakening, he lamented that he had no one with whom to discuss his questions or struggles related to Christianity. Though he was largely self-taught, God began to provide a steady series of friends and mentors who greatly influenced Newton in his spiritual life and ministry.

---

76. Newton, *A Monument to the Praise of the Lord's Goodness, and to the Memory of Dear Eliza Cuningham*, in *Works* (1985), 5:101–26.

77. Newton, *A Monument to the Praise of the Lord's Goodness, and to the Memory of Dear Eliza Cuningham*, in *Works* (1985), 5:125.

78. Cecil, *Life of John Newton*, 85.

Dr. David Jennings (1691–1762)

One of Newton's earliest spiritual influences was his mother's pastor, Dr. David Jennings. He was the minister of the Independent Meeting at Old Gravel Lane, Wapping. He was friends with two other influential pastors, Isaac Watts and Samuel Brewer. Aitken theorizes that young Newton might have been influenced by a sermon that Jennings preached on Philemon, which echoes the first line of his "Amazing Grace." Jennings declared, "We have in this epistle a memorable instance of the richness and freeness of the grace of God, for the encouragement of the meanest and vilest sinners to fly to him for mercy."[79]

While it is difficult to determine with any certainty the influence that Pastor Jennings had upon Newton in his boyhood, it is clear that he exerted a great influence following his conversion. Newton first reached out to Jennings while he was on his first voyage as captain of the *African*, a slave trade ship. He continued to exchange letters with his childhood pastor until Jennings died in 1762. There is no doubt that Jennings reinforced the Reformed doctrines Newton first learned in catechism as a boy, including God's providence over all things. Newton's letters to him between 1752 and 1756 reflect a strong theme of God's providence, particularly as it relates to suffering. For example, Newton remarks, "My infirmities are little less prevalent than formerly, yet I daily see more plainly that his grace shall in the end be sufficient for me, and that my weakness may be a means of perfecting and displaying his glorious strength: most gladly therefore with St. Paul I will rather glory under my infirmities, since when I am thus weak, then I am strong."[80] Newton's comments reflect a growing understanding of God's redemption of trials for the purpose of sanctification and growth. This subject later became a dominant theme of his letters of pastoral care.

Jennings' most significant influence on Newton was likely not the message of his correspondence but its manner. Jennings was Newton's first spiritual pen pal. This relationship provided Newton with a spiritual mentor and demonstrated to him the power and effectiveness of the personal, written letter for spiritual advice and pastoral care.[81] Perhaps this early

---

79. Aitken, *John Newton*, 28.

80. Newton, "Letters to David Jennings."

81. Newton expressed his longing to Jennings for a spiritual mentor with whom he could correspond with regarding more significant topics of life and religion: "I seldom think myself more happy than when writing to a Pious and experienced person to whom I can enlarge on subjects very different from the light impertinence which is for the most part understood by the phrase of a polite letter." Newton, "Letters to David Jennings."

influence motivated Newton's future practice of offering spiritual counsel through letter writing.[82] Regardless, he considered Jennings his first spiritual mentor, the "most worthy person" he could regard as "patron."[83]

Captain Alexander Clunie (d. 1770)

During the early days of his correspondence with Jennings, Newton's second voyage as captain on the *African* led him again to the island of St. Kitts in the British Virgin Islands. In response to his many prayers for spiritual guidance, God used this occasion to introduce Newton to Captain Alexander Clunie. Clunie was also a ship captain and a mature believer who was a member at Stepney Independent Meeting in London, pastored by Samuel Brewer. During Newton's month-long stay in St. Kitts, Newton and Clunie spent many hours together in theological conversation. Clunie "evangelized" Newton and "reformed how he practiced his faith."[84] Newton wrote, "He encouraged me to open my mouth in social prayer; he taught me the advantage of Christian converse; he put me upon an attempt to make my profession more public, and to venture to speak for God."[85] After years of being self-taught in religion, Newton found in Clunie a "prayer partner, mentor, and spiritual director."[86]

Clunie made two chief contributions to the life and theology of Newton. First, Clunie helped Newton understand the security of the covenant of grace. Newton often connected the afflictions of life as occasions for God's preserving grace, believing that God both uses difficulties to refine the believer and to demonstrate His protective power in safeguarding the believer through trials. But it was Clunie who first helped Newton understand the doctrine of God's preserving grace. Newton wrote, "But now I began to understand the security of the covenant of grace, and to expect to be preserved, not by my own power and holiness, but by the mighty power and promise of God, through faith in an unchangeable Saviour."[87]

---

82. Grant Gordon identified Newton's letter-writing relationship with Jennings as a key factor that shaped Newton as a pastoral counselor. See Gordon, "John Newton," 68.
83. Cecil, *Life of John Newton*, 20.
84. Aitken, *John Newton*, 124.
85. Newton, *Narrative*, in *Works* (2015), 1:74.
86. Aitken, *John Newton*, 124.
87. Newton, *Narrative*, in *Works* (2015), 1:75.

Second, Clunie connected Newton to a solid community of Reformed believers at Stepney Chapel in London. Through this connection, Newton met Samuel Brewer, the minister at Stepney. Brewer would likewise become a close friend and mentor to Newton. Brewer directed Newton to listen to several preachers in the greater London area, which exposed Newton to some of the ablest preachers of the evangelical movement. Most significantly, Brewer provided Newton with a letter of introduction to George Whitefield, who would profoundly affect Newton's young faith.[88]

George Whitefield (1714–70)

George Whitefield was the most significant preacher of the Evangelical Revival in England and was the finest preacher heard by Newton.[89] The two first met in June of 1755. In September, Newton enjoyed fourteen encounters with Whitefield, including opportunities to listen to him preach, meet with him privately, and share meals.[90] He was in the company of Whitefield so often that he earned the title "Young Whitefield."

Though impossible to determine with certainty, one theme from Whitefield's sermons may have impacted Newton's theological understanding of suffering during the formative years of his Christian life. Whitefield taught the sanctifying effect of various trials, which would become a key topic in Newton's letters. In a sermon entitled "Glorifying God in the Fire," Whitefield proclaimed:

> God Almighty knows, we are often purged more in one hour by a good sound trial, than by a thousand manifestations of his love. It is a fine thing to come purified, to come pardoned out of the furnace of affliction; it is intended to purge us—to separate the precious from the vile; the chaff from the wheat; and God, in order to do this, is pleased to put us into one fire after another, which makes me love to see a good man under afflictions, because it teaches something of the work of God in the heart.[91]

Whitefield continued his sermon by describing various ways believers could glorify God in the day of trial.

---

88. Aitken, *John Newton*, 128.
89. Aitken, *John Newton*, 128.
90. Aitken, *John Newton*, 134.
91. Whitefield, "Glorifying God in the Fire," in Buckland, *Selected Sermons*, 130.

Using similar language, Newton once wrote to a friend about the refining effects of Polly's illness upon their faith. He wrote, "The Lord has been pleased to put us in the fire; but, blessed be his name, we are not burnt. Oh, that we may be brought out refined, and that the event may be to the praise of his grace and power!"[92] There are many parallels between Whitefield's sermon and Newton's theology of suffering.[93] At a time when Newton was vigorously active in his faith and at a highly impressionable time in his theological development, there is no doubt that George Whitefield had a massive impact on his life. Aitken writes, "Newton deepened his faith with the help of some influential mentors and preachers, of whom the most important was the celebrated Methodist leader, George Whitefield."[94]

Following his time with Whitefield in September of 1755, Newton wrote home to his wife: "I cannot say how much I esteem him and hope to my dying day I shall have reason to bless God on his behalf."[95]

Thomas Haweis (1734–1820)

Thomas Haweis was an Anglican minister at Oxford who met Newton around 1760. While earlier biographers largely ignored Haweis's influence on Newton's life, more recent works have demonstrated the significant role that he played in Newton's ordination to the Church of England.[96] While this achievement was perhaps Haweis's most considerable influence upon Newton, he played another role in Newton's life. Haweis discovered a series of eight letters Newton had written to Benjamin Fawcett regarding some of the "nautical and spiritual experiences in his adventurous life as a seafarer."[97] Haweis encouraged Newton to expand these letters and publish them as his spiritual autobiography. Later published in 1764 as *An Authentic Narrative*, the work instantly spread Newton's name and story throughout Europe.[98]

92. Newton, *Works* (1985), 6:62.

93. For further evidence of this fact, compare Reinke's chapter on trials (chapter 9) in *Newton* with Whitefield's sermon.

94. Aitken, *John Newton*, 127. See Aitken's development of this point on pages 127–32.

95. Newton, *Works* (1985), 5:503.

96. For an overview of Haweis's influence, see Wood, "Influence of Thomas Haweis," 187–202.

97. Aitken, *John Newton*, 166.

98. The book went through five editions in the first six months and became a frequently quoted source in "tracts, sermons and religious magazines." It was translated into

Without the strategic work of Haweis, it is likely that Newton would not have been ordained in the Church of England or landed as curate at Olney, which would have dramatically changed the course of Newton's life. However, unknowingly, Haweis also directed the future of Newton's pastoral care. Having acquired a copy of Newton's original letters to Fawcett, Haweis realized the spiritual benefit that Newton's letters could be to encourage the spiritual health of others. Newton's "plain and easy" style of weaving spiritual commentary with significant life events from his past would become the same formula he employed to minister to dozens of future recipients who would receive letters of pastoral encouragement.

William Bull (1738–1814)

William Bull was the minister at the Independent Church at Newport-Pagnell, a few miles from Olney where Newton was curate. The two quickly became lifelong friends and spiritual "soulmates." While Polly was Newton's "best friend" and William Cowper his closest friend outside of his marriage, William Bull was a close second. Aitken wrote that his friendship with Bull was "one of the warmest friendships in Newton's life, second only in its closeness after his relationship with William Cowper."[99] Bull often taught at Newton's midweek prayer meeting, and the two frequently met to enjoy theological discussion and mutual encouragement.

Aitken argues that Bull played a "paternal" role in Newton's life, helping him sort out his various ministerial priorities and encouraging him to resume hymn writing following Cowper's suicide attempt, which brought the hymn-writing endeavor to a halt.[100] But Bull's most significant contribution to Newton's pastoral care ministry appears to be his sermons, as Newton would often use Bull's sermon material as content for his letters. Aitken explains, "Newton frequently took up the themes of his friend's teachings in his voluminous correspondences, both with Bull himself (to whom he wrote over 120 letters) and with others."[101] The two would often exchange sermon outlines, aiding one another in pulpit work.[102] While Bull's sermons

---

multiple languages in Europe and gained influence in the American continent as well. See Aitken, *John Newton*, 185.

99. Aitken, *John Newton*, 244.
100. Aitken, *John Newton*, 244.
101. Aitken, *John Newton*, 245.
102. Cecil, *Life of John Newton*, 268.

are unavailable for investigation, it is evident that the topic of "trials" was a frequent theme of correspondence between the two. Some of the content on suffering that Newton employs in his pastoral letters to others may have come from his correspondence with Bull.[103]

The Shaping of Newton's Life and Theology: Authors and Books

Newton's life experiences and critical figures were not the only shaping influences on his life and theology; several authors and particular books also influenced him. Hindmarsh provides a convenient list of texts drawn from Newton's diary between 1725–56.[104] Newton's habit was to read from a broad range of authors, especially early in life.[105] Yet, later in his ministry, a study of his letters reveals which authors and books were of the most significant influence. Therefore, this section will focus on those authors and books that were particularly impactful in Newton's life.

Authors

Isaac Watts (1674–1748)

The earliest author of influence upon John Newton was Isaac Watts. Watts was a friend of Newton's childhood pastor, David Jennings. He is most well known as a hymn writer and as pastor at John Owen's former church, Mark Lane Independent Meeting Hall. Newton's mother utilized the catechisms for children and the hymnbook developed by Dr. Watts in her rearing of Newton. Young John Newton had memorized these books by the time he was four years old.[106] These works anchored Newton in Reformed theology and awakened what would become a lifelong endeavor of hymn writing. Dr. Watts's hymnal for children influenced Newton to spend much of his

---

103. Many of Newton's letters to William Bull include themes of trials and suffering. See Newton, *One Hundred and Twenty Nine Letters*, 124, 178, 233–34, 256–59, 277, 284, 305.

104. Hindmarsh, *English Evangelical Tradition*, 332–36. Hindmarsh also provides summaries and some quotes from Newton's diary entries that demonstrate how Newton responded to the book.

105. Hindmarsh, *English Evangelical Tradition*, 79.

106. Aitken, *John Newton*, 27.

ministry later writing weekly hymns for children that would aid them in internalizing scriptural truth.[107] Later in life, Newton read a treatise by Watts on the influence of divine love upon the "passions," which particularly resonated with his experience.[108]

John Owen (1616–83)

A second author who particularly impacted Newton was the Puritan John Owen. Owen was the foremost theologian of the Puritan era. He was Cromwell's chaplain, vice-chancellor of Oxford, and later minister at Leadenhall Street (Mark Lane Independent Meeting Hall). Newton once wrote to a friend, "We are favoured with many excellent books in our tongue; but I with you agree in assigning one of the first places (as a teacher) to Dr. Owen."[109] In 1754, as Newton was growing in his new faith, he read Owen's most famous work on the person of Christ, *Christologia*. Up until this time, Newton had been convinced of the doctrine of God's providence in saving him and preserving him, but his Christology remained relatively underdeveloped.[110] However, a key emphasis on the person of Christ would later be a dominant theme of Newton's letters of spiritual counsel to others.[111]

What brought about this new development in Newton's theology? Reading Owen's *Christologia* may have created the initial spark of interest that aided Newton to grow in his understanding of the doctrine of Christ. Hindmarsh, citing Newton's diary entry in 1754, wrote that Newton's reading of *Christologia* "led him to pray for more knowledge of the mystery of godliness in Christ."[112] While Owen's work does not intend to address Christ's role in the believer's sanctification, it is interesting to note that Newton

---

107. Aitken, *John Newton*, 188.

108. Hindmarsh, *English Evangelical Tradition*, 335.

109. Newton, *Works* (1985), 2:101.

110. This fact can be observed in his *Authentic Narrative*. In his final letter of the *Narrative*, he states that he "devoted his life" to "know nothing but Jesus Christ and him crucified" (*Narrative, Works* [2015], 1:80). The large amount of discretionary time he enjoyed at Liverpool would allow him to engage in this pursuit. But up until this season, he writes relatively little about communion with Christ, which would be a dominant theme of his later years.

111. For example, see Reinke's chapters, "The Daily Discipline of Joy in Jesus" and "Christ-Centered Holiness" in *Newton*, 67–90, 127–40.

112. Hindmarsh, *English Evangelical Tradition*, 333.

made this application.¹¹³ In one of his sermons on Handel's *Messiah*, Newton elaborates: "An eminent divine [John Owen in his *Christologia*] points out some special seasons in the Christian life, in which he thinks the peculiar pressures of the soul may obtain the most sensible and immediate relief, by direct application to the Saviour."¹¹⁴ By this, Newton means that it is appropriate in certain seasons of life for the believer to pray to Christ, because He is a sympathetic High Priest, to find relief from the soul's pressures that are often created by trials or suffering.¹¹⁵ Thus it appears that Owen's work had a significant impact on Newton's understanding of the doctrine of Christ as it relates to a believer's sanctification, particularly in trials.

Owen would continue to be an influence throughout Newton's life. Hindmarsh states that Newton considered Owen "among the foremost teachers of theology."¹¹⁶ Newton later mentions Owen's exposition of Ps 130 as being "the most moving address to sinners I ever met with" and calls Owen's work on the Holy Spirit "the epitome, if not the master-piece of his writings."¹¹⁷ Though the "great champion of free grace, Dr. Owen" significantly shaped Newton's theology, Newton confessed that his style was "something obscure."¹¹⁸ But it was one of Owen's contemporaries, Richard Baxter, whose aim was to speak "as plain as we can," who would further shape Newton's practical theology and provide for him an exemplary model of pastoral care.

Richard Baxter (1615–91)

Richard Baxter was a third influential author in Newton's life. The Puritan writers of the previous century had a profound impact on Newton's theology and ministry, as demonstrated through his comments about authors like Owen and Baxter. But these writers had different purposes to Newton.

---

113. Owen, *Works*, 1:2–272. Owen's treatise does address Christ's role as High Priest, but his aim is not directed toward Christian sanctification. Newton, however, took this doctrine and applied it to believers who were suffering. See Newton, *Works* (1985), 2:20. See also Reinke, who demonstrates Newton's application of Christ's role as High Priest to the believer's sanctification in trials, in *Newton*, 57.

114. Newton, *Works* (1985), 4:578.

115. Newton makes this same point in his essay "Thoughts on the Doctrine of the Holy Trinity," in *Works* (1985), 6:441.

116. Hindmarsh, *English Evangelical Tradition*, 81.

117. Newton, *Works* (1985), 2:54, 1:180, 2:101.

118. Newton, *Works* (1985), 1:180; Hindmarsh, *English Evangelical Tradition*, 81, 333.

John Newton's Theology of Suffering and Its Application to Pastoral Care

Hindmarsh states, "Owen was, he felt, among the foremost teachers of theology but suffered from a style 'something obscure'; in contrast, Baxter had 'rather cloudy' sentiments in divinity but was a superb pastor and man of deep spirituality. Owen was a doctrinal authority; Baxter was read for spiritual inspiration."[119]

Baxter was the vicar at Kidderminster and a prolific writer of the Puritan era. He is most famous for his systematic approach to pastoral care, where he regularly visited members of his church for spiritual instruction and counseling. Baxter's example influenced Newton's regular practice of visiting members of his church in Olney for pastoral care.[120] Similarly, Baxter's writings shaped Newton's pastoral care in both content and purpose. While Newton acknowledged Baxter's limitations and weaknesses, he nonetheless felt that he was "one of the greatest men of his age; and perhaps, in fervor, spirituality, and success, more than equal, both as a minister and a Christian, to some twenty, taken together, of those who affect to undervalue him in this present day."[121] Newton specifically mentions reading Baxter's *The Saints' Everlasting Rest*, *Dying Thoughts*, and *A Call to the Unconverted*, noting that his works were superior to the modern compositions.[122] Baxter also produced *A Christian Directory*, a voluminous piece of pastoral counseling in which he applied biblical truth to hundreds of various life scenarios or "cases of conscience."[123] Though not mentioned by name, Newton states that he read other practical works of Baxter. While Baxter wrote to a general Christian audience, Newton would direct his pastoral care to specific individuals, though he later published many of these private letters to benefit the broader community. Though Newton's style is very different and much less directive, Baxter's emphasis on Christian spirituality, particularly his emphasis on biblical truth applied to specific life challenges, directed and shaped Newton's focus on pastoral care in his ministry.[124]

---

119. Hindmarsh, *English Evangelical Tradition*, 81.

120. "'My afternoons are generally spent visiting the people, three or four families a day.' He emphasized his determination to 'converse singly' with individuals for an hour at a time, keeping careful record of these appointments." Aitken, *John Newton*, 187. Baxter kept detailed records of his visits, as did Newton.

121. Newton, *Works* (1985), 1:667.

122. Newton, "Letter to William Wilberforce."

123. Baxter, *Christian Directory*, in *Practical Works* 1.

124. An additional influence was one of the founding members at the Eclectic Society, Eli Bates, who wrote a book on Baxter's writings, *Selections from the Works of Baxter*. See Aitken, *John Newton*, 290, 386.

John Bunyan (1628-88)

A third Puritan who influenced Newton was John Bunyan. A Nonconformist preacher, Bunyan was imprisoned for refusing to cease preaching publicly following the Act of Uniformity in 1662. While in prison, he wrote his most famous work, *The Pilgrim's Progress*. Tony Reinke has convincingly demonstrated the many ways that Bunyan affected Newton.[125] Several strands of influence relate to Newton's theology of suffering and pastoral care. First, Bunyan's autobiography, *Grace Abounding to the Chief of Sinners*, impacted Newton as he and Bunyan shared a similar past. Reinke explained, "Newton, the 'African blasphemer,' was a monster of sin, whose debaucheries made even sailors blush. Bunyan, the 'village rebel,' was a man who breathed obscenities and once was rebuked by a prostitute for his swearing. . . . Each was converted by free grace. Neither forgot it."[126] Reinke further explains how they followed similar paths in education, pastoral ministry, and creative uses of "popular cultural mediums" to maximize their care and spiritual influence upon other believers.[127]

Newton's letters reflect two specific themes that came from Bunyan's autobiography.[128] First, Bunyan noted how prison allowed him to know Jesus "as more real and apparent. . . . Here I have seen him and felt him indeed." Reflecting this theme, Newton wrote that "in affliction [Christ] allows his people to have fellowship with him" and thus know Him better.[129] Second, Bunyan found that trials "kept him from trusting in himself and moved him to 'look to God, through Christ, to help me, and carry me through this world.'"[130] Echoing Bunyan, Newton wrote that "it is thus by looking to Jesus, that the believer is enlightened and strengthened, and grows in grace and sanctification" and "by these experiences [trials] the believer is weaned more from self, and taught more highly to prize and more absolutely rely on him."[131]

125. Reinke, *Newton*, 27-29, 188.

126. Reinke, *Newton*, 28-29.

127. Spurgeon said of Bunyan and Newton, "Both of them had been ringleaders in sin before they became leaders in the army of the Redeemed," and "no man in his senses will venture to assert that there was anything in Newton or Bunyan why they should engross the regard of the Most High." As quoted in Reinke, *Newton*, 28-29.

128. Marylynn Rouse identifies these themes in an appendix to Cecil's biography of Newton. See Cecil, *Life of John Newton*, 270.

129. Newton, *Works* (1985), 1:230.

130. As quoted in Cecil, *Life of John Newton*, 270.

131. Newton, *Works* (1985), 2:487, 1:443.

The second influence that impacted Newton's pastoral care theology in regard to his view of the Christian life and his perspective on trials was Bunyan's work, *The Pilgrim's Progress*. Newton had read this book so many times, he admitted to his friend Alexander Clunie, that he had practically memorized it.[132] Newton taught the basics of the Christian life every week to the disadvantaged people in Olney using Bunyan's work.[133] Regarding trials, Newton used Bunyan's section called "The Enchanted Ground" to illustrate how trials awaken believers from spiritual slumber. He wrote, "We live on an enchanted ground, are surrounded with snares, and if not quickened by trials, are very prone to sink into formality or carelessness. It is a shame it should be so, but so it is, that a long course of prosperity always makes us drowsy."[134] Newton's use of Bunyan's classic became so well known that he was later asked to write a preface to the 1776 edition of the book. Marylynn Rouse sums up Bunyan's influence on Newton when she writes, "Many of Bunyan's thoughts and attitudes became evident in Newton's own life."[135]

John Flavel (1628–91)

One final Puritan author who influenced John Newton was John Flavel. When Newton was still captain of the *African* and growing in his faith, he wrote to his boyhood pastor David Jennings regarding the need for a resource to teach Christian doctrine to sailors. In the letter, he references John Flavel's book, *Navigation Spiritualized: A New Compass for Seaman*. This work was one of several treatises Flavel wrote to minister to sailors.[136] Before his ejection in 1622, Flavel was a minister at the seaside town of Dartmouth, and many of his parishioners were sailors. Perhaps Newton was initially attracted to Flavel because of his unique writings to seamen. In any case, Flavel's works so helped Newton that he would later recommend "any of his works" to his young friend William Wilberforce.[137]

The letter to Wilberforce specifically mentions two additional books by Flavel (beyond his *Navigation*), which reveal themes found in many of

132. Newton, *Christian Correspondent*, 129.
133. Reinke, *Newton*, 28.
134. Newton, *Aged Pilgrim's Triumph*, 33. Cf. Reinke, *Newton*, 188.
135. Cecil, *Life of John Newton*, 270.
136. Other titles include *A Caution to Seaman: A Dissuasive Against Several Horrid and Detestable Sins* and *The Seaman's Companion: Six Sermons on the Mysteries of Providence as Relating to Seaman; and the Sins, Dangers, Duties and Troubles of Seaman*.
137. Newton, "Letter to William Wilberforce."

Newton's letters. The first work is his *Mystery of Providence*. The doctrine of providence was a key component of Newton's theology of suffering. One can hear the echoes of Flavel's seminal work on providence in the pastoral counsel that Newton offered to people in trials. For example, Flavel states that "our hearts may be established and kept steady under *calamitous and adverse providences*," and "afflictive providences are of great use to the people of God."[138] He then articulates several ways that "calamitous" providences benefit the believer.[139] Similarly, Newton wrote, "It is still needful that they pass through many tribulations. . . . They are not the tokens of God's displeasure, but fatherly chastisements, and tokens of his love, designed to promote the work of grace in their hearts and to make them partakers of his holiness."[140] Leaning on Flavel, Newton taught that believers should see the "great use" that afflictive providences bring to the people of God.

A second work by Flavel mentioned by Newton is his *Keeping the Heart*, originally titled *A Saint Indeed: Or, the Great Work of a Christian Opened and Pressed*. Newton's letters reflect several themes from Flavel's work. For example, Flavel wrote: "What better method could Providence take to accomplish thy desire [to have corruptions mortified] than pulling from under thy head that soft pillow of creature-delights on which you rested before?"[141] A century later, Newton counseled a sufferer using similar language, noting that God sometimes removes earthly provisions so that "we may lean only and entirely upon our beloved."[142]

Flavel also wrote that believers suffer much less than their sins deserve: "The knowledge of myself, and the consideration of what I deserve for my sins, which is eternal torment; when with this knowledge I arrive at my lodging, however unprovided I find it, methinks, it is much better than I deserve."[143] Similarly, Newton stated, "The Lord afflicts us at times: but it is always a thousand times less than we deserve."[144]

---

138. Flavel, *Works*, 4:487.

139. Flavel emphasizes the need for believers to submit to providence in suffering, a common theme of Newton's letters. See especially Newton, *Works* (1985), 1:249–50, 2:432–37.

140. Newton, *Works* (1985), 4:238.

141. Flavel, *Keeping the Heart*, 45.

142. Newton, *Letters*, 81.

143. Flavel, *Keeping the Heart*, 48.

144. Newton, *Works* (1985), 2:151.

Tony Reinke identifies an influence that Flavel's work had on Newton's view of sanctification.[145] Newton often counseled suffering believers to "look to Christ" in suffering since trials facilitate spiritual growth as Christians behold the person and work of Christ. He wrote, "It is thus by looking to Jesus, that the believer is enlightened and strengthened, and grows in grace and sanctification. . . . By beholding we are gradually formed into the resemblance of Him whom we see, admire, and love."[146] Perhaps Newton was leaning on Flavel, who wrote: "The more frequent and spiritual your converse and communion with Christ is, the more of the beauty and loveliness of Christ will be stamped upon your spirits, changing you into the same image, from glory to glory."[147]

Newton's favorite topic in pastoral care was human nature, or what he called "anatomy," the study of the human heart.[148] While Newton admits that much of his understanding came from his observations of people and his interactions with them, Flavel also shaped his thinking. Flavel often wrote about the heart's various dynamics and responses, particularly in the context of trials and suffering. For example, he wrote *Preparation for Suffering* to equip believers to respond to suffering in godly ways.[149] One of his more significant works was *Pneumatologia: A Treatise on the Soul of Man*, in which he articulates the mechanics and dynamics of the inner man.[150] He also wrote specific treatises about particular heart challenges, such as *A Practical Treatise on Fear: Its Varieties, Uses, Causes, Effects and Remedies*.[151]

Flavel may have been the most significant Puritan influence on Newton's theology of suffering and was undoubtedly one of his favorite authors.[152] Newton held Flavel in such high esteem that he recommended "any" of his works as solid, reliable, and helpful.[153]

---

145. Reinke, *Newton*, 156–57.

146. Newton, *Works* (1985), 2:487.

147. Flavel, *Works*, 2:224. The passage underlying this point in both Flavel and Newton was 2 Cor 3:18, a favorite passage of both authors.

148. Newton, *Works* (1985), 1:478.

149. Flavel, *Works*, 6:3.

150. Flavel, *Works*, 2:475.

151. Flavel, *Works*, 3:239.

152. Cosby's analysis of Flavel's doctrine of suffering closely follows Newton's doctrine as developed in chapter 2 of this work. See Cosby, *Suffering and Sovereignty*, chapters 4–5.

153. Newton, "Letter to William Wilberforce."

Books

While the authors mentioned previously were the most significant sources of influence, specific books also shaped Newton's theology. He read widely and broadly, especially early in life.[154] In 1752, just a few years after his conversion, Newton read four books that gave him "a further view of Christian doctrine and experience" and were "an important influence on his spiritual development."[155] Two of these books seemed to provide a unique shaping influence on his view of pastoral care and his theology of suffering. The first book was entitled *Some Remarkable Passages in the Life of Colonel James Gardiner* by Philip Doddridge.[156] Writing to his boyhood pastor David Jennings, Newton said that this book "has affected me more frequently and sensibly than all the books I ever read."[157] Newton notes in his diary how the book specifically affected him.[158] One way is that Colonel Gardiner's life story and conversion shared many parallels to his own story, including a similar background of ungodliness, checks of conscience that brought superficial and temporary change, and eventually a dramatic conversion story. Though Newton could not have appreciated this fact in 1752, it must have been stunning to him in later years that his own life would continue to follow Colonel Gardiner's story in multiple ways: Colonel Gardiner also had a wife with a delicate and broken constitution (with whom he exchanged many letters of great affection); he used letters to share his life story (some are referenced in the book); he was away from family for long periods; he taught religion to his soldiers (as Newton would later do with his sailors); and he lost a child, which Gardiner considered his "greatest trial" (similar to Newton's loss of his adopted niece). Gardiner's emphasis on a "personal life of faith" was potentially an additional influence. Newton notes in his diary that Gardiner's significant spiritual growth brought him to repentance over his relatively "small improvement."[159] Doddridge

---

154. See his recorded reading list in Hindmarsh, *John Newton*, 332–36. Hindmarsh makes the point that Newton's reading was "eclectic" (79).

155. Newton, *Works* (2015), 1:67; Aitken, *John Newton*, 116. The books were *The Life of God in the Soul of Man* (1677) by Henry Scougal, *Meditations Among the Tombs* (1746) by James Hervey, *Some Remarkable Passages in the Life of Colonel James Gardiner* (1747) by Philip Doddridge, and *The Life of Sir Matthew Hale* (1749) by Gilbert Burnet.

156. Doddridge, *Some Remarkable Passages*.

157. Newton, "Letters to David Jennings."

158. Entries for July 19, 1752 and July 17, 1753 in Newton, "Diaries 1751–1807."

159. Newton, "Diaries 1751–1807."

and Gardiner exchanged several letters from their meeting in 1739 until Gardiner's death in 1745. The letter writing was mutually edifying and may have influenced Newton's future habit of writing letters as a means of spiritual care and encouragement.

The second book that affected Newton was Henry Scougal's *The Life of God in the Soul of Man*, published in 1677.[160] Like many of Newton's most influential works, Scougal wrote this treatise as a personal letter to a friend; it was not initially intended for publication. Scougal was a professor of divinity at Aberdeen University. It was his practice to assemble his students every Sunday evening to have "pious discourses" and hold private counseling meetings with them.[161] Though Newton does not elaborate specifically on how the book affected him, perhaps Newton followed Scougal's example when he formed a similar practice at his church in Olney. Like Flavel, Scougal emphasized the need to "look to Jesus" as the primary practice that leads to sanctification. He wrote, "The true way to improve and ennoble our souls is, by fixing our love on the divine perfections, that we may have them always before us, and drive an impression of them on ourselves, and 'beholding with open face, as in a glass, the glory of the Lord, we may be changed into the same image, from glory to glory.'"[162] Newton often quoted from this same verse, stating that believers should "look to Jesus" for their sanctification in trials.[163]

Newton regularly called the afflictions of life God's "love tokens" since God designed them for the believer's good. Likewise, Newton spoke of his need to "kiss the rod" of his trial since it was "sweetened with abundant mercies."[164] He utilizes language similar to Scougal, who wrote:

> A person moulded into this temper [a settled joy and love for God] would find pleasure in all the dispensations of Providence: temporal enjoyments would have another relish, when he should taste the divine goodness in them, and consider them as tokens of love sent by his dearest Lord and Maker; and chastisements, though they be not joyous but grievous, would hereby lose their sting, the rod as well as the staff would comfort him—he would snatch a kiss

---

160. Scougal, *Life of God*.

161. Scougal, *Life of God*, 32. "He thought that ministers should not miss a day in which they do not treat *personally* and in *private* with some of their people about the affairs of their souls"; 36–37.

162. Scougal, *Life of God*, 71.

163. Newton, *Works* (1985), 2:487.

164. Newton, *Works* (1985), 4:238–39, 2:142.

from the hand that was smiting him, and gather sweetness from that severity.[165]

Likewise, Newton seems to echo Scougal when he speaks of some of "our dearest friends" being taken from us so that believers would not lean too heavily on the things in this world. Scougal wrote, "If any earthly comforts have got too much of your heart . . . and the dearest of these are removed out of the world, so that you must raise your mind toward heaven when you would think upon them. Thus God hath provided that your heart may be loosed from the world, and that he may not have any rival in your affection."[166] Similarly, Newton wrote, "But when some of our dearest friends are taken from us, the lives of others threatened, and we ourselves are brought low with pain and sickness, then we not only say but feel that this must not, cannot be our rest."[167] Newton even wrote about his affection for his wife potentially interfering with adoration for God: "And now it should be our great concern and prayer, that our love may not be inordinate, or irregular; nor interfere with what we owe to the great Lover of our souls."[168] While Newton does not explicitly mention the effect of *The Life of God in the Soul of Man* on his own life, it is clear that there are parallels of language and similar themes that demonstrate Scougal's influence on Newton's theology of suffering.

Conclusion

Newton's life was one of "many dangers, toils, and snares." God used many of these challenging near-death experiences to impress upon him the reality of His saving and preserving providence. This discovery was the first piece of Newton's theology of suffering. Over time, various people and particular authors would further shape his understanding of God's redemptive purposes in trials and the sanctifying work of Christ as He draws them to Himself through various difficulties. These factors helped create an overall doctrine of suffering that would form the backbone of his pastoral care theology to hurting people. Some of his mentors used the medium of letters to minister to Newton, which created an appreciation for the shepherding

---

165. Scougal, *Life of God*, 78–79.
166. Scougal, *Life of God*, 115.
167. Newton, *Works* (1985), 2:197.
168. Newton, *Works* (1985), 5:551–52.

effectiveness of written correspondence. As Newton entered pastoral ministry in 1764, these shaping influences equipped him to become the foremost pastoral counselor of the eighteenth century.

2

Newton's Theology of Suffering

JOHN NEWTON'S LIFE AND ministry emphasized Christian spirituality, the dynamics of a believer's ongoing relationship with God.[1] This theme grew out of the evangelical movement of his time, which largely focused on communion with God and personal holiness.[2] Newton's model of pastoral care

---

1. Chapter 1 demonstrated how certain writers, such as Henry Scougal, John Bunyan, and John Flavel influenced Newton's theology of suffering in the context of Christian spirituality. James Gordon states that Christian spirituality in Newton's day emphasized "lived doctrine centered on Christ, and moral renewal after the image of Christ." See Gordon, *Evangelical Spirituality*, 4. The evangelical emphasis on "lived doctrine centered on Christ" flowed from the movement's emphasis on "conversionism" (the "belief that lives needed to be changed") and "crucicentrism" (a "stress on the sacrifice of Christ on the cross"). These are two of the four qualities identified by Bebbington as the "special marks of evangelical religion." See Bebbington, *Evangelicalism in Modern Britain*, 2–3.

2. For Newton, communion with God and personal holiness were the same pursuit. A believer becomes like Christ by beholding Him. Reinke notes, "Newton is clear: we become by beholding. 'By beholding we are gradually formed into the resemblance of him whom we see, admire, and love.'" Reinke, *Newton*, 131. Gordon expands on this point: "Frequent prayer and a constancy of devotion reinforce the sense of the immediacy of God in daily life.... In the process of sanctification, openness to God and inner alertness to his voice as mediated through the Scriptures, promote the development of Christian taste and nourish and inform the Christian mind." Gordon, *Evangelical Spirituality*, 87. Gordon provides a concise but relatively thorough overview of Newton's understanding of communion with God and the pursuit of holiness. See Gordon, *Evangelical Spirituality*, 86–89. His work also distinguishes the common features of evangelical spirituality in the broader movement from the unique facets of individual writers, such as Newton.

arose from this theme since he believed that spiritual counseling was merely the practice of helping fellow believers grow in conformity to Christ and in their relationship with God in the context of daily life. As Newton gained more experience in pastoral ministry, he often ministered to people in various occasions of suffering. Newton believed that the trials and afflictions of life were not to be viewed as mere annoyances and distractions to Christian spirituality but were instead the fundamental way that God works to grow believers in their walks with Him.[3] In other words, Newton's doctrine of suffering was a crucial component in his doctrine of sanctification and thus a primary theme in his approach to pastoral care, since his ministry of counseling endeavored to promote Christian growth, conformity to Christ, and communion with God. To better understand Newton's doctrine of suffering and its impact on his pastoral care ministry, this chapter demonstrates that five essential doctrines formed the foundation of his theology of affliction.[4]

God's Sovereign Goodness: The Character of God and the Interpretation of Suffering

Newton's affirmation of Calvinism formed the foundation of his doctrine of suffering. This affirmation of divine providence over "all things" anchored his doctrine of suffering to the character of God. Newton described God's providence simply with the phrase "the Lord reigns." He explained that "every event in the kingdom of providence and of grace is under his rule. His providence pervades and manages the whole and is as minutely attentive to every part as if there were only that single object in his view."[5]

Newton understood that God's control of all things worked in concert with His wisdom, care, and grace in such a way that everything "works for good" as a "token of his love." He wrote:

> [The believer's] faith upholds him under all trials, by assuring him, that every dispensation is under the direction of his Lord; that chastisements are a token of his love; that the season, measure, and

---

3. This chapter will demonstrate the validity of this point in Newton's theology.

4. See appendix A for an index of key biblical passages that Newton used to build his theology of suffering. The main texts are referenced throughout this chapter. For the purpose of this work, the phrases "theology of suffering," "theology of affliction," and "theology of trials" are used synonymously.

5. Newton, *Letters*, 238.

continuance of his sufferings, are appointed by Infinite Wisdom, and designed to work for his everlasting good; and that grace and strength shall be afforded him, according to his day.[6]

Newton punctuated his affirmations of God's providence with reminders of God's character. Specifically, he often mentions five qualities: goodness, wisdom, love, grace, and care.[7] Newton wrote, "The sovereignty of God toward his people is not arbitrary, but connected with a wisdom which can make no mistakes and a love which can give no unnecessary pain to those for whom he died upon the cross."[8] On another occasion, Newton affirms God's goodness in trials when he quotes Nah 1:7, applying it to the chronic and difficult nature of his wife's illness: "However, upon trial, I can confirm what I then said, and assure you, upon new and repeated experience, that the Lord is good, a stronghold in the day of trouble, and he knoweth them that put their trust in him."[9] Newton also interpreted his suffering as an expression of God's care. He wrote to a fellow minister: "Every day almost I meet with occasions of admiring the wisdom, care, and faithfulness of our Great Shepherd intimating and adjusting his dispensations exactly to our need and state."[10] Finally, Newton affirmed that God's grace and His sovereignty are inseparable. He explained, "But the Lord's appointments, to those who fear him, are not only sovereign but wise and gracious. He has connected their good with his own glory, and is engaged, by promise, to make all things work together for their advantage."[11] In summary, Newton believed that a good, wise, loving, caring, gracious God controls all things

---

6. Newton, *Works* (1985), 1:169.

7. (1) Goodness: Newton, *Works* (1985), 1:442, 1:455–56, 2:436–37, 2:31, 2:23, 2:34, 5:539. (2) Wisdom: Newton, *Works* (1985), 1:169, 1:442, 1:455, 1:226–27, 2:197–99, 2:31–33, 2:23, 2:174, 2:19–21; Newton, *Aged Pilgrim's Triumph*, 174; Newton, *Twenty-Five Letters*, 117; Newton, *Letters*, 50, 92, 201, 224, 407, 414. (3) Love: Newton, *Works* (1985), 6:425, 1:169, 1:442, 1:621, 2:31–33, 2:217, 2:19–21, 4:238–39; Newton, *Aged Pilgrim's Triumph*, 174; Newton, *Twenty-Five Letters*, 116–17; Newton, *Letters*, 50, 91, 201, 221, 279, 407, 414. (4) Grace: Newton, *Works* (1985), 6:224, 6:338, 1:169–70, 2:228, 2:231, 2:433, 2:197–99, 2:22–23, 2:217–20, 2:146–48, 2:174, 2:34–36, 4:238; Wilberforce, *Correspondence*, 1:139; Newton, *Twenty-Five Letters*, 85; Newton, *Letters*, 71, 99, 215–16, 366. (5) Care: Newton, *Works* (1985), 2:146–48; Newton, *Aged Pilgrim's Triumph*, 135; Newton, *Letters*, 414.

8. Newton, *Aged Pilgrim's Triumph*, 174.

9. Newton, *Works* (1985), 6:62.

10. Newton, *Letters*, 414.

11. Newton, *Works* (1985), 1:249.

such that they always accomplish His purpose to glorify Himself in doing good for His people.

When believers embrace God's sovereignty over trials, interpreted through the lens of these attributes, it transforms their outlook on the difficulty. In a letter to a struggling Christian, Newton described the perspective of a believer convinced of God's sovereign goodness in times of trial: "He would willingly acquiesce in all the dispensations of Divine Providence. He believes that all events are under the direction of infinite wisdom and goodness, and shall surely issue in the glory of God and the good of those who fear him."[12]

Sometimes, Newton encountered believers who struggled to affirm God's providence over all things. Writing to one such individual, he insists that

> The Lord reigns. He who once bore our sins, and carried our sorrows, is seated upon a throne of glory and exercises all power in heaven and on earth. Thrones, principalities, and powers bow before him. Every event in the kingdoms of providence and of grace is under his rule. His providence pervades and manages the whole and is as minutely attentive to every part as if there were only that single object in his view.[13]

He challenged his fellow Calvinists who were eager and zealous to defend the doctrine of divine election but struggled to submit to God's sovereignty when it came to their own daily trials:

> The doctrine of God's sovereignty . . . is no less fully assented to by those who are called *Calvinists*. We zealously contend for this point in our debates with the *Arminians*; and are ready to wonder that any should be hardy enough to dispute the Creator's right to do what he will with his own. . . . But, alas! how often do we find ourselves utterly unable to apply [the doctrine of sovereignty], so

---

12. Newton, *Works* (1985), 1:249.

13. Newton, *Letters*, 237–38. Newton continues: "From the tallest archangel to the meanest ant or fly, all depend on him for their being, their preservation, and their powers. He directs the sparrows where to build their nests, and to find their food. He overrules the rise and fall of nations, and bends, with an invincible energy and unerring wisdom, all events; so that while many intend nothing less, in the issue their designs all concur and coincide in the accomplishment of his holy will. He restrains with a mighty hand the still more formidable efforts of the powers of darkness; and Satan with all his hosts cannot exert their malice a hair's-breadth beyond the limits of his permission. This is he who is the head and husband of his believing people. How happy are they whom it is his good pleasure to bless! How safe are they whom he has engaged to protect!"

as to reconcile our spirits to those afflictions which he is pleased to allot us![14]

Newton also noted that believers tend to focus on "second causes and immediate instruments of events" and thus fail to see God's specific orchestration in every situation. He explained, "We are prone to fix our attention upon the second causes and immediate instruments of events; forgetting that whatever befalls us is according to his purpose, and therefore must be right and seasonable in itself, and shall in the issue be productive of good."[15] The solution, wrote Newton, was to see God's wise and gracious hand in all things: "Though he put forth his hand, and seem to threaten our dearest comforts, yet when we remember that it is *his* hand, when we consider that it is *his* design, *his* love, *his* wisdom, and *his* power, we cannot refuse to trust him."[16] He wrote that these "second causes" are merely instruments in God's hands, a perspective that brings peace to the believer.[17] "When I consider all second causes and instruments as mere saws and hammers in the workman's hands, and that they can neither give us pleasure or pain, but as our Lord and Saviour is pleased to employ them, I feel a degree of peace and composure."[18]

The affirmation of God's wise, gracious providence was the staple doctrine of Newton's theology of suffering. He possessed unshakable confidence in God's control of all things, coupled with a conviction that God is wise, good, loving, gracious, and disposed to care for His people. This perspective led Newton to believe and to counsel that God can only bring about what is truly best for His children.[19]

14. Newton, *Works* (1985), 1:248. Emphasis original.

15. Newton, *Works* (1985), 1:456.

16. Newton, *Works* (1985), 6:33. Emphasis original. "How happy are they who can resign all to him, see his hand in every dispensation, and believe that he chooses better for them than they possibly could for themselves." Newton, *Works* (1985), 1:456.

17. Surprisingly, Newton does not address the problem of theodicy directly. However, given the influence of Puritans like John Flavel upon his life, it is likely that he held a similar view. Cosby summarizes Flavel's view: "Flavel is careful not to assign evil to God. Rather, God permits it, restrains it, overrules it—for His glory and the good of His people.... Can God, then, be found 'guilty' of evil? Again, Flavel answers in the negative. God... may permit and govern evil without being the 'author' of evil." Cosby, *Suffering and Sovereignty*, 52, 54.

18. Newton, *Letters*, 360–61.

19. "He believes that all events are under the direction of infinite wisdom and goodness, and shall surely issue in the glory of God and the good of those who fear him." Newton, *Works* (1985), 1:443.

The Work of Christ: How Jesus Helps Believers Who Are Suffering

John Newton centered his life and ministry upon the person and work of Jesus. Reinke argues that the core of Newton's counsel, the "center" and "core message" of the Christian life, was the all-sufficiency of Jesus Christ.[20] Newton himself affirmed the centrality of Jesus to his own life and ministry in several of his works. For example, he wrote, "I trust the great desire of my soul is that Christ may be all in all to me, that my whole dependence, love, and aim, may center in him alone."[21] Writing to his beloved pastor-friend, William Bull, he asserted, "It is not worthwhile to preach unless we preach Jesus and him crucified. Ah, his name is powerful and precious indeed! May he be our theme in the pulpit and in the parlour, living and dying."[22] Newton summarized his Christocentric emphasis by simply stating to a friend, "'*None* but Jesus,' that is my motto."[23]

As Newton's Christology was central to all of his life and ministry, it was essential to his theology of trials and afflictions.[24] While his affirmation of God's gracious providence was the staple precept forming the framework of his doctrine of suffering, the person and work of Christ was the center. In particular, his view of how Christ assists the struggling believer heavily influenced him. The sufficiency of Jesus was the bedrock of his belief system. He often cited 2 Cor 12:9, where Jesus responds to the apostle Paul regarding his afflicting thorn in the flesh: "My grace is sufficient for you, for power is perfected in weakness."[25] Writing to a friend in affliction, Newton

---

20. Reinke, *Newton*, 30. Reinke's conclusion is not inconsistent with the previous paragraph that concluded that God's providence was the staple doctrine of Newton's theology of suffering. Reinke is making a much broader statement about Newton's overall emphasis in the Christian life. But the two topics often went together in Newton's counsel: he affirmed God's gracious providence in suffering, demonstrating that suffering is purposeful and guided by the wise hand of the heavenly Father. This formed the framework of his doctrine of affliction. Then, he pointed sufferers to Christ, showing that Jesus is a sufficient help for suffering, which was his central theme and goal.

21. Newton, *Twenty-Five Letters*, 57.

22. Newton, *One Hundred and Twenty Nine Letters*, 207–8.

23. Newton, *Works* (1985), 6:42.

24. As an Anglican minister, Newton subscribed to the Thirty-Nine Articles of Religion of the Church of England which articulate a Nicean/Chalcedonian Christology (Article Two). See Bray, *Documents*, 286.

25. Newton, *Works* (1985), 2:316, 1:621. Reinke argues that "few (if any) Bible passages more clearly shaped [Newton's] thinking of the Christian life than Paul's testimony of grace in the Christian life in 2 Cor 12:7–10." Reinke, *Newton*, 42–43.

summarized how trials serve the purpose of growing the believer by demonstrating the sufficiency of Jesus:

> I trust you find the name and grace of Jesus more and more precious to you: his promises more sweet, and your hope in them more abiding; your sense of your own weakness and unworthiness daily increasing; your persuasion of his all-sufficiency to guide, support, and comfort you, more confirmed. You owe your growth in these respects, in a great measure, to his blessing upon those afflictions which he has prepared for you and sanctified to you. May you praise him for all that is past and trust him for all that is to come.[26]

In his letters, Newton identifies four chief ways that Christology affects how the believer responds to suffering: the role of Jesus as High Priest, His role as the "disposer" of trials, how "looking to Christ" brings transformation, and the need for believers to consider Christ's suffering.

Jesus: The Sympathetic High Priest

Newton reminded his readers that Jesus is a sympathetic High Priest who feels for them in their suffering:

> It is a comfortable consideration, that he with whom we have to do, our great High Priest, who once put away our sins by the sacrifice of himself, and now forever appears in the presence of God for us, is not only possessed of sovereign authority and infinite power, but wears our very nature, and feels and exercises in the highest degree those tendernesses and commiserations, which I conceive are essential to humanity in its perfect state.[27]

As genuinely human and divine, Jesus can "feel" the weaknesses of His people and is thus enabled to sympathize with them in their struggles and trials.[28] Newton coined the term "experimental sympathy" to describe this

---

26. Newton, *Works* (1985), 2:220.
27. Newton, *Works* (1985), 2:20.
28. Influenced by the English Puritans, Newton held to the "classical" position that explains Christ's sympathy and His being "touched with our infirmities" as a function of the incarnation. Newton's use of emotional language should not be understood to affirm more modern views which challenge the classical view concerning God's impassibility and simplicity. For an overview of Puritan Christology, see Beeke and Jones, *Puritan Theology*, 335–45. For a more specific understanding of Christ's sympathy from a Puritan perspective, see Goodwin, *Heart of Christ*, 123–58. For an introduction of the modern debate surrounding classical theism, see Dolezal, *All That Is in God*.

unique characteristic of the God-man: "Still more, besides his benevolence, he has an experimental sympathy. He knows our sorrows, not merely as he knows all things, but as one who has been in our situation, and who, though without sin himself, endured when upon earth inexpressibly more for us than he will ever lay upon us."[29] And Newton asserted that the knowledge of Christ's experiential sympathy ought to be a great source of encouragement to believers undergoing difficulties. He explained:

> Alas! what a preposterous, strange, vile creature should I appear to an angel, if he knew me as I am! It is well for me that Jesus was made lower than the angels, and that the human nature he assumed was not distinct from the common nature of mankind, though secured from the common depravity; and because he submitted to be under the law in our name and stead, though he was free from sin himself, yet, sin and its consequences being (for our sakes) charged upon him, he acquired, in the days of his humiliation, an experimental sympathy with his poor people. He knows the effects of sin and temptation upon us, by that knowledge whereby he knows all things; but he knows them likewise in a way more suitable for our comfort and relief, by the sufferings and exercises he passed through for us. Hence arises encouragement.[30]

Christ's experiential knowledge of human weaknesses and temptation enables Him to minister the appropriate "comfort and relief" to the suffering Christian.

Jesus: The Supreme Disposer of Trials

Newton asserted further that Jesus does not simply sympathize with humanity because of His human nature, He is also the "supreme disposer" of the believer's trials and sovereignly "adjusts" them according to His wisdom. Newton wrote:

> When we further consider, that he who thus suffered in our nature, who knows and sympathizes with all our weakness, is now the Supreme Disposer of all that concerns us, that he numbers the very hairs of our heads, appoints every trial we meet with in number, weight, and measure, and will suffer nothing to befall us but what

---

29. Newton, *Works* (1985), 2:20–21.
30. Newton, *Works* (1985), 1:511–12.

> shall contribute to our good;—this view, I say, is a medicine suited to the disease, and powerfully reconciles us unto every cross.[31]

In other words, believers find divine comfort and spiritual "medicine" in their suffering as they remember that Jesus not only sympathizes with them as the Son of Man but "appoints" every detail of every trial in light of His understanding, dispensing each aspect of every difficulty solely for their good. In this view, Newton combines his knowledge of the providence of Christ with the truth of Rom 8:28, that "all things" work together for the believer's good. He particularly liked to emphasize this perspective in trials.

Newton once wrote to a friend who was ill that he wished he could cure or prevent the disease. But he then corrected himself, admitting that perhaps his "intention" would be better than his "judgment." He explained: "Every indisposition, both as to the season, degree, and continuance, is of his appointment likewise. When he sees it needful to remind us of our frailty and our dependence upon him, he will do it. And when his gracious end in sending affliction is answered, he will remove it."[32] Newton went on to explain that believers thus convinced of this perspective will be encouraged that "every changing dispensation is to them an effect of the same unceasing care and attention toward them."[33] In other words, Christ's providence, coupled with His aim to produce "good," is an ongoing expression of His care for His people. Trials, no less than comforts, are indications of Christ's loving attention to believers.

Jesus: Become Like Him by Beholding Him

In Newton's theology, suffering is a critical component of sanctification, the doctrine of spiritual growth. God designs trials as a means of promoting the maturity of His children. Newton believed that believers must actively "look to Christ" in their suffering as their chief comfort. But this admonition must be understood in the context of Newton's view of sanctification. He often said, in light of 2 Cor 3:18, that the believer "becomes" more like Christ by

---

31. Newton, *Works* (1985), 6:5. In a similar letter, he wrote: "When our spirits are overwhelmed within us, he knows our path, and adjusts the time, the measure of our trials, and every thing that is necessary for our present support and seasonable deliverance, with the same unerring wisdom and accuracy as he weighed the mountains in scales and hills in a balance, and meted out the heavens with a span." Newton, *Works* (1985), 2:20.
32. Barlass, *Sermons on Practical Subjects*, 570.
33. Barlass, *Sermons on Practical Subjects*, 570.

"beholding" Christ in His Word. Tony Reinke summarizes Newton's viewpoint as follows: "We become by beholding."[34] Newton explains: "It is thus by looking to Jesus, that the believer is enlightened and strengthened, and grows in grace and sanctification. . . . By beholding we are gradually formed into the resemblance of Him whom we see, admire, and love."[35] When Newton uses the phrase "look to Christ," he means that the believer ought to think about, meditate upon, and even "picture" in his mind's eye the work of Christ for him.[36] In a hymn entitled "Looking Unto Jesus," Newton explains how a believer can meditate upon various aspects of the life, death, and resurrection of Jesus.[37] But this process must be guided by Scripture. In his exposition of 2 Cor 3:18, Newton explained:

> The word of God is a glass in which the goodness and beauty of the Lord Jesus are manifested to the eye of faith by the light of the Holy Spirit. In this wonderful glass the whole object is not seen at once, but every view we take strengthens the sight to discover something not perceived before: and the prospect is not only affecting, but transforming; by beholding we are gradually formed into the resemblance of Him whom we see, admire, and love.[38]

Newton often related this general perspective of sanctification to the particular challenge of trials. When tempted to be overwhelmed or discouraged, he gave this advice to believers: "Look to Jesus." He wrote:

> So when a sense of sin prevails, and the tempter is permitted to assault us with dark and dreadful suggestions, it is easy for us to say, "Be not afraid"; but those who have tried, well know that looking to Jesus is the only and sure remedy in this case;—if we can get a

---

34. Reinke, *Newton*, 131.

35. Newton, *Works* (1985), 2:487.

36. Newton held that the imagination ought to be utilized in meditation, but it must be guided by Scripture. Though there was some diversity, this was the position of the English Puritans. Some Puritans, like Joseph Hall, believed that meditation should be limited to Scripture. Other Puritans, such as John Bunyan, applied imagination more broadly to many aspects of the Christian life, but Bunyan maintained that such use must be directed by Scripture. Newton, who was influenced by Bunyan's writings, seems to lean more toward the latter view. For more on Newton's use of the imagination, see Reinke, *Newton*, 72–74. For an overview of the topic in a Puritan perspective, see Beeke, "Puritan Practice of Meditation," in Beeke and Jones, *Puritan Theology*, 889–907. Regarding the two main views of the Puritans on the use of imagination in meditation and a particular look at Bunyan's view, see Kaufmann, *Pilgrim's Progress and Traditions*.

37. Newton, *Works* (1985), 3:454–55.

38. Newton, *Works* (1985), 2:487.

sight of him by faith, as he once hung between the two thieves, and as he now pleads within the vail [sic], then we can defy sin and Satan, and give our challenge in the Apostle's words, "Who is he that condemneth? It is Christ that died, yea, rather, that is risen again; who also maketh intercession for us."[39]

Newton taught that the spiritual discipline of "looking to Jesus" has a sanctifying effect, especially in seasons of difficulty. He wrote, "To view him by faith, as living, dying, rising, reigning, interceding, and governing for us . . . will enable us to endure any cross, to overcome all opposition, to withstand temptation, and to run in the way of his commandments with an enlarged heart."[40] Thus Newton's counsel to sufferers is summed up in one phrase: "Look to Jesus." He concluded, "The best advice I can send, or the best wish I can form for you, is, that you may have an abiding and experimental sense of those words of the apostle, which are just now upon my mind,—'LOOKING UNTO JESUS.' The duty, the privilege, the safety, the unspeakable happiness, of a believer, are all comprised in that one sentence."[41]

Jesus: His Suffering and the Believer's Suffering

As believers look to Jesus, Newton often encouraged sufferers to meditate specifically on the differences between Christ's sufferings and their own, recognizing that their sufferings are "intermixed with an abundance of mercies." He writes, "But how different were his sufferings from yours? There is no sting in your rod, nor wrath in your cup; your pains and infirmities do not cause you to sweat blood, nor are you left to cry out, 'My God, my God, why hast thou forsaken me?'"[42] With this advice, Newton did not intend to minimize the afflicting experiences of God's people but rather to contrast their experiences with that of Christ and to highlight the many provisions and graces that believers enjoy even in seasons of trials.

Newton also reminded sufferers that there is a unique fellowship with Christ to be sought and enjoyed in their trials. Leaning on Phil 3:10, he noted that this fellowship is one of the many mercies available to the believer in difficulties. He explained, "In whatever states his people are, they may by faith have fellowship with him in their sufferings, and he will by sympathy

---

39. Newton, *Works* (1985), 6:5.
40. Newton, *Aged Pilgrim's Triumph*, 34. See also Newton, *Letters*, 47–48.
41. Newton, *Works* (1985), 6:4. Emphasis original.
42. Newton, *Works* (1985), 6:72.

and love have fellowship and interest with them in theirs."[43] Believers experience the unique love and sympathy of their High Priest through the experience of suffering, which should bring hope and encouragement in their difficulties. Furthermore, the call of Christ for believers to share in His sufferings is motivated by His love for His people since Christ is desirous for greater fellowship with His children. Newton states, "He suffered, being tempted; and because he loves you, he calls you to a participation of his sufferings."[44] Further, he references Col 1:24, reminding believers that they are called to follow Christ's example in his suffering and to "fill up" his afflictions with their own experiences. Newton encourages his fellow sufferers:

> But in affliction he allows his people to have fellowship with him; thus they fill up the measure of his sufferings, and can say, As he was, so are we in the world. Marvel not that the world hates you, neither marvel that Satan rages against you. Should not the disciple be as his Lord? Can the servant expect or desire peace from the avowed enemies of his Master? We are to follow his steps; and can we wish, if it were possible, to walk in a path strewed with flowers, when his was strewed with thorns?[45]

43. Newton, *Works* (1985), 2:21

44. Newton, *Works* (1985), 1:230.

45. The full paragraph is worth quoting at length: "By enduring temptation, you, as a living member of the body of Christ, have the honour of being conformed to your Head. He suffered, being tempted; and because he loves you, he calls you to a participation of his sufferings, and to taste of his cup: not the cup of the wrath of God; this he drank alone, and he drank it all. But in affliction he allows his people to have fellowship with him; thus they fill up the measure of his sufferings, and can say, As he was, so are we in the world. Marvel not that the world hates you, neither marvel that Satan rages against you. Should not the disciple be as his Lord? Can the servant expect or desire peace from the avowed enemies of his Master? We are to follow his steps; and can we wish, if it were possible, to walk in a path strewed with flowers, when his was strewed with thorns? Let us be in nothing terrified by the power of our adversaries; which is to them an evident token of perdition, but to us of salvation, and that of God. To us it is given, not only to believe in Christ, but also to suffer for his sake. If we would make peace with the world, the world would let us alone; if we could be content to walk in the ways of sin, Satan would give us no disturbance; but because grace has rescued us from his dominion, and the love of Jesus constrains us to live to him alone, therefore the enemy, like a lion robbed of his prey, roars against us. He roars, but he cannot devour; he plots and rages, but he cannot prevail; he disquiets, but he cannot destroy. If we suffer with Christ, we shall also reign with him: in due time he will bruise Satan under our feet, make us more than conquerors, and place us where we shall hear the voice of war no more for ever." Newton, *Works* (1985), 1:230–31. In another letter, he wrote: "Jesus despised, reproached, neglected, opposed, and betrayed; and his people admired and caressed: he living in the want of all things, and they filled with abundance: he sweating blood for anguish, and they strangers

Finally, Newton encouraged believers to remember that Christ suffered for them and because of their sin.[46] Meditation on this truth produces encouragement, endurance, and hope in times of trials. He reminded a suffering friend: "Such considerations as these, together with the remembrance of what he suffered for us, are always at hand to compose our souls under troubles, and will be effectual according to the degree of faith."[47] Similarly, he wrote to another struggler: "The thoughts of what we have deserved at his hands, and what Jesus suffered for our sakes, when applied by his Holy Spirit, have a sovereign efficacy to compose our minds, and enable us to say, 'Not my will, but thine be done.'"[48] Meditation on the suffering of Christ for believers not only encourages perseverance in difficulties but transforms experiences of affliction into opportunities for joy. Newton explained, "A lively impression of his love, or of his sufferings for us, or of the glories within the veil, accompanied with a due sense of the misery from which we are redeemed; these thoughts will enable us to be not only submissive, but even joyful, in tribulations."[49]

The doctrine of Christ was the center of Newton's theology and a key component in his understanding of trials and suffering. His greatest desire was to know Christ and to counsel others in such a way that they would know Him as well. He wrote, "I trust the great desire of my soul is that He may be all in all to me, that my whole dependence, love, and aim may center in Him alone."[50]

Suffering Redeemed: How God Works to Benefit Believers Through Suffering

Newton not only emphasized the person and work of Christ in his ministry, he also loved to speak specifically of the work of Christ in redemption. When ministering to suffering Christians, he often brought hope and encouragement by pointing to the ways that Jesus redeems afflictions to

---

to distress: how unsuitable would these things be! How much better to be called to the honour of filling up the measure of his sufferings!" Newton, *Works* (1985), 2:218.

46. Newton, *Works* (1985), 1:230–31, 1:274, 1:452, 2:396, 2:486, 4:14–15, 6:33, 6:72, 6:227, 6:333, 6:425; Newton, *Letters*, 277–79.

47. Newton, *Works* (1985), 6:33.

48. Newton, *Works* (1985), 6:217.

49. Newton, *Works* (1985), 1:621.

50. Newton, *Twenty-Five Letters*, 56–57.

accomplish His good purposes.[51] Newton wrote of six main ways that God utilizes suffering to benefit His people.

To Demonstrate Insufficiency Such that Believers Lean on Christ

Newton believed that God uses suffering as a chief tool to accomplish His purpose of sanctifying believers. In Newton's theology, sanctification aims at two goals that bring glory to God: communion with Christ and conformity to Christ. The first pursuit, communion with Christ, is demonstrated chiefly in the believer's continual reliance upon Christ.[52] The second pursuit, conformity to Christ, manifests itself in spiritual fruit and Christlike character.[53] To accomplish these ends, God transforms and redeems the brokenness, sin, and suffering in the lives of His people.

The first and primary way God utilizes suffering, according to Newton, is by making believers feel their weaknesses, inadequacy, and utter dependence so that they lean solely and continually on Christ. This process reveals and magnifies the sufficiency of Jesus, bringing Him glory. Newton wrote, "We have no sufficiency in ourselves, but we have all-sufficiency in Him."[54] But to realize this perspective, believers must first know their insufficiency. Newton stressed the need for Christians not just to know their weakness but to *feel it* experientially. He wrote:

> The Lord permits us to feel our weakness, that we may be sensible of it; for though we are ready in words to confess that we are weak, we do not so properly know it, till that secret, though unallowed, dependence we have upon some strength in ourselves is brought to the trial, and fails us. To be humble, and, like a little child, afraid of taking a step alone, and so conscious of snares and dangers around us, as to cry to him continually to hold us up that we may be safe, is the sure, the infallible, the only secret of walking closely with him.[55]

---

51. As a small sample to substantiate this trend, see Newton, *Works* (1985), 6:33, 6:72–73, 6:223–24, 6:488, 6:264, 6:338, 1:169–70, 1:693, 1:213–14, 1:525, 1:235, 1:249–50, 1:442, 1:226–27, 1:621–22, 2:436–37, 2:197–99, 2:22, 2:217–20, 2:34, 5:539.

52. Newton, *Works* (1985), 1:442–43, 1:622–23; Newton, *Letters*, 81, 366.

53. Newton, *Works* (1985), 6:72, 1:230–31, 2:24, 2:217.

54. Newton, *Works* (1985), 6:348.

55. Newton, *Works* (1985), 1:693.

One means, noted Newton, that the Lord often uses to accomplish this goal is to remove other "supports" that believers look to and lean upon, such that they might depend entirely on Him:

> When faith and knowledge are in their infancy, the Lord helps this weakness by cordials and sensible comforts; but when they are advanced in growth he exercises and proves them by many changes and trials, and calls us to live more directly upon his power and promises in the face of all discouragements, to hope even against hope, and at times seems to deprive us of every subsidiary support, that we may lean only and entirely upon our beloved.[56]

In suffering, God aims to demonstrate the believer's insufficiency to magnify the sufficiency of Jesus. Newton summarized it this way: "It is by the experience of these evils within ourselves [revealed through trials], and by feeling our utter insufficiency, either to perform duty, or to withstand our enemies, that the Lord takes occasion to show us the suitableness, the sufficiency, the freeness, the unchangeableness of his power and grace."[57] As believers "feel" their insufficiency through trials, they correspondingly feel their need for the sufficiency of Christ's mercy and grace. This dynamic drives believers to lean more on Christ. Newton explained:

> I trust you find the name and grace of Jesus more and more precious to you: his promises more sweet, and your hope in them more abiding; your sense of your own weakness and unworthiness daily increasing; your persuasion of his all-sufficiency to guide, support, and comfort you, more confirmed. You owe your growth in these respects, in a great measure, to his blessing upon those afflictions which he has prepared for you and sanctified to you. May you praise him for all that is past, and trust him for all that is to come.[58]

God also uses trials to lead believers to a heartier pursuit of the spiritual disciplines and other exercises of faith, which develop further dependence upon and trust in the Lord. For example, Newton wrote that trials can "quicken" prayer: "By affliction prayer is quickened, for our prayers are very apt to grow languid and formal in a time of ease."[59] Newton observed

---

56. Newton, *Letters*, 81.
57. Newton, *Letters*, 71.
58. Newton, *Works* (1985), 2:220.
59. Newton, *Works* (1985), 2:197. Newton even advised others on how they should pray during a trial: "Pray for a tender conscience, and a dependent spirit. Watch against

that this "ease" does not usually promote such exercise or dependence, but trials drive the believer to such pursuits. He wrote, "Activity and strength of grace is not ordinarily acquired by those who sit still and live at ease, but by those who frequently meet with something which requires a full exertion of what power the Lord has given them."[60]

Similarly, God redeems afflictions to promote the reading and understanding of Scripture. Newton wrote, "Affliction greatly helps us to understand the Scriptures, especially the promises; most of which being made to times of trouble, we cannot so well know their fulness, sweetness, and certainty, as when we have been in the situation to which they are suited, have been enabled to trust and plead them, and found them fulfilled in our own case."[61] Newton argues that trials are a necessary ingredient for knowing the "fulness, sweetness, and certainty" of many biblical promises, which are often given in the context of suffering. He maintains that Christians need to experience the reality of God's promise worked out in affliction to know them truly. Writing to William Bull, Newton shared his conviction from his own life about "experimental" theology: "I have not only read these gracious promises and believe them to be true, but I have tried them, and found them to be true."[62]

Newton maintained that God provokes believers to more active expressions of faith and dependence through various afflictions, which demonstrate their insufficiency and display the sufficiency of Christ. These transformational dynamics accomplish God's will that believers depend more on Him. Newton summarized this perspective to a suffering friend: "When great trials are in view, we run simply and immediately to our all-sufficient Friend, feel our dependence, and cry in good earnest for help."[63]

---

the motions of self; they are subtle and various. Let no engagements prevent you from reserving seasons of retirement for prayer, and reading the Scriptures. The best company, the best public ordinances, will not compensate for the neglect of these." Newton, *Works* (1985), 5:522.

60. Newton, *Works* (1985), 2:198.

61. Newton, *Works* (1985), 2:197.

62. Newton, *One Hundred and Twenty Nine Letters*, 257. In context, Newton describes the "promises" he has in mind: "All your concerns are in the hands of Him who is infinitely wise, good, and powerful; that to him belong the issues from death; that diseases come and go at his command; that he does all things well; that he can sweeten the most bitter medicines; his wisdom prescribes for our good; that he is so near, so kind, so all-sufficient, as to enable us to rejoice under our heaviest trials; that the time is short; and the Lord will make amends for all, etc., etc." (256–57).

63. Newton, *Works* (1985), 1:622.

Like a mother "weaning" her children, God uses trials to wean believers from self so that they lean on Christ: "By these experiences the believer is weaned more from self, and taught more highly to prize and more absolutely to rely on him, who is appointed unto us of God, Wisdom, Righteousness, Sanctification, and Redemption."[64] The sufficiency of Christ and the insufficiency of self, demonstrated chiefly through experiences of suffering, form the bedrock of Newton's model of sanctification. Since sanctification was a chief goal of Newton's pastoral care, this point demonstrates an essential link between his theology of suffering and his ministerial care.[65]

To Wean Believers from the World

Not only does God wean believers from relying on self, but He endeavors to rescue them from worldliness and an excessive attachment to the things of this life. Newton frequently used the analogy of the Israelites coming out of Egypt into the promised land, noting that they would not have longed for Canaan if their arrangement in Egypt had been satisfying and comfortable. He wrote:

> The Lord, therefore, who knew their weakness and their undue attachment to a country which was not to be their rest, was pleased first to imbitter Egypt to them, and then the news of a Canaan provided for them was welcome. And thus he deals with his people still. Our affections cleave inordinately to the present life. Notwithstanding the many troubles we meet with, sufficient, as it should seem, to wean us from such a state of vanity and disappointment, we can but seldom feel ourselves, in good earnest, desirous to be gone; how much less should we be so if every thing went smooth with us? It is happy for us if we have suffered enough to make us desire a better country.[66]

The Lord would have believers desire a better country, and thus trials and disappointments in this present world help create that desire. Newton described the present life as the "school of the cross" in which "his daily providential dispensations are suited to wean our attachment from

---

64. Newton, *Works* (1985), 1:443–44.

65. Chapter 3 will demonstrate that Newton aimed to facilitate sanctification as a chief goal of his pastoral care ministry.

66. Newton, *Works* (1985), 6:223. Cf. Heb 13:7–16.

every thing here, and to convince us that this cannot be our rest."[67] This perspective, when embraced, transforms a believer's outlook to realize that many of life's losses are "choicest mercies" that elicit thankfulness to God. Newton explained to one such individual who had experienced a difficulty, "I sympathize with all your complaints; but if the Lord is pleased to make them subservient to the increase of your sanctification, to wean you more and more from this world, and to draw you nearer to himself, you will one day see cause to be thankful for them, and to number them amongst your choicest mercies."[68]

As painful as it may be to hear, Newton wrote that even attachment to the dearest relationships in life cannot be a believer's ultimate satisfaction. He counseled one who had recently lost a dear family member: "But when some of our dearest friends are taken from us, the lives of others threatened, and we ourselves are brought low with pain and sickness, then we not only say but feel that this must not, cannot be our rest."[69] Seeking to practice the same principle himself, Newton wrote to his wife that their marital love would not be an inordinate competition with a love for God:

> The Lord has given us a sufficiency of mutual affection, which has been strengthened by a long series of endearments and kind offices, and by a near participation in the comforts and trials of life. And now it should be our great concern and prayer, that our love may not be inordinate, or irregular; nor interfere with what we owe to the great Lover of our souls.[70]

While thankful for God's good gifts, believers should ultimately lean on the Giver alone. Thus, God uses trials to wean believers from the world such that they will lean more on Christ.

To Refine Faith and Conform Believers to Christ

As believers rely more on Christ instead of worldly supports, their faith grows and matures. Newton understood that God uses trials to refine, test, confirm, and strengthen a believer's faith. Leaning on Job 23:10 and Heb 12:11, Newton wrote:

---

67. Newton, *Works* (1985), 6:488.
68. Newton, *Works* (1985), 2:135.
69. Newton, *Works* (1985), 2:197.
70. Newton, *Works* (1985), 5:551–52.

Newton's Theology of Suffering

> The afflictions which at present are not joyous but grievous, shall, when we have been duly exercised by them, yield the peaceable fruits of righteousness. I trust the Lord gives you a measure of patience and submission to his holy will; if so, every thing shall be well; and when he has fully tried you, you shall come forth as gold. . . . How unspeakably better is it to be chastened of the Lord now, than to be left to ourselves for a season, and at last condemned with the world.[71]

When Newton's wife became gravely ill, he wrote to a friend: "The Lord has been pleased to put us in the fire; but, blessed be his name, we are not burnt. Oh, that we may be brought out refined, and that the event may be to the praise of his grace and power!"[72]

These refinements always serve to conform believers to Christ. Growth in Christlikeness is a "grand theme" of Newton's doctrine of suffering and a frequent point of his counsel. Referencing Heb 12, he wrote that God afflicts "not for his pleasure but for our profit, that we may be made partakers of his holiness."[73] Referencing a believer's union to Jesus, he wrote, "By enduring temptation, you, as a living member of the body of Christ, have the honour of being conformed to your Head."[74] Newton further indicated that even temptations thus redeemed serve the purpose of sanctification: "As by temptations we are conformed to the life of Christ, so likewise, by the sanctifying power of grace, they are made subservient to advance our conformity to his image."[75]

Newton understood that the sanctifying effect of trials produces Christlike character. Still, believers must actively lean on the power of the Lord in their afflictions for the development of this character. He explained:

> Many of our graces likewise cannot thrive or shew themselves to advantage without trials; such as resignation, patience, meekness, long-suffering. . . . It is so in the Christian life: activity and strength of grace is not ordinarily acquired by those who sit still and live at ease, but by those who frequently meet with something which requires a full exertion of what power the Lord has given them.[76]

---

71. Newton, *Works* (1985), 6:216–17. For similar language, see also 1:654, 6:194, 6:62, 2:21, 6:59, 2:25, 6:72, 4:486.
72. Newton, *Works* (1985), 6:62.
73. Newton, *Works* (1985), 6:223.
74. Newton, *Works* (1985), 1:230.
75. Newton, *Works* (1985), 1:230.
76. Newton, *Works* (1985), 2:198.

Thus redeemed, Newton taught that believers should see trials as "honorable" because they transform believers more into the likeness of Jesus.[77] In Newton's theology, suffering drives people away from self-dependence to Christ-dependence, and as they behold Him more in the Scriptures, they are transformed into His image. He wrote:

> It is thus by looking to Jesus, that the believer is enlightened and strengthened, and grows in grace and sanctification, according to that passage of St. Paul, "We all with open face," or unvailed [sic] face, "beholding as in a glass the glory of the Lord, are changed into the same image, from glory to glory, as by the Spirit of the Lord," 2 Cor 3:18. The word of God is a glass in which the goodness and beauty of the Lord Jesus are manifested to the eye of faith by the light of the Holy Spirit. In this wonderful glass the whole object is not seen at once, but every view we take strengthens the sight to discover something not perceived before: and the prospect is not only affecting, but transforming; by beholding we are gradually formed into the resemblance of Him whom we see, admire, and love.[78]

To Relate to Other Sufferers

Not only does suffering help believers comfort others who suffer, but it helps them to develop a heart of sympathy and compassion toward others in their afflictions. The apostle Paul wrote to the Corinthians that God comforts the afflicted so that they can comfort others in their distress (2 Cor 1:3–4). Newton often made this point to other ministers. He asserted that other pastors would be more effective in counseling sufferers as they themselves endured suffering. Newton wrote to a fellow minister, "By our own sufferings we learn likewise (the Lord sanctifying them to that end) to sympathize with the afflicted, and to comfort them from the experiences we have had of the Lord's goodness and faithfulness to ourselves."[79] This sympathy represents "the mind of Christ" produced in the believer:

> It is by our own sufferings we learn to pity and sympathize with others in their sufferings: such a compassionate disposition, which excites our feelings for the afflicted, is an eminent branch of the mind

---

77. Newton, *Works* (1985), 2:24.
78. Newton, *Works* (1985), 2:487.
79. Newton, *Works* (1985), 6:264.

> which was in Christ. But these feelings would be very faint, if we did not in our experience know what sorrows and temptations mean.[80]

Thus, God redeems suffering by softening the hearts of believers toward others who suffer and equips them, as they find help and comfort in Christ, to share and minister that encouragement of Christ to other sufferers.

To Reveal Hidden Sins

God also redeems suffering by employing it to reveal the hearts of believers. The more believers see and experience the indwelling sin in their hearts, the more Jesus's grace and mercy are made manifest. God designs trials to reveal the believer's insufficiency and highlight the sufficiency of Christ. Newton maintained that God accomplishes this goal by exposing more of the Christian's depravity and "vileness." Newton wrote, "If we were not vile and worthless beyond expression, the exceeding riches of his grace would not have been so gloriously displayed."[81]

To help believers understand this purpose of God in trials, Newton often wrote of how suffering served the aim of God in revealing hidden sins in the heart that need transformation:

> Afflictions do us good likewise, as they make us more acquainted with what is in our own hearts, and thereby promote humiliation and self-abasement. There are abominations which, like nests of vipers, lie so quietly within, that we hardly suspect they are there till the rod of affliction rouses them: then they hiss and shew their venom. This discovery is indeed very distressing; yet, till it is made, we are prone to think ourselves much less vile than we really are, and cannot so heartily abhor ourselves and repent in dust and ashes.[82]

---

80. Newton, *Works* (1985), 2:198. Elsewhere, Newton wrote: "Whoever is truly humbled will not be easily angry, will not be positive and rash, will be compassionate and tender to the infirmities of his fellow-sinners, knowing, that, if there be a difference, it is grace that has made it, and that he has the seeds of every evil in his own heart; and, under all trials and afflictions, he will look to the hand of the Lord, and lay his mouth in the dust, acknowledging that he suffers much less than his iniquities have deserved. These are some of the advantages and good fruits which the Lord enables us to obtain from that bitter root, indwelling sin." Newton, *Works* (1985), 1:452.

81. Newton, *Works* (1985), 2:81.

82. Newton, *Works* (1985), 2:198–99.

Seen in this light, afflictions are divine rescue operations; first to arouse and reveal, then to rescue believers from hidden wickedness and unseen venomous sin.

Similarly, Newton wrote that God desires to bring believers into a "humble frame of spirit" that depends on Jesus alone. Trials accomplish this goal when they serve to expose sin. He explained, "But how shall we attain this humble frame of spirit? It must be, as I said, from a real and sensible conviction of our weakness and vileness, which we cannot learn (at least I have not been able to learn it) merely from books or preachers. The providence of God concurs with his Holy Spirit in his merciful design of making us acquainted with ourselves."[83] In other words, God works through His providence to reveal believers' indwelling sin, which develops humble dependence upon Christ.

Newton shared with others his own struggle in this regard. In one instance of Polly's many seasons of illness, Newton wrote to a friend regarding their experience:

> I hope we may say, the Lord drew near in the day of distress, and gave us some degree of peaceful resignation to his will. Yet the evil heart of impatience and unbelief had room to show itself, (I speak for one,) and I have the greatest reason to lie ashamed in the dust, and cry "Unclean, unclean." But truly God is good; he considers our frame; he remembers we are but dust: he delighteth in mercy, and therefore we are not consumed.[84]

Even in revealing hidden sins, God desires to show mercy and bring about the believer's transformation. Thus, Newton maintains that the Lord's sovereign design in the exposure of wickedness through affliction is a mechanism of the believer's sanctification.

To Rejoice, Not Just Endure

When believers begin to see and experience God's redemptive hand in their suffering, they are enabled to endure their afflictions better. However, Newton challenged Christians to go a step further. Following Scripture, he maintained that believers ought to rejoice in their sufferings in light of God's redemptive mercies. He wrote:

---

83. Newton, *Works* (1985), 1:693–94.
84. Newton, *Works* (1985), 6:62.

> If the Lord is pleased to put forth his power in us, he can make the heaviest [trial] light. A lively impression of his love, or of his sufferings for us, or of the glories within the veil, accompanied with a due sense of the misery from which we are redeemed; these thoughts will enable us to be not only submissive, but even joyful, in tribulations.[85]

Believers who rejoice in their difficulties and trials glorify God and display Christ's sufficiency.

God designs a redemptive purpose in affliction. The transformation of suffering to accomplish good purposes was the core of Newton's doctrine of suffering and the central theme of his counsel to believers living in trials. Newton maintained that God uses suffering to magnify the sufficiency of Christ by exposing the insufficiency of believers to bring them into a humble, dependent trust in Him.

In summary, Newton believed that every trial was guided by the wise providence of God. He maintained that Christ was sufficient for every trial. He believed that sanctification is God's goal for every believer and that He uses trials to accomplish it. His primary redemptive work, according to Newton, is to demonstrate the believer's insufficiency through suffering in order to highlight and magnify the sufficiency of Christ. In addition, Newton regularly taught that believers need to view their difficulties from a biblically informed, divine perspective.

A Divine Perspective: How Christians Should Interpret Their Suffering

As believers come to see God's redemptive purposes in suffering, their outlook on suffering undergoes a transformation. Not only did Newton counsel others by highlighting God's good goals in their trials, but he also brought hope by helping them to adopt a divine perspective on their difficulties. Newton identified eight essential perspectives that undergirded his theology of suffering and guided his counsel to struggling believers.

---

85. Newton, *Works* (1985), 1:621. Cf. 2:34–36.

The School of the Cross

Newton compared the Christian life to a "school" where pupils (believers) are educated in experiential theology and learn to lean less on themselves and more on Christ. The metaphor of the "school" was Newton's favorite illustration of the believer's experience. He used terms such as "the school of the cross," "the school of Christ," "the school of the Great Teacher," "the school of disappointment," "the school of experience," or sometimes simply "school."[86] Leaning on Heb 12, Newton aimed to help struggling believers understand that afflictions are part of God's spiritual education curriculum, growing them in maturity and Christ-dependence. He wrote to a fellow struggler:

> I suppose you are still in the school of the cross, learning the happy art of extracting real good out of seeming evil, and to grow tall by stooping. The flesh is a sad untoward dunce in this school: but grace makes the spirit willing to learn by suffering; yea, it cares not what it endures, so sin may be mortified, and a conformity to the image of Jesus be increased.[87]

Newton admitted that believers are "poor, slow scholars" in this school, yet they need to view every moment of life as designed by God to teach spiritual lessons. He explained, "His providence and wisdom have so disposed things, in subserviency to the purposes of his grace, that the whole world around them is as a great school; and the events of every day, with which they are connected, have a tendency and suitableness, if rightly improved, to promote their instruction."[88]

Tokens of Love: Disguised Mercies

In his pastoral letters to people, Newton frequently referred to trials as "love tokens" from God and even wrote a hymn titled with this exact phrase.[89] Leaning on Heb 12:1–11, Newton encouraged suffering people to view their afflictions as "love expressions" of a heavenly Father who trains believers for holiness. He writes:

---

86. Newton, *Works* (1985), 2:47, 2:217, 2:226, 5:177, 5:182, 6:347.
87. Newton, *Works* (1985), 2:217.
88. Newton, *Works* (1985), 4:178.
89. Newton, *Works* (1985), 3:456.

> And though they are still in a state of discipline, for the mortification of sin yet remaining in them; and though, for the trial, exercise, and growth of their faith, it is still needful that they pass through many tribulations; yet none of these are strictly and properly penal. They are not the tokens of God's displeasure, but fatherly chastisements, and tokens of his love, designed to promote the work of grace in their hearts and to make them partakers of his holiness.[90]

Because some Christians were prone to see difficulties as divine expressions of punishment, Newton urged them to view troubles as God's fatherly training for righteousness. In a different letter, he called his readers to view trials as "tokens of divine love ... no less than comforts."[91] Afflictions are, in reality, "disguised mercies," designed for the good of believers.[92] He wrote, "How seasonable and important at such a time is the mercy which, under the disguise of an affliction, gives an alarm to the soul, quickens us to prayer, makes us feel our own emptiness, and preserves us from the enemy's net."[93] Writing somewhat tongue-in-cheek, Newton informed a fellow minister that "tokens of love" are called "affliction in the language of mortals."[94]

---

90. Newton, *Works* (1985), 4:238.

91. Newton, *Works* (1985), 1:442.

92. Newton relies primarily upon Heb 12:10–11 as his main rationale for this perspective. He writes, "Years of health are mercies—intervals of sickness are mercies likewise—to the flesh they are not joyous but grievous; but there is a need-be for them, and peaceful fruits of righteousness to be gathered from them, if not immediately yet afterward (Heb 12:11). Afflictions are either small daily medicines which our Physician and best friend sees that our spiritual maladies require, or they are furnaces to prove and purify our graces; or, lastly, they are occasions which his providence appoints for the clearer manifestation of his power and love to us, in us, and by us. When he darkens our sky, and brings a cloud over us, it is a ground on which he designs to paint his covenant rainbow. The rainbow is a beautiful and wonderful appearance, but it is never seen in fair weather. If we had gone to heaven as upon a carpet, without meeting one rough step or strong blast all the way, still we should have been losers." As quoted in Beeke and Jones, *Puritan Theology*, 44. For more development on Newton's point that trials are "love tokens," see Reinke, *Newton*, 191–92.

93. Newton, *Works* (1985), 6:264. In a similar way, he wrote: "What a mercy it is to know that all is in safe hands; that sickness and health, comfort or affliction, life or death, are all equally in the inventory of a believer's privileges,—all equally blessings, though some in one view are more apparently so, and some are sent more under a disguise to do us good; so that, perhaps, we are afraid of them, and would willingly, if we could, prevent them from coming; but they are the Lord's messengers, they have a gracious errand to deliver, and therefore they must have admittance." Newton, *Letters*, 84.

94. Newton, *Letters*, 414.

John Newton's Theology of Suffering and Its Application to Pastoral Care

For Christians, suffering is covert love and disguised mercy, designed by a caring heavenly Father for their spiritual wellbeing.

Light Afflictions in Light of Eternity

Newton held a third transformative perspective regarding the nature of trials. In sum, believers should view temporal and material trials in light of eternal and heavenly rewards. Applying 2 Cor 4:17, he wrote that believers ought to have a "humble confidence," knowing that "the heaviest afflictions are light, and the longest momentary, compared with that far more exceeding and eternal weight of glory, to which he is leading us by them."[95] When Newton's wife became gravely ill, he shared with a friend: "Therefore let us not fear: whatever sufferings may be yet appointed for us, they shall work together for our good; and they are but light and momentary in comparison of that exceeding and eternal weight of glory to which we are drawing nearer every hour."[96] For this perspective to be helpful in suffering, believers must have a clear picture of the joys and mercies that await them in heaven. Newton often referenced Rev 21:4, which states that God will one day wipe away every tear from the eyes of believers, putting away death, pain, mourning, and crying forever. With this truth in mind, he encouraged Christians to counsel others in this way: "We can tell them, that, at the worst, the sufferings of the present life are not worthy to be compared with the glory that shall be revealed; and that therefore, under the greatest pressures, they should so weep as those who expect in a little time to have all their tears wiped away." Weighty, glorious, eternal realities transform present-day burdens into momentary, light afflictions that will one day be removed forever.

The "Need-Be" of Trials

In a broken world, suffering can seem random and meaningless. But Newton believed that trials were full of divine purpose, produced by a good, all-wise God for the benefit of His children. Newton employed a memorable phrase to drive home this point: there is a "need-be" for trials.[97] He wrote,

---

95. Newton, *Works* (1985), 6:425.
96. Newton, *Works* (1985), 6:63.
97. Newton, *Works* (1985), 1:619, 6:99, 2:21, 6:143, 1:178, 6:216, 6:264, 6:90, 6:73,

"But, when we are afflicted, it is because there is a need-be for it. [God] does it not willingly. Our trials are either salutary medicines, or honourable appointments, to put us in such circumstances as may best qualify us to show forth his praise."[98] In other words, trials always have a divinely ordained purpose. They are not accidents, random acts, or moments of bad luck or fate. Instead, God designs difficulties for the spiritual benefit of His children. Newton's letters articulate some of these benefits. For example, by afflictions, "prayer is quickened," scriptural study is strengthened, and graces, such as "patience, meekness [and] long-suffering," are enhanced.[99]

For believers, suffering is always a purposeful and needed work of God to grow them into Christlikeness and further equip them for service. There is always a "need-be" to suffering.

Suffering Less than Our Sins Deserve

It is easy for believers to interpret their suffering as though they were innocent bystanders affected by unjust affliction. However, Newton often encouraged them to remember that their suffering was much less than their sins deserve. He wrote to a young woman, "You have been sick, nigh unto death, but the Lord has raised you up: may he enable you to consider sin as the source and cause of every sorrow; and that the afflictions the Lord sends, however trying to the flesh, are light, compared with what sin deserves."[100] To another sufferer, he offered a similar perspective: "The Lord afflicts us at times: but it is always a thousand times less than we deserve."[101]

On this same theme, Newton often contrasted the undeserved, unspeakably more severe nature of Christ's sufferings with the suffering of believers. He wrote:

> It pleased the Father to bruise him. . . . How different the cup he drank himself, from that which he puts into our hands! His was unmixed wrath and anguish; but all our afflictions are tempered and sweetened with many mercies. Yet we suffer, at the worst, unspeakably less than we deserve; but he had done nothing amiss.

2:217, 6:338, 1:443, 1:691, 1:249, 4:156. Though a frequent term of Newton, it is uncertain if he coined the term or borrowed it from others.

98. Newton, *Works* (1985), 6:338.
99. Newton, *Works* (1985), 2:197.
100. Newton, *Works* (1985), 6:444.
101. Newton, *Works* (1985), 2:151.

> Now let our pains be all forgot;
> Our hearts no more repine;
> Our sufferings are not worth a thought,
> If, Lord, compared with thine.[102]

In other words, Newton believed that believers are comforted in their own suffering by meditating on the sufferings of Christ, which were much more severe than theirs and utterly undeserved.

A Multiplicity of Mercies

Just as believers are prone to be blind to the sufferings that their sins rightly deserve, they also tend to miss the incredible mercies they enjoy that are eclipsed by their difficulties. Newton directed afflicted believers to the multitude of mercies that surrounded them in their afflictions. He wrote:

> Then, again, our trials are intermixed with abundance of mercies; temporal mercies which appear exceedingly valuable to those who feel the want of them, and have a load of poverty, neglect, &c. superadded to grievous pains and sicknesses to struggle with; but, especially, spiritual mercies. In a time of sickness we may see in the strongest light the privilege of being a believer, to have a right to cast ourselves and our all upon the covenant mercies of God in Christ.[103]

Newton often stressed that the "abundance of mercies" in difficulties are abundant proofs of God's love toward believers: "The innumerable comforts and mercies with which he enriches even those we call darker days, are sufficient proofs that he does not willingly grieve us: but when he sees a need-be for chastisement, he will not withhold it because he loves us; on the contrary, that is the very reason why he afflicts."[104]

God always wraps the afflictions of believers in numerous mercies that soften the sting of the trial and assure them of His goodness and love toward them. Newton longed for believers to have eyes to see these tender mercies in their suffering.

---

102. Newton, *Works* (1985), 6:214.
103. Newton, *Works* (1985), 6:72.
104. Newton, *Works* (1985), 2:21.

Newton's Theology of Suffering

The Post of Affliction Is the Post of Honor

In his pastoral ministry, Newton employed a variety of metaphors to communicate biblical truths and illustrate theological points. He observed that Christians often view their trials as God's condemning penalties when, in fact, they are redemptive mercies for their benefit. Like Job's friends, Christians are prone to view their difficulties as God's punishment rather than occasions of spiritual privilege. To aid believers to adopt this perspective, Newton utilized this analogy:

> Long observation convinces me, that the temptations which some endure are not chastisements brought upon them by unfaithfulness, or for any thing remarkably wrong in their spirit or walk; I often rather consider that in his warfare, as in worldly wars, the post of danger and difficulty is the post of honour, and as such assigned to those whom he has favoured with a peculiar measure of his grace.[105]

When Christians pray for opportunities to serve God and maximize their lives for His praise and glory, He often answers their prayers favorably by assigning them to difficult situations of strategic ministry. Newton explained:

> Where the Lord gives this desire [to most glorify and praise the Lord] he will gratify it; and as afflictions, for the most part, afford the fairest opportunities of this kind, therefore it is, that those whom he is pleased eminently to honour are usually called, at one time or another, to the heaviest trials; not because he loves to grieve them, but because he hears their prayers, and accepts their desires of doing him service in the world.[106]

Newton encouraged believers in such a state to consider it an honor and privilege that God would call them to such a position: "Should we, therefore, not account it an honour and a privilege, when the Captain of our salvation assigns us a difficult post? since he can and does (which no earthly commander can) inspire his soldiers with wisdom, courage, and strength, suitable to their situation."[107]

---

105. Newton, *Works* (1985), 1:628.
106. Newton, *Works* (1985), 2:35.
107. Newton, *Works* (1985), 2:35–36.

John Newton's Theology of Suffering and Its Application to Pastoral Care

Resign All to Him

Newton's final perspective on suffering is perhaps his most foundational and critical point, as it formed what he believed to be God's ultimate purpose in suffering. He desired that all believers would "resign all to Him," to trust Him with every part of their lives ultimately. He wrote:

> If every event, great and small, is under the direction of his providence and purpose; and if he has a wise, holy, and gracious end in view, to which every thing that happens is subordinate and subservient; then we have nothing to do, but with patience and humility to follow as he leads, and cheerfully to expect a happy issue. The path of present duty is marked out; and the concerns of the next and every succeeding hour are in his hands. How happy are they who can resign all to him, see his hand in every dispensation, and believe that he chooses better for them than they possibly could for themselves![108]

Newton often encouraged suffering Christians to "resign all to Him" or "submit" to God's daily designs. But it is essential to understand his meaning. Christian resignation is not the same as fatalism, since believers affirm that God "has a wise, holy, and gracious end in view" and believe that "he chooses better for them than they possibly could for themselves." Nor does Newton intend to promote Christian stoicism, an emotional indifference to trials. In a different letter, he clarifies his meaning:

> Christian resignation is very different from that stoical stubbornness which is most easily practised by those unamiable characters whose regards centre wholly in self; nor could we in a proper manner exercise submission to the will of God under our trials, if we did not feel them. He who knows our frame is pleased to allow, that afflictions for the present are not joyous, but grievous. But to them that fear him he is near at hand, to support their spirits, to moderate their grief, and in the issue to sanctify it; so that they shall come out of the furnace refined, more humble, and more spiritual.[109]

In other words, the believer who resigns all to God is not indifferent or void of appropriate feelings of grief. In a similar letter, Newton noted that even the Lord Jesus wept at the tomb of Lazarus, demonstrating that godly feelings, reasonable in their season, are not inconsistent with a humble

---

108. Newton, *Works* (1985), 1:456.
109. Newton, *Works* (1985), 2:25.

submission to the will of God in difficulties.[110] However, God sanctifies these moments to "moderate" grief and keep the believer from spiraling into "anguish and bitterness of sorrow."[111]

Avoiding the errors of both fatalism and stoicism, Newton taught that Christian resignation was a humble, quiet acceptance of all life's challenges, built upon a robust trust in Christ, which actively affirms His goodness, care, and wisdom to bring about His good purposes. Newton explained, "Let us pray for submission to the will of God, and that we may welcome every event, from a sense of his hand being concerned in it, and a persuasion (which his promises warrant) that, some way or other, all shall conduce to our final advantage."[112] Not only did Newton possess this desire for others, but he also prayed for it in himself. He wrote, "The Lord has promised to direct, moderate, sanctify, and relieve every trial of every kind. I long to have a more entire submission to his will, and a more steadfast confidence in his word, to trust him and wait on him, to see his hand and praise his name in every circumstance of life great and small."[113]

For Newton, Christian "resignation" was the end goal since the term encapsulated the core dynamics of how a healthy Christian should respond to trials.[114] His aim was that believers would find happiness in fully trusting Him as sovereign over all things and as the One who is ultimately wise to choose what is truly best for them.

---

110. "The Lord, who knows our frame, does not expect or require that we should aim at a Stoical indifference under his visitations. He allows, that afflictions are at present not joyous, but grievous; yea, he was pleased when upon earth to weep with his mourning friends when Lazarus died." Newton, *Works* (1985), 2:32.

111. Newton, *Works* (1985), 2:32. "But he has graciously provided for the prevention of that anguish and bitterness of sorrow, which is, upon such occasions, the portion of such as live without God in the world; and has engaged, that all shall work together for good, and yield the peaceable fruits of righteousness. May he bless you with a sweet serenity of spirit, and a cheerful hope of the glory that shall shortly be revealed." Newton, *Works* (1985), 2:32.

112. Newton, *Works* (1985), 5:540.

113. Newton, *Letters*, 63.

114. In his three letters on Christian growth and sanctification, Newton names "resignation" as a chief mark of what he believed to be the final stage of a believer's maturity. See Newton, *Works* (1985), 1:214. He also names "resignation" as a chief mark of the "mind of Christ"; Newton, *Works* (1985), 2:186, 4:206. In his other letters, Newton regularly names "resignation" as a mark of mature Christianity. See Newton, *Works* (1985), 1:170, 1:456, 1:523, 1:538, 2:25–28, 2:186, 2:514, 5:554–55, 5:571–72, 6:55, 6:62, 6:72, 6:143, 6:197, 6:238, 6:245.

Satan and Temptation in the Context of Trials

Two additional, and closely related, subjects must be explored to understand fully Newton's theology of suffering, since they tie in so closely with his understanding of afflictions. In *Letters on Religious Subjects*, Newton included a letter entitled "On Temptation," articulating his viewpoint of Satan and temptation. Newton believed that "temptations, in their own nature, are grievous and dreadful, yet when, by the grace of God, they are productive of these [spiritually valuable] effects, they deserve to be numbered among the 'all things which are appointed to work together for the good of those who love him.'"[115] These spiritually beneficial effects include items mentioned previously, such as revealing hidden sins, proving faith, quickening prayer, conformity to Christ, and promoting greater dependence upon the Lord.[116] Beyond these, Newton added two additional values of redeemed suffering.

God's Design in Allowing Temptations and Assaults from Satan

First, the Lord intends to use temptation to prevent greater evils. Newton wrote, "I doubt not, however burdensome your trials may at some seasons prove, you are enabled, by your composed judgment, to rejoice in them, and be thankful for them. You know what you suffer now; but you know not what might have been the consequence, if you had never smarted by the fiery darts of the wicked one."[117] Second, temptations display the power, wisdom, and grace of God in supporting a believer when he is pushed, through temptation, beyond his own strength to persevere. Newton often illustrated this principle by borrowing the picture from Exodus of the burning bush that was not consumed. He explained, "This emblem is generally applicable to the state of a Christian in the present life, but never more so than when he is in the fire of temptation."[118]

In Newton's theology, the temptations of believers and the works of Satan overlap significantly. Though he identifies some particular temptations unique to Satan, he usually makes no distinctions.[119] But Newton

---

115. Newton, *Works* (1985), 1:227.
116. Newton, *Works* (1985), 1:227, 230–32.
117. Newton, *Works* (1985), 1:227.
118. Newton, *Works* (1985), 1:228.
119. Newton wrote, "It is not always easy, nor is it needful, exactly to draw the line between the temptations of Satan and our own corruptions: but sometimes it is not

asserted that there were specific reasons that God allows His children to be tempted by Satan. Using the example of Job, Newton explained several of these purposes:

> The Lord, for the vindication of Job's integrity, and for the manifestation of his own faithfulness and power in favour of his servant, was pleased to give Satan leave to try what he could do. The experiment answered many good purposes: Job was humbled, yet approved; his friends were instructed; Satan was confuted, and disappointed; and the wisdom and mercy of the Lord, in his darkest dispensations towards his people, were gloriously illustrated. This contest and the event were recorded for the direction and encouragement of his church to the end of time.[120]

Further, the Lord allows Satan to assault believers as it provides an occasion to display the power and strength of God made perfect in weakness.[121] Leaning on a favorite passage, 2 Cor 12, Newton wrote to the Rev. John Campbell, "Messengers from Satan and thorns in the flesh are *gifts* and mercies if they preserve us from being exalted above measure."[122]

---

impossible to distinguish them." As one example, Newton mentions the situation when a believer is tempted to blaspheme the name of Christ. He wrote, "When a child of God is prompted to blaspheme the name that he adores, or to commit such evils as even unsanctified nature would recoil at; the enemy has done it." Newton, *Works* (1985), 1:234.

120. Newton, *Works* (1985), 1:228–29.

121. Newton used this analogy to demonstrate the point: "We handle vessels of glass or china with caution, and endeavour to preserve them from falls and blows, because we know they are easily broken. But if a man had the art of making glass malleable, and, like iron, capable of bearing the stroke of a hammer without breaking, it is probable, that, instead of locking it carefully up, he would rather, for the commendation of his skill, permit many to attempt to break it, when he knew their attempts would be in vain. Believers are compared to earthen vessels, liable in themselves to be destroyed by a small blow; but they are so strengthened and tempered by the power and supply of Divine grace, that the fiercest efforts of their fiercest enemies against them may be compared to the dashing of waves against a rock. And that this may be known and noticed, they are exposed to many trials; but the united and repeated assaults of the men of the world, and the powers of darkness, afford but the more incontestable demonstration, that the Lord is with them of a truth, and that his strength is made perfect in their weakness." Newton, *Works* (1985), 1:229–30.

122. Newton, *Letters*, 370.

John Newton's Theology of Suffering and Its Application to Pastoral Care

Satan's Strategies Against Believers

Writing to his dear friend, the Rev. William Bull, Newton made this observation: "[Satan] is always ready to fish, as we say, in troubled waters, and to assault believers when under the pressure of great trials."[123] Thus, trials are a strategic occasion for the enemy to gain a foothold in the life of the Christian. To help believers see through these efforts, Newton articulated several strategies of Satan and particular opportunities that he often utilizes to tempt, distract, and disquiet God's people when facing various trials. First, Satan works to "hide from them the Lord's designs in permitting him thus to rage."[124] Perhaps this point explains why Newton regularly reminded sufferers of God's good intentions to redeem their afflictions for good. Second, Satan tempts believers during trials to "utter impatient speeches, which do but aggravate their distress."[125] Newton cites both Job and Jeremiah, who maintained their spiritual integrity until they began to speak. He gave this counsel to afflicted believers: "We cannot prevent dreadful thoughts from arising in our hearts; but we should be cautious of giving them vent, by speaking unadvisedly."[126] Third, Satan works to convince believers that every corruption they feel must of necessity arise from their hearts. For example:

> When a child of God is prompted to blaspheme the name that he adores, or to commit such evils as even unsanctified nature would recoil at; the enemy has done it, and shall be answerable for the whole guilt. The soul in this case is passive, and suffers with extreme reluctance what it more dreads than the greatest evils which can affect the body.[127]

Fourth, the enemy aims to drive believers away from the throne of grace in prayer, particularly in moments of temptation. Newton explained, "By discontinuing prayer, we give the enemy the greatest encouragement possible; for then he sees that his temptations have the effect which he intends by them, to intercept us from our stronghold."[128] Satan also works this strategy on the other side of temptation, when a believer falls into sin, keeping

123. Newton, *One Hundred and Twenty Nine Letters*, 181.
124. Newton, *Works* (1985), 1:233.
125. Newton, *Works* (1985), 1:233.
126. Newton, *Works* (1985), 1:234.
127. Newton, *Works* (1985), 1:234.
128. Newton, *Works* (1985), 1:234–35. Newton adds, "But so long as prayer is restrained, our burden is increased."

him from the throne of grace in confession.[129] If this strategy fails, Satan will resort to critiquing the believer's attempts at prayer, which weary him and create inappropriate guilt. Fifth, since Satan cannot destroy a believer, he endeavors to stir up worry through dreadful suggestions. Newton experienced this affliction personally when his adopted niece, Betsy "Eliza" Catlett, went through a season of depression. He wrote to William Bull, "She is in a deep melancholy, and her distress is probably aggravated by the dreadful suggestions of that enemy who, when he is permitted, is always ready to worry those whom he may not destroy."[130] Newton related her experience to his good friend, William Cowper, who went through multiple protracted seasons of depression and experienced overwhelming thoughts of God's condemnation.[131] Sixth, Satan tempts believers to be lazy and rest in their battle with sin. Newton liked to employ scenes from John Bunyan's work *The Pilgrim's Progress* to illustrate his teachings. To explain this strategy of Satan, he used Bunyan's picture of the "Enchanted Ground," a deceptive place of rest where pilgrims are tempted to stop and sleep. In such cases, trials awaken believers from the temptation of spiritual slumber. He wrote, "We live on an enchanted ground, are surrounded with snares, and if not quickened by trials, are very prone to sink into formality or carelessness."[132] For Newton, the affliction of Eliza's depression served this purpose. He wrote, "Perhaps Satan was spreading a net for my feet, or preparing a spell to lull me to sleep upon the enchanted ground—and the Lord has in this way interposed to disappoint his malice."[133]

---

129. "If the enemy surprises you, and your heart smites you, do not stand astonished as if there was no help, nor give way to sorrow as if there was no hope, nor attempt to heal yourself; but away immediately to the Throne of Grace, to the great Physician, to the compassionate High Priest, and tell him all. Satan knows, that if he can keep us from confession, our wounds will rankle; but do you profit by David's experience, Ps 32:3–5." Newton, *Works* (1985), 2:48–49.

130. Newton, *One Hundred and Twenty Nine Letters*, 305. Newton discusses the same situation in his letters to the Coffin family.

131. Writing about Cowper's situation, Newton relied specifically on the example of Job to substantiate his understanding of Satan's influence, particularly Job 7:14–15 and 16:11–14. He seems to apply this same understanding to Betsy's condition as well. See Newton, "Letter to Rev. Samuel Greatheed," 1.

132. Newton, *Aged Pilgrim's Triumph*, 33.

133. Newton, *Letters of John Newton*, 90.

Satan's Power and Influence

Newton was clear that God must permit Satan to afflict and tempt believers. He is on a chain that cannot be broken.[134] The devil has the most influence on unbelievers since "the heart while unrenewed is his workshop," though the renewed hearts of believers are at risk as well.[135] For believers, Newton maintained that the devil's chief means of influence comes through the imagination. He explained, "His temptations may be considered under two heads—the terrible and the plausible."[136] In the former temptation, Satan attacks humble Christians with tender consciences like a roaring lion, filling their minds with "dark and horrible thoughts," displacing their peace and leaving them distressed in what is clearly a satanic assault. In the latter temptation, he subtly attacks careless and self-dependent Christians as an angel of light, striving to trap them in faulty judgments and misguided conduct. Regarding this second approach, Newton wrote that Satan's "motions are so insinuating, and so connatural to the man of sin within us, that they cannot be easily distinguished from the workings of our own thoughts."[137]

While medicine was primitive in Newton's day, he observed that Satan seemed to have more influence over the imaginations of people with "nervous disorders" and other physical maladies. Newton also held that specific individuals experiencing various forms of bodily weakness are more prone to overt attacks of the enemy. For example, his adopted niece, Eliza Catlett, suffered for a year with an indigestion disorder, which had a significant adverse effect on her "nervous system." Newton then explained, "By the Lord's permission, [this effect] has given Satan an open door to fill her imagination with horrible thoughts concerning God and his word. He persuades her that all her former religious profession was hypocrisy; that the Lord has now deserted her, cut her off, and set her up as a mark of his endless displeasure, etc."[138]

Newton had ministered to so many people of weak constitution, he thought of himself as a sort of "*doctor* to persons troubled in mind," in

---

134. "Satan will try to hinder and disturb you; but he is in a chain which he cannot break, nor go a step farther than he is permitted." Newton, *Works* (1985), 1:698.

135. Newton, *Letters*, 319.

136. Newton, *Letters*, 319.

137. Newton, *Letters*, 319.

138. Newton, *Letters of John Newton*, 89.

that he understood their condition.¹³⁹ In his most specific description, he explained:

> The human frame is the medium of the soul's perceptions, and when the animal spirits, or nervous fluid, or by whatever name the physicians please to call that *hidden inscrutable something* which pervades and influences the constitution, is affected in a certain way—it is to the mind, what a colored glass is to the eye, it gives a tincture to every object. Yes it opens a door to the enemy, and gives him access to the imagination. I cannot explain this, but I have no doubt of the fact.¹⁴⁰

In such cases, Newton's solution, as with every other form of affliction and suffering, was to look to Christ alone for help and healing. Speaking of his dear Eliza, he wrote, "My trial is great, but the all-sufficient Lord is my support. I am sure this affliction did not spring out of the ground. . . . I aim to resign her and myself into his hands, and to hope that all will work for his glory and our final benefit."¹⁴¹

In his sermon "Death Swallowed Up in Victory," Newton reminded his listeners that Satan is a defeated foe and will one day be put away forever. He preached:

> How much have some of them suffered from his subtle wiles and his fiery darts! from his rage as a roaring lion, from his cunning as a serpent lying in their path, and from his attempts to deceive them under the semblance of an angel of light! 2 Cor 11:14. But now they are placed out of his reach. Death and Satan are swallowed up. The victory is complete. The wicked one shall never have access to touch or disturb them any more.¹⁴²

Conclusion

John Newton's theology of suffering formed the backbone of his spirituality since it was intimately linked to the believer's sanctification. Newton's goal in pastoral care was to help Christians in the challenges and difficulties of life by assisting believers to mature in their communion with Christ and

---

139. Newton, *Letters of John Newton*, 42.
140. Newton, *Letters of John Newton*, 43.
141. Newton, *One Hundred and Twenty Nine Letters*, 305, 309.
142. Newton, *Works* (1985), 4:485.

conformity to Christ. These pursuits emerged directly from his theology of suffering. This chapter has identified the five doctrinal distinctives that formed the basis of this theology.

First, Newton believed that God's wise, gracious providence guides every moment of life, including suffering. Afflictions are not random or purposeless, but governed by the good purposes of the heavenly Father. This doctrine formed the framework of his system. Second, Christ is a sympathetic High Priest to believers who suffer. As believers turn to Him for help in their difficulties, He demonstrates His all-sufficiency in the midst of their own insufficiency. This process draws believers into more *communion with Christ*. Third, God redeems suffering by using it to sanctify believers, conforming them to the image of Christ. This point demonstrates the crucial link between suffering and sanctification. God intends to draw believers to lean more on Christ, seeing his complete sufficiency and being transformed more into His likeness. He accomplishes these sanctifying goals through the vehicle of trials and suffering. Thus, believers are shaped in *conformity to Christ*. Fourth, as believers begin to interpret their own suffering as God's kind, transformative work, it brings comfort and encouragement to their difficulties. Finally, while Satan has significant influence in the lives of believers, God overrules his intentions for good to further strengthen believers and to magnify the sufficiency of Jesus. Newton concludes, "When trials are in view, we run simply and immediately to our all-sufficient friend, feel our dependence and cry in good earnest for help. . . . Here, indeed, we may expect some trials and difficulties, but His grace shall be sufficient to support and comfort, to sanctify and deliver."[143]

The structure of Newton's doctrine of affliction not only supported his spirituality, it served to shape, inform, and direct his model of pastoral care and counseling. The next chapter will develop this essential connection.

---

143. Newton, *Works* (1985), 1:662; Newton, *Twenty-Five Letters*, 85.

3

Newton's Pastoral Care

JOHN NEWTON MAINTAINED A diverse pastoral ministry in his forty-three years of ministerial service. While his clerical duties included regular preaching, mentoring, prayer meetings, children's education, missionary endeavors, pastoral training, and ecumenical meetings, his pastoral care and hymn writing are likely his most impactful achievements.[1] This chapter will focus on Newton's pastoral care ministry and demonstrate that his theology of suffering formed an essential structure that served to shape, inform, and direct his model of pastoral care and counseling.

Overview of John Newton's Pastoral Care Ministry

Newton began his first pastorate in Olney on May 27, 1764. From these earliest days of ministerial life, he prioritized the spiritual care of his people. After several months into his curacy at Olney, he wrote to Lord Dartmouth, "My afternoons are generally spent visiting the people, three or four families a day."[2] Aitken adds that "he was a most diligent pastoral visitor. He

---

1. This chapter does not focus on Newton's influence as a hymn writer. For information on this topic, see Aitken, *John Newton*, chapters 30–33; Huntly, "Newton and Cowper," 29–33; Rouse, "Introduction to the Olney Hymns."
2. Letter from John Newton to Lord Dartmouth, dated February 11, 1765 (Legge, *Historical Manuscripts Commission*, 175).

emphasized his determination to 'converse singly' with individuals for an hour at a time, keeping a careful record of these appointments. He also offered spiritual counsel to several parishioners each week in his vicarage study."[3] Newton exemplified skill in casuistry, applying biblical truth to various life situations.[4] Hindmarsh explains that "there were sin-sick souls to be comforted and unfeeling profligates to be upbraided. All of this required that he be a skilled casuist. It was in routine visits and emergency pastoral calls that he sought to enforce and to apply his public teaching to the particular cases of individuals in the parish."[5] As his affection and skill became more well known, many traveled to Olney to meet with him in his home. Bull states that "his friendly and hospitable home . . . was a place to which the troubled and tempted resorted."[6]

Some authors, such as Cecil, did not regard Newton as an exceptionally gifted preacher. Cecil writes that "he did not generally aim at accuracy in the *composition* of his sermons, nor at any *address* in the delivery of them. His utterance was far from clear, and his attitudes ungraceful."[7] However, Newton's shepherding care and pastoral fondness delivered through his preaching made him both effective with and loved by the people. Cecil explains, "He possessed, however, so much affection for his people, and so much zeal for their best interests, that the defect of his manner was of little consideration with his constant hearers; at the same time, his capacity and habit of entering into their trials and experience, gave the highest interest to his ministry among them."[8] In other words, Newton's love and care for his people, particularly his ability to connect with his hearers in their suffering, endeared the people to him and allowed him significant influence concerning the care of souls.

Newton not only prioritized spiritual counsel in formal duties like preaching and pastoral visits, but he also engaged in pastoral care during informal settings. John Campbell, the pastor of the Congregational Church

---

3. Aitken, *John Newton*, 187.

4. "Casuistry" may be defined as the "art of moral theology applied with biblical integrity to various cases that a person is confronted with in his conscience or life." Beeke and Jones, *Puritan Theology*, 927.

5. Hindmarsh, *English Evangelical Tradition*, 204.

6. Newton, *Letters*, x–xi.

7. Cecil, *Life of John Newton*, 193.

8. Cecil, *Life of John Newton*, 193. Further, "the parent-like tenderness and affection, which accompanies his instruction, made them prefer him to preachers, who, on other accounts, were much more generally popular." Cecil, *Life of John Newton*, 193.

in Kingsland and friend of Newton, recorded dozens of Newton's "conversational remarks" in casual circumstances with various people.[9] These informal comments demonstrate that Newton made the most of every opportunity to care for souls.[10] For example, Campbell reported that Newton responded to a person struggling in a season of difficulty, "Crosses are good things! God does most good to man by them—they humble him, they bring him to know his dependence on God."[11] Whether formal or informal, in season or out of season, Newton could be found caring for the souls of people.

However, Newton's letter-writing ministry was his favorite and most effective means of pastoral care.[12] He believed that God had called him specifically to the care of souls through written correspondence. William Jay records Newton's thoughts on this point: "I rather reckoned upon doing more good by some of my other works than by my 'Letters,' which I wrote without study, or any public design; but the Lord said, 'You shall be most useful by them'; and I learned to say, 'Thy will be done! Use me as Thou pleases, only make me useful.'"[13] Newton learned the value of spiritual advice through letters he received in his own life from the mentoring pen of early influences like David Jennings and Alexander Clunie.[14] Later, Newton wrote his autobiography as a series of letters to his friend, Thomas Haweis. The publication of his *Authentic Narrative* became an instant success, demonstrating to Newton the potential spiritual influence of writing correspondence.

The "familiar letter" was a favored tool of correspondence in the evangelical movement of the eighteenth century. It mainly served as a vehicle for "religious conversation," where the "focus of the letters was on personal spirituality."[15] Newton utilized this "paper converse" to provide spiritual

9. Campbell, *Letters and Conversational Remarks*. Many of these conversational remarks reflect similar themes from his formal letters of counsel and care.

10. There are other similar collections of informal remarks made by Newton in additional works. Cecil includes a section of his *Memoirs* entitled "Remarks Made by Mr. Newton, in Familiar Conversation" in Newton, *Works* (1985), 1:99–108. William Jay's autobiography contains a similar piece; see Jay, *Autobiography*, 303–22.

11. Jay, *Autobiography*, 163.

12. Packer called Newton the "greatest pastoral letter-writer of all time." As quoted in Murray, "John Newton," 7.

13. Jay, *Autobiography*, 317.

14. For more information on how these and other mentors shaped his early life as a believer, see chapter 1.

15. Hindmarsh, *English Evangelical Tradition*, 243. He goes on to conclude, "The familiar letter was a particularly fitting genre for spiritual direction" (245).

care to people, especially those beyond the walls of his congregation in Olney. Aitken explains that the letters "started out as Newton's personal replies to a number of correspondents who wrote to him seeking his spiritual advice on topics of general interest."[16] Encouraged by the success of his autobiography, Newton began submitting copies of some of these letters to a gospel magazine where they were published under the pseudonym "Omicron." The gospel magazine letters became so popular they were later published as a stand-alone volume.[17] Thus, Newton transformed the common mode of communication via letters and "pioneered a new form of ministry—spiritual direction by published correspondence."[18]

As Newton's published letters circulated, various readers began writing to him, seeking his counsel regarding their own questions and personal struggles. His pastoral care expanded greatly as the needs in his congregation were compounded by outside requests for spiritual advice. Newton's comments to William Bull demonstrate the extent of his pastoral care activity at Olney:

> I have seldom one hour free from interruption. Letters come that must be answered, visitants that must be received, business that must be attended to. I have a good many sheep and lambs to look after, sick and afflicted souls dear to the Lord. . . . Among those various avocations night comes before I am ready for noon and the week closes when according to the state of my business it should not be more than Tuesday.[19]

This trend continued and increased throughout his life and ministry. At seventy years old, Newton lamented, "I am so overwhelmed with correspondence though I wrote more than forty while abroad, I have nearly as many by me that should be answered, if I could find time, and almost every post adds to their number."[20]

Newton published five hundred pastoral letters during his lifetime, "making him the leading evangelical commentator on religious subjects

---

16. Aitken, *John Newton*, 241.

17. Aitken, *John Newton*, 22.

18. Aitken, *John Newton*, 244. Aitken may overstate the case a bit here as James Hervey had published *Theron and Aspio* which employed some of the same elements as Newton's letters.

19. Newton, *One Hundred and Twenty Nine Letters*, 6.

20. As quoted in Gordon, "John Newton," 105.

in Britain."[21] Following his death, another five hundred letters were published.[22] The large number of letters available for study yields clear insights regarding Newton's pastoral care practice. The previous chapter demonstrated that Newton's theology of suffering played a critical role in his understanding of the Christian life and the doctrine of sanctification. This chapter will show that his biblically informed view of trials formed an essential structure in his content and pastoral care method.

Pastoral Care Is Applied Theology

The letters of John Newton demonstrate that his pastoral care practice consisted of the careful, wise, compassionate application of his theology to the particular struggles and situations of people. In other words, Newton's spiritual counsel derived from his doctrinal convictions. Gordon explains that "he had come to some very definite theological conclusions, and he then consciously used these to influence his interpretation of life situations and to provide appropriate counsel."[23]

Newton's emphasis on practical theology and "experimental" spirituality derived from the influences of Puritan theology and the evangelical movement of the eighteenth century. As demonstrated in the previous chapters, Puritans like John Flavel and Richard Baxter shaped Newton's understanding of Christian doctrine, biblical spirituality, and pastoral care. Though Newton rarely used the term, he believed and practiced the Puritan concept of casuistry, the "art of moral theology applied with biblical integrity to various cases that a person is confronted with in his conscience or life."[24] For the Puritans, pastoral care was the application of biblical theology to life for God's glory. Likewise, the spirituality of the evangelical movement of Newton's day emphasized "lived doctrine centered on Christ," the application

---

21. Aitken, *John Newton*, 244.
22. Reinke, *Newton*, 23.
23. Gordon, "John Newton," 91.
24. Beeke and Jones, *Puritan Theology*, 927. Though Newton practiced casuistry, he held to a much simpler form. Whereas Puritan pastors like Richard Baxter and William Perkins produced larger volumes aimed at addressing every conceivable "case of conscience" a Christian might experience, Newton's formula emphasized gospel simplicity. He wrote, "A simple desire of pleasing God, and adorning the gospel, will preclude many cases of minute casuistry, which occupy little and trifling minds." Newton, *Works* (1985), 6:409.

of theology to life.²⁵ In Newton's ministry, his doctrinal convictions regarding suffering influenced his pastoral care in five specific ways.

Five Pathways of Effective Ministry in Pastoral Care

First, Newton's doctrine shaped his direction of care when counseling those who were suffering. The five doctrinal distinctives that form Newton's theology of suffering establish five unique pathways in which ministers of the gospel can travel to care for hurting people.²⁶ Each avenue of ministry directs pastors to God-ordained purposes in pastoral care, such as bringing encouragement or facilitating sanctification. While significant overlap exists, Newton seemed to employ each element of his doctrine of suffering to produce a specific goal of pastoral care.

Sovereign Goodness Brings Stability

The trials and difficulties of life are disorienting and destabilizing to those who endure them. Newton emphasized God's good, gracious, wise character revealed in His providential control of all things to address this reality. He wrote, "But the Lord's appointments, to those who fear him, are not only sovereign but wise and gracious. He has connected their good with his own glory, and is engaged, by promise, to make all things work together for their advantage."²⁷ He ministered this doctrine to people facing trials to bring a sense of stability to their situations, enabling them to trust the Lord better. Notice how Newton connected God's sovereignty to stability and then to trust: "Though he put forth his hand, and seem to threaten our dearest comforts, yet when we remember that it is *his* hand, when we consider that it is *his* design, *his* love, *his* wisdom, and *his* power, we cannot refuse to trust him."²⁸ For Newton, the doctrine of divine sovereignty, directed by

---

25. Gordon, *Evangelical Spirituality*, 4.

26. By way of review, the five doctrinal distinctives established in the previous chapter are the sovereignty of God, the work of Christ, the redemption of suffering, divine perspectives on suffering, and the work of Satan in temptation.

27. Newton, *Works* (1985), 1:249.

28. Newton, *Works* (1985), 6:33. "How happy are they who can resign all to him, see his hand in every dispensation, and believe that he chooses better for them than they possibly could for themselves." Newton, *Works* (1985), 1:456.

God's good, wise character, enables believers to find a sturdiness in their suffering, enabling them to trust "his hand" that is working for their good.

Newton believed so strongly that the sovereignty of God was essential to his ministry to suffering people that virtually every letter he wrote to struggling believers either specifically addresses the doctrine in some way or otherwise assumes it.[29] Thus, this belief was the staple conviction of his theology of suffering. His view of "sovereign goodness" formed a backbone or framework of his counsel to hurting people, the "persuasion of his wisdom, holiness, sovereignty and goodness."[30] In contrast to some modern conventions of religious care that view God as good and loving but unable to control the calamities of life,[31] Newton counseled his people to see that "afflictions spring not out of the ground, but are fruits and tokens of Divine love, no less than his comforts; that there is a need-be, whenever for a season he is in heaviness."[32] He often referenced Rom 8:28, encouraging strugglers that God was entirely in control of their calamities and was always working for their good through them.[33] Newton's habit demonstrates that the pastor's counsel to suffering people regarding the role of God is directly related to the minister's perspective of God's control and God's character (specifically, His goodness and wisdom). Theology drives pastoral care. Only faithful biblical theology fuels accurate, helpful pastoral counseling. And it is only divine doctrine, ministered with skill and wisdom on the part of the pastor, that brings spiritual stability to disoriented Christians.

Christology Brings Consolation and Closeness

When a pastor ministers to suffering people, where does he direct their focus and attention? Newton had only one answer: Jesus. He wrote:

> The best advice I can send, or the best wish I can form for you, is, that you may have an abiding and experimental sense of those words of the apostle, which are just now upon my mind,—"*looking*

---

29. Reinke argues that Newton's view of God's sovereignty in trials is an "important theme" of his letters to suffering people. Reinke, *Newton*, 181.

30. Newton, *Works* (1985), 1:455.

31. For an example of this erroneous perspective of God as impotent and not in control of all things, see Kushner, *When Bad Things Happen*.

32. Newton, *Works* (1985), 1:443.

33. Newton, *Works* (1985), 2:436, 6:99, 6:338, 6:5, 6:62–63, 1:69–70, 1:249–50, 1:442, 2:436–37, 2:33, 2:24, 2:147–48.

> *unto Jesus.*" The duty, the privilege, the safety, the unspeakable happiness, of a believer, are all comprised in that one sentence.[34]

For Newton, meditation on Christ, communion with Christ, and fellowship with Christ through the Scriptures should describe both the gaze and practice of the suffering believer. But Newton had specific goals in mind when he directed hurting Christians toward Christ. First, he used truths about Christ's role in suffering to encourage and counsel Christians facing difficulties. He wrote:

> It is a comfortable consideration, that he with whom we have to do, our great High Priest, who once put away our sins by the sacrifice of himself, and now forever appears in the presence of God for us, is not only possessed of sovereign authority and infinite power, but wears our very nature, and feels and exercises in the highest degree those tendernesses and commiserations, which I conceive are essential to humanity in its perfect state.[35]

For Newton, encouragement to hurting people is not accomplished by pithy admonitions and wishful hopes. Instead, the consolations of Christ Himself, the "man of sorrows" who was "tempted in all things," bring about the greatest encouragements to believers in suffering.

Second, Newton ministered the doctrine of Christ to Christians facing difficulties to enhance their communion with Christ. In his theology, suffering plays a crucial role in Christian sanctification, drawing believers into a more significant relationship with Jesus. Newton endeavored to strengthen their friendship with Christ by encouraging them to look to Him. His favorite phrase was simply "Look to Jesus." For Newton, the practice of "looking to Jesus" directs the sufferer's focus and draws him ever closer to Christ, building his relationship with Him. As they look to Christ, Newton emphasized the unique "fellowship" that Christians may enjoy as they specifically draw near to Him in their difficulties. Newton explained, "In whatever states his people are, they may by faith have fellowship with him in their sufferings, and he will by sympathy and love have fellowship and interest with them in theirs."[36] According to Newton, God's goal in this design is to bring about

---

34. Newton, *Works* (1985), 6:4.
35. Newton, *Works* (1985), 2:20.
36. Newton, *Works* (1985), 2:21

greater fellowship with Christ: "He suffered, being tempted; and because he loves you, he calls you to a participation of his sufferings."[37]

While sovereignty formed the framework of his theology of suffering, Christology was the cornerstone.[38] His pastoral admonishments to turn to Christ in suffering were not thoughtless sentiments but intentional, calculated efforts of pastoral care designed to bring consolation and greater communion with the Savior.

Redemption Reorients and Repurposes

As believers draw near to Christ and are stabilized by a trust in His sovereign goodness over their trials, they are further enabled to see and understand some of God's purposes in suffering. In Newton's theology, suffering was always redemptive, meaning Christ's work extends to transform "all things" in life to accomplish His good purposes (Rom 8:28). Newton endeavored to care for people in suffering by showing them how God was using their difficulties for their benefit. These transformative dynamics of trials produce encouragement and hope as believers come to see God's good purposes worked out in their afflictions.

In one particular letter, Newton cataloged several ways God redeems suffering for the benefit of believers, such as enhancements to prayer and Bible reading, opportunities to see Christ's sustaining power, the proving of faith, the development of Christian character, the growth of sympathy toward other sufferers, and the discovery of hidden sins.[39] He concluded his letter by revealing his pastoral purpose in sharing these perspectives: "I would enumerate all the good fruits which, by the power of sanctifying grace, are produced from this bitter tree. May we, under our several trials, find them all revealed in ourselves, that we may not complain of having suffered in vain."[40] In other words, Newton's ministerial goal went beyond mere education of God's purposes in trials. He challenged afflicted believers to not "waste" their suffering by failing to benefit from it. Thus, he aimed to encourage believers not merely to endure suffering, but to see, embrace, and realize the good purposes of God by experiencing the transformative work He intends through it.

---

37. Newton, *Works* (1985), 1:230.
38. See Reinke, *Newton*, 30.
39. Newton, *Works* (1985), 2:195–99.
40. Newton, *Works* (1985), 2:199.

Newton's pastoral care emphasized one particular redemptive theme above the others: God's chief purpose in trials is to demonstrate the insufficiency of believers in order to reveal the depths of Christ's sufficiency so that they will lean solely on Him.[41] Hence, the centrality of Christology in Newton's system is directed toward this redemptive purpose, that believers would experience the sufficiency of Jesus in their suffering. Newton explained:

> The Lord permits us to feel our weakness, that we may be sensible of it; for though we are ready in words to confess that we are weak, we do not so properly know it, till that secret, though unallowed, dependence we have upon some strength in ourselves is brought to the trial, and fails us. To be humble, and, like a little child, afraid of taking a step alone, and so conscious of snares and dangers around us, as to cry to him continually to hold us up that we may be safe, is the sure, the infallible, the only secret of walking closely with him.[42]

This process leads to the discovery that "we have no sufficiency in ourselves, but we have all-sufficiency in Him."[43]

Not only do pastors provide perspective on suffering to believers who are afflicted, they wisely and gently turn their attention from the suffering to the good benefits that God is working through their difficulties. Newton's counsel to suffering people consisted primarily in assisting them to see and embrace His redemptive purposes for their good.

Biblical Perspectives Produce Hope

Newton aimed to bring biblical hope to suffering Christians through his pastoral care. True to his convictions, he understood that true hope was a derivative of theology applied to life. Thus, his method to bring encouragement to afflicted believers was rooted in the practice of assisting them to have a biblically renewed outlook on their difficulties. As noted in the

---

41. "When faith and knowledge are in their infancy, the Lord helps this weakness by cordials and sensible comforts; but when they are advanced in growth he exercises and proves them by many changes and trials, and calls us to live more directly upon his power and promises in the face of all discouragements, to hope even against hope, and at times seems to deprive us of every subsidiary support, that we may lean only and entirely upon our beloved." Newton, *Letters*, 81.

42. Newton, *Works* (1985), 1:693.

43. Newton, *Works* (1985), 6:348.

previous chapter, Newton encouraged suffering Christians to see difficulties as God's "love tokens" designed for their good. He wrote:

> And though they are still in a state of discipline, for the mortification of sin yet remaining in them; and though, for the trial, exercise, and growth of their faith, it is still needful that they pass through many tribulations; yet none of these are strictly and properly penal. They are not the tokens of God's displeasure, but fatherly chastisements, and tokens of his love, designed to promote the work of grace in their hearts and to make them partakers of his holiness.[44]

As noted in the previous chapter, he often reminded afflicted believers that there is always a "need-be" for trials. Newton explained, "But, when we are afflicted, it is because there is a need-be for it. [God] does it not willingly. Our trials are either salutary medicines, or honourable appointments, to put us in such circumstances as may best qualify us to show forth his praise."[45] Newton used this phrase intentionally to bring a perspective of purpose and thus generate hope in the lives of people disoriented by various trials.

Newton aimed to bring hope by relating other perspectives as well, reminding Christians that they are enrolled in "Christ's school," that their trials are always sweetened with "many mercies" (if they could only see them), and that their difficulties are comparatively "light" in relation to eternity and in regard to what their sins genuinely deserve.[46] But his favorite perspective that he shared with afflicted believers related to God's goal that they would "resign all to Him." Newton explained how this perspective brings hope: "Let us pray for submission to the will of God, and that we may welcome every event, from a sense of his hand being concerned in it, and a persuasion (which his promises warrant) that, some way or other, all shall conduce to our final advantage."[47] In other words, Christians find hope and encouragement in their trials by understanding that God desires their humble submission to His will, trusting Him supremely, and believing that He intends it to their "advantage."

Newton understood that there is significant sustaining power in perspective. He recognized that a lack of hope in difficulties directly results

---

44. Newton, *Works* (1985), 4:238.
45. Newton, *Works* (1985), 6:338.
46. For more on these themes, see chapter 2.
47. Newton, *Works* (1985), 5:540.

from how Christians view their circumstances. Thus, his pastoral care endeavored to reorient the thinking of believers to adopt biblical outlooks on their problems which, as they are embraced, produce hope and encouragement.

Insight Informs and Instructs

Newton believed that Christians face three enemies: the world, the flesh, and the devil, which are "combined against our peace."[48] Of these three, he counseled most often about remaining sin (the flesh) and the schemes of Satan. Since the primary strategy of these enemies is deceit, Newton aimed to provide biblical insight about the operations of the flesh and the devil so that believers could identify and guard themselves against the tricky efforts of these foes.

In his letter "On Temptation," Newton provided suffering Christians with spiritual intelligence about the enemy's strategies, such as Satan's efforts to blind believers to God's good designs in their trials, to keep them from prayer, to encourage laziness in their battle with sin, and to lead them to fear or faulty judgment regarding their circumstances.[49] As in many of his letters to individuals, Newton reminded his readers in this letter of God's "designs" in their temptation, such as to prevent greater evils; to manifest His power, wisdom, and grace; to conform believers to Christ; to increase their sympathy toward other sufferers; and to root out self-dependence and self-righteousness.[50] Among other purposes already mentioned, Newton communicated this information to Christians to provide spiritual insight regarding the nature of temptation. In light of this information, he counseled them to pay attention and keep watch. He wrote, "I shall, however, mention some things by which, ordinarily, Satan maintains his advantage against them in these circumstances, that they may be upon their guard as much as possible."[51]

Watchfulness was a common theme of Newton's letters to those who were suffering.[52] For him, watchfulness entails an ongoing awareness of the

48. Newton, *Works* (1985), 1:192.
49. Newton, *Works* (1985), 1:226–35.
50. Newton, *Works* (1985), 1:227–32.
51. Newton, *Works* (1985), 1:233.
52. Newton, *Works* (1985), 6:15, 6:52, 6:40, 6:115, 1:651, 1:527, 1:433, 1:195, 6:272, 2:531, 6:26.

tactics of indwelling sin and the devil, such that a believer can engage in constant vigilance, persisting in prayer and spiritual practices to avoid falling into sin. True to his theology, Newton saw watchfulness as ultimately another occasion for a believer to trust in Christ's provision and grace. Notice how Newton connected the themes of watchfulness, constant dependence on Christ, and prayer in this advice he gave to Miss K:

> I hope you will remember, that all your comfort and prosperity depends upon keeping near to him who is the sun, the shield, the life of his poor children, and that neither experiences, knowledge, nor attainments, can support us, or maintain themselves, without a continual supply from the fountain. This supply is to be kept up by constant prayer, and prayer will languish without continual watchfulness.[53]

In other words, the wellbeing of a believer, especially in the context of trials, depends upon "keeping near" to Christ for "a continual supply" of His provisions, and this effort only occurs by "constant prayer" that is provoked by "continual watchfulness" regarding the tactics of Satan.[54]

Not only did Newton aim to bring stability, consolation, purpose, and hope to those he counseled, he also purposed to make them more mindful of spiritual temptations and urged them to be constantly on guard against them.

Through his example, Newton demonstrated that a minister's purposes in pastoral care, whether to instruct or encourage, derive specifically from his own biblical doctrine that is ministered with wisdom to bring about the divinely intended purpose. In this regard, Newton exemplified how the "power of Christ" provides the believer everything "for life and godliness," which comes through the agency of His "precious and magnificent promises" (2 Pet 1:2–4). The five components of Newton's doctrine of suffering thus establish five pathways of care that provide specific provisions to those in need.

Expectations in Pastoral Care

Newton's theology of suffering not only provides paths of specific instruction and ministry in pastoral care but also reveals some of his expectations

---

53. Newton, *Works* (1985), 6:16.

54. In context, Newton is warning Miss K (Anna Kenyon of Yeadon) about Satan, who "watches with envy and rage to find an opening by which to assault" believers. Newton, *Works* (1985), 6:15.

regarding counseling. What sort of results should a pastor expect if his counseling is successful? How quickly should he anticipate seeing results? Newton held to the classic Reformed position of progressive sanctification that a believer grows in spiritual maturity not instantly but by degrees over time.[55] Though he was sympathetic to the Methodist movement, he held to his Puritan roots regarding sanctification. Thus, he rejected the Methodist concept of Christian perfectionism, a stance that led him to part ways with his friend, John Wesley.[56]

Newton's most helpful work on sanctification is a series of three letters that are loosely based upon Mark 4:28.[57] But even these letters demonstrate that his understanding of Christian growth was built mainly around his doctrine of affliction. Specifically, Newton's theology of suffering informed his thinking about the pace of Christian growth in counseling and set realistic benchmarks for what could be achieved through pastoral counseling.

The Pace of Growth in Pastoral Care

Newton often spoke of the need for believers not just to know sound doctrine but to possess a "heart knowledge" as gospel promises are experienced in life. He called this "experimental knowledge" and viewed it as a mark of spiritual health and maturity.[58] Because Christian maturity comes through

---

55. Bunyan's *The Pilgrim's Progress* was the work on sanctification that Newton alluded to and quoted from the most, making it likely the most significant resource on the subject in his life. See Reinke, *Newton*, 27–29.

56. Hindmarsh writes, "While Newton had been able to suppress his differences with Wesley over predestination, the extent of the atonement, and final perseverance, he was not able to accept the behavior of Wesley's followers in the wake of the perfectionism revival. The claim to perfection, however hedged about by talk of grace, seemed in many cases no more than an enthusiastic self-righteousness that belied trusting wholly in the merits of Christ for redemption. . . . He could not . . . make any rapprochement with Wesley's growing stress upon perfectionism. The behavior of [Wesley's] followers raised the specter of a Pelagianism that lay outside his understanding of evangelical theology, unduly stressing human agency in salvation." Hindmarsh, "'Middle-Man,'" 43.

57. The three letters are entitled "A; or, Grace in the Blade," "B; or, Grace in the Ear," and "C; or, The Full Corn in the Ear." Newton, *Works* (1985), 1:197–217.

58. Newton likely inherited this view of experimental knowledge from the Puritans. For example, Thomas Boston describes experimental knowledge as "a real feeling of the beauty and excellency, and efficacy of divine truth on the heart." He later defines this knowledge as "an inward and spiritual feeling of what we hear and believe concerning Christ and his truths, whereby answerable impressions are made on our souls." Boston, *Whole Works*, 2:645–46. Thomas Brooks taught that experimental knowledge was

applying doctrine in life experiences and not through knowledge alone, the pastoral counselor should recognize that progress in counseling will often take time because sanctification usually is slow. Reflecting on his own journey, Newton wrote, "Candour will always allow much for inexperience. I have been thirty years forming my own views; and, in the course of this time, some of my hills have sunk, and some of my valleys have risen: but, how unreasonable would it be to expect all this should take place in another person; and that, in the course of a year or two."[59]

Newton's view of God's providence also influenced his convictions about experimental theology through afflictions, thus shaping his perspective on the pace of pastoral counseling and the progress of spiritual growth. He gave this advice to another pastor: "We may grow wise apace in opinions, by books and men; but vital, experimental knowledge can only be received from the Holy Spirit, the great instructor and comforter of his people."[60] He then explained that God "does not teach all at once, but by degrees. Experience is his school; and by this I mean the observation and improvement of what passes within us and around us in the course of every day."[61]

Newton then establishes this connection to pastoral care: "We are ready to expect that others should receive upon our word, in half an hour's time, those views of things which have cost us years to attain. But none can be brought forward faster than the Lord is pleased to communicate inward light."[62] In other words, the gospel minister ought to be patient with people in pastoral care, recognizing that God must work and that He does so according to His timetable, not the counselor's timetable. As pastors remember the length of years in their own journeys toward godliness, they will set more realistic expectations of progress for those under their care.

---

knowledge that "springs from a spiritual sense and taste of holy and heavenly things." He contrasts knowledge that is only understood "notionally" from knowledge that is experienced "feelingly." Like Newton, Brooks linked the acquisition of experimental knowledge to experiences in life as doctrines are worked out in application such that they are affirmed and "felt." Brooks, *Complete Works*, 2:436–37. Newton particularly believed that experimental knowledge was gained through trials (see Newton, *Works* [1985], 2:20–23, 2:174–76, 3:102, 6:142) and was a mark of spiritual maturity (1:674, 2:210, 2:100, 1:432, 1:379, 1:188, 1:533, 2:374, 2:583).

59. Newton, *Works* (1985), 1:101.
60. Newton, *Works* (1985), 2:100.
61. Newton, *Works* (1985), 2:100.
62. Newton, *Works* (1985), 1:101.

John Newton's Theology of Suffering and Its Application to Pastoral Care

Realistic Benchmarks in Pastoral Care

The reality that sanctification is often slow did not lead Newton to conclude that progress in spiritual growth must be minimal. Instead, he believed pastors should gauge advancement in Christian maturity by specific, measurable marks. Writing to Lord Dartmouth, he articulated five "branches of blessedness," or attainable attributes of Christian maturity, to which believers "in a humble attendance upon the Lord . . . *may be* while upon the earth."[63] First, Newton explained that believers are capable of possessing a "clear, well-grounded, habitual persuasion of our acceptance in the Beloved," meaning they may enjoy an assurance of their salvation.[64] Second, Christians can achieve "a conscience void of offense," which keeps them from continuing in an unrepentant state for known sin.[65] Third, they may experience true, "real communion with the Lord."[66] For example, Newton used the illustration of a person reading Scripture "not as an attorney may read a will . . . but as the heir reads it, as a description and proof of his interest."[67] Fourth, maturing believers may gain a "power of reposing ourselves and our concerns upon the Lord's faithfulness and care."[68] Newton explained that this frame of spirit manifests itself in two ways: through "a reliance upon him" that he will provide, protect, and guide; and by a "submission to his will, under all events which, upon their first impression, are contrary to our own views and desires."[69] Finally, growing Christians ought to attain a "spirit cheerful and active for the Lord's service."[70] Motivated out of thankfulness, a child of God desires to "devote his strength and influence" in service to Him.[71]

It is intriguing to note that Newton's maturity benchmarks are elsewhere described as specific byproducts of redeemed suffering.[72] In other words, Newton believed and taught that God primarily uses afflictions to

63. Newton, *Works* (1985), 1:519.
64. Newton, *Works* (1985), 1:520.
65. Newton, *Works* (1985), 1:521.
66. Newton, *Works* (1985), 1:522.
67. Newton, *Works* (1985), 1:522.
68. Newton, *Works* (1985), 1:523.
69. Newton, *Works* (1985), 1:523.
70. Newton, *Works* (1985), 1:524.
71. Newton, *Works* (1985), 1:524.
72. For evidence of this point, see chapter 2, especially the section "Suffering Redeemed."

produce these facets of Christian growth in His children. For example, he believed that trials serve to develop a believer's assurance of salvation:

> Assurance grows by repeated conflict, by our repeated experimental proof of the Lord's power and goodness to save; when we have been brought very low and helped, sorely wounded and healed, cast down and raised again, have given up all hope, and been suddenly snatched from danger, and placed in safety; and when these things have been repeated to us and in us a thousand times over, we begin to learn to trust simply to the word and power of God, beyond and against appearances: and this trust, when habitual and strong, bears the name of assurance.[73]

Pastors can learn from Newton's example. Newton's theology of suffering provided both content for his counsel to others and shaped how he thought about the pace of counseling and clear marks of progress in spiritual growth. Rather than setting up artificial timelines and superficial measures, ministers of the gospel should let clear, biblical principles inform and establish the practical benchmarks of pastoral care.

Not only did Newton's theology inform his expectations in pastoral care, it also influenced his anthropology. Specifically, his paradigm for understanding suffering equipped him to better understand people in the context of pastoral care.

Understanding People in Pastoral Care

In his divinity studies, Newton admitted that his favorite subject of study was "anatomy," his term for the "study of the human heart."[74] Indeed, his careful observations of people in various states and life situations equipped him to minister to them better through pastoral care. Some writers, such as Reinke, believe that the real genius of Newton's pastoral care was his ability to "apply the treasures of divine truth to each of the manifold circumstances faced in the Christian life."[75] Through his example of studying

---

73. Newton, *Works* (1985), 2:176.

74. Newton, *Works* (1985), 1:478.

75. "Newton was a spiritual doctor, and his chosen specialty, as he called it, was cardiology, the careful and exhaustive study of the human heart's response to every conceivable situation and condition in this life. From his experience as a diagnostician of the heart, Newton labored to apply the treasures of divine truth to each of the manifold circumstances faced in the Christian life. . . . Newton was a keen-eyed student of the human heart who eagerly leaned into the human experience. In this sense he was, and

people through the lens of Scripture, pastors can learn three essential lessons about ministerial counseling.

First, pastors must spend time with their people if they desire the knowledge for effective soul care ministry. Writing to a younger clergyman, James Coffin, Newton explained his experience with his parishioners at Olney:

> I was their official teacher from the pulpit; but I taught them chiefly by what I first learned from them in the course of the week, by visiting and conversing with them from house to house. Indeed I learned more from them than from all my great folios and quartos! In their artless, simple talk, I saw more of the workings of the heart, the power of grace, and the devices of Satan—than any books could show me.[76]

It is no surprise that Newton regularly and systematically visited people in his congregation, met with individuals privately for counseling, and opened his home frequently for spiritual conversation. He wrote that these visits offered him more spiritual insight than his books.[77] It was this knowledge that enabled him to excel in pastoral care. His ministry to his people was effective because he spent time with them. A pastor cannot be effective in his ministry of pastoral care by books alone. He must learn from and be with his people.

Second, pastors ought to develop the art of studying people as they spend time with them. Newton's habit was to engage in the study of people constantly. Quoting Newton, Cecil recalled, "'A minister,' he used to say, 'wherever he is, should be always in his study. He should look at every man, and at every thing, as capable of affording him some instruction.'"[78] When spending time with his parishioners at Olney, Newton stated that he gained insight into the heart, the workings of grace, and the devices of Satan. However, his favorite subject of study, by far, was the interworkings of the human heart. He explained in a different letter, "Anatomy is my favourite branch: I mean, the study of the human heart, with its workings and counter-workings, as it is differently affected in a state of nature or of grace, in the different seasons of prosperity, adversity, conviction, temptation,

---

remains, one of the church's most perceptive and practical theologians on the Christian life." Reinke, *Newton*, 27.

76. Newton, *Letters of John Newton*, 54.
77. Newton, *Letters of John Newton*, 54.
78. Newton, *Works* (1985), 1:92.

sickness, and the approach of death."[79] Newton understood that people are active responders to life, not passive participants. He advised that ministers should study the dynamics of human hearts as actively interpreting, engaging, and responding to various circumstances and situations. He especially stressed the value of such observations in states of trials and difficulties, such as "adversity, conviction, temptation, sickness, and the approach of death." He wrote elsewhere:

> For about six weeks past, I have had occasion to spend several hours of almost every day with the sick and the dying. These scenes are to a minister like walking the hospitals to a young surgeon. The various cases which occur, exemplify, illustrate, and explain, with a commanding energy, many truths, which may be learned indeed at home, but cannot be so well understood, or their force so sensibly felt, without the advantage of experience and observation.[80]

Following his theology of suffering, Newton believed that the heart is most clearly revealed, and thus better understood, in times of trial.[81]

As ministers study people's hearts as active responders in various life situations, Newton recommended focusing on two areas. First, they should observe how different people reside in different stages of spiritual maturity. Writing to another young pastor, he advised:

> I would advise you to study the living as well as the dead, or rather more. Converse much with experienced Christians and exercised souls. You will find advantage in this respect, not only from the wise, but from the weak of the flock. In the course of your acquaintance, you will meet with some in a backsliding state, some under temptations, some walking in darkness, others rejoicing in the light, &c. Observe how their spirits work, what they say, and how they reason in their several cases; what methods and arguments you find most successful in comforting the feeble-minded, raising up those who are cast down, and the like, and what answers they return.[82]

---

79. Newton, *Works* (1985), 1:478. Grant Gordon lists a few examples of the observations made by Newton, such as the tendencies of young believers, the struggle of watching others suffer, and the nature of grief. See Gordon, "John Newton," 92.

80. Newton, *Works* (1985), 1:477–78.

81. Newton, *Works* (1985), 1:227, 2:199. See also chapter 2 for additional examples.

82. Newton, *Works* (1985), 1:143.

John Newton's Theology of Suffering and Its Application to Pastoral Care

Newton developed his anthropology through this process. His continuous practice of observation, guided by his biblical understanding of people, led him to see different stages of spiritual growth, such as some who are "backsliding," others "under temptations," and still others "rejoicing in the light." In a different set of letters, Newton outlined three stages of spiritual maturity, in which believers manifest certain tendencies, meet specific challenges, and achieve particular results.[83] Following Newton's pattern, ministers will better serve people in pastoral care when they identify their specific stage in spiritual development.

Second, as pastors study people and observe different phases of Christian maturity, they should examine their findings against the Bible and their hearts. Newton continued his advice to the young pastor with this admonition:

> Compare these [observations of people] with the word of God, and your own heart. What you observe of ten persons in these different situations, may be applied to ten thousand. For though some circumstances vary, the heart of man, the aids of grace, and the artifices of Satan, in general, are universally the same. And whenever you are to preach, remember, that some of all these sorts will probably be before you, and each should have something said to their own peculiar case.[84]

Newton derived his spiritual "cardiology," the study of human hearts, from the analysis of these three sources: observations of people, the word of God, and his own heart. While he always maintained that the Scriptures were the foundational authority, he recognized that the truths of the Bible are best utilized in pastoral care as they are understood in the context of real life and experiences. Thus, "experimental knowledge" connected biblical truth and effective pastoral care.

The third essential lesson that can be learned from Newton about ministerial counseling is that pastors should utilize their conclusions about people to direct shepherding efforts. Newton believed that the observations made of a few individuals could be extrapolated to thousands since "the heart of man, the aids of grace, and the artifices of Satan, in general, are

---

83. Newton, *Works* (1985), 1:197–217.

84. Newton, *Works* (1985), 1:144. This quote demonstrates that Newton held to the primacy of Scripture as the authority for understanding people. Though he stressed the importance of observing human behavior in pastoral care, he is clear that such observations must be examined through the lens of Scripture and confirmed by the Scripture. His biblical understanding of suffering made him a keen observer of people.

universally the same."[85] Newton advised, "Observe how their spirits work, what they say, and how they reason in their several cases; what methods and arguments you find most successful in comforting the feeble-minded, raising up those who are cast down, and the like, and what answers they return."[86] His advice underlines the need for wisdom in pastoral care. While Scripture provides the divinely inspired counseling content, the pastor must apply biblical truth with insight and discernment based upon the person's uniqueness and situation. Likewise, when a pastor is engaged in public ministry, he should be careful to follow this advice as well.[87] Newton's habit simply follows the advice of Scripture, which recognizes that different types of people possess different spiritual needs and thus require particular counsel (1 Thess 5:14).

Newton's pastoral practice hinged on a reciprocal pastoral skill, where time and observations with his people provided him with the insight he needed to minister effectively to them. He maintained that pastoral shepherding, whether private or public, should be directed by the wisdom of keen human observation or spiritual "anatomy," which guides care uniquely and effectively to people.

These observations demonstrate that Newton's theology shaped his observations about people and influenced his anthropology as he engaged in pastoral care. His doctrine of affliction also affected him personally, as he experienced his own seasons of suffering. These individual trials produced valuable lessons for his ministry to others.

The Value of Personal Affliction in Pastoral Care

Throughout his ministry, Newton engaged with other pastors in many different contexts: he wrote letters, started the Eclectic Society meeting, and helped establish a pastoral training school.[88] Consistent with the other facets of his ministry, Newton's theology of suffering played a foundational role in his pastoral ministry perspective and his advice to fellow ministers.

---

85. Newton, *Works* (1985), 1:144.

86. As Newton wrote, "And whenever you are to preach, remember, that some of all these sorts will probably be before you, and each should have something said to their own peculiar case." Newton, *Works* (1985), 1:144.

87. Newton, *Works* (1985), 1:144.

88. For more information about the establishment of the Eclectic Society and the school for pastors, see Aitken, *John Newton*, 284 and 289–93.

John Newton's Theology of Suffering and Its Application to Pastoral Care

Newton admitted that the benefits of afflictions were a "frequent and favourite" topic in his pastoral ministry.[89] Though he confessed that his own "path for many years has been smooth, and [his] trials, though [he had] not been without trials, comparatively, [were] light and few," the reality of Newton's story reveals that he lived through "many dangers, toils, and snares."[90] He came close to death over a dozen times before his conversion, was a slave in Guinea for eighteen months, lost his adopted daughter to tuberculosis, endured the heartache of his other adopted daughter's stay in a mental asylum, walked with his wife through her decades of chronic illnesses and near-death experiences, and grieved over his friend Cowper's suicide attempts and decades-long depression. Through these experiences and many others, Newton came to see the benefits of afflictions as God redeems them for good. He also learned that suffering brings particular personal advantages to the pastor. Writing to a fellow pastor, he stated that God purposely "appoints his ministers to be sorely exercised, both from without and within."[91] Specifically, Newton identifies five benefits of sanctified trials for the pastor.

First, God ordains seasons of afflictions to the pastor to squelch his own pride and self-sufficiency. Newton understood that pastors are particularly vulnerable to temptations of all sorts as they are at the "forefront" of the battle. He explained to a minister friend:

> How seasonable and important at such a time is the mercy which, under the disguise of an affliction, gives an alarm to the soul, quickens us to prayer, makes us feel our own emptiness, and preserves us from the enemy's net. These reflections are applicable to all the Lord's people, but emphatically so to his ministers. We stand in the fore-front of the battle. The nature of our employment exposes us to peculiar dangers; more eyes are upon us; our deviations are more observed, and have worse effects, both with respect to the church and the world, than if we were in private life.[92]

Writing to the Rev. W. B. Cadogan, who had just recovered from a severe illness, Newton theorized as to the Lord's purposes for the trial:

---

89. For an exhaustive list of benefits that come through suffering, see chapter 2.

90. Newton, *Works* (1985), 2:22. For an overview of some of these personal trials, see chapter 1.

91. Newton, *Letters*, 45.

92. Newton, *Works* (1985), 6:264.

Newton's Pastoral Care

> Whatever we seem to be in the eyes of men, we are nothing in his sight further than we are humbled and abased in our own. It requires much discipline to keep pride down in us, even considered only as Christians, more as ministers, still more as ministers conspicuous for ability and usefulness.... But the Lord, by leaving you a little to yourself, has provided you with something to reflect on, which I trust will be a sanctified means of keeping you less dependent upon yourself.[93]

Newton knew this struggle personally as he approached the end of life and saw his usefulness beginning to diminish. Recalling a quote from Puritan Cotton Mather that he had read some fifty years earlier, he shared it with a fellow pastor: "My usefulness was the last idol I was willing to part with, but now I can part with that, and am content to be laid aside and forgotten, so that he may be glorified."[94] Newton understood that ministers were particularly prone to the wiles of "Mr. Self" (as he called it). Thus, God employs afflictions to deflate ministers, help them feel their weaknesses, and move them to lean on Christ and His sufficiency alone.[95]

Second, God employs times of difficulty for ministers to keep them from ministerial backsliding. Writing again to Rev. Cadogan, he noted:

> What the Lord appeared to have done for you and by you had given you a near place in my heart, and nothing appears to me so awful as a minister, who having given for a time proofs of a zeal for God and love for souls, afterwards declines and dies away from the good cause. Oh! My dear sir, ought we not, and by the grace of God shall we not think it vastly more desirable to be afflicted with all the afflictions of Job, to be stoned to death, or to be buried alive, rather than to be left to such a conduct as might stumble the weak and encourage the wicked?[96]

In other words, Newton believed that his friend's serious illness was a means of keeping him from declining and dying away from the "good cause" of gospel ministry.

Third, Newton taught that God uses trials in the life of ministers to develop sympathy in them toward others who are suffering. Writing to Rev. S, he explains, "By our own sufferings we learn likewise (the Lord sanctifying

---

93. Newton, *Letters*, 415.
94. Mather, as cited in Newton, *One Hundred and Twenty Nine Letters*, 295.
95. Newton, *Works* (1985), 1:452, 1:622–23; Newton, *Letters*, 81, 366.
96. Newton, *Letters*, 415.

them to that end) to sympathize with the afflicted, and to comfort them from the experiences we have had of the Lord's goodness and faithfulness to ourselves."[97] When Newton's friend William Bull experienced a season of ongoing anxiety over a dangerous journey undertaken by Bull's son, Newton sympathized, "I know, by repeated experience, how busy imagination is at such a time in contriving and foreboding the worst that can happen."[98] Newton's own repeated experiences of similar trials and difficulties enabled him to be sympathetic rather than judgmental toward his friend's situation.

Newton maintained that God not only uses trials to develop sympathy among his servants but specifically ordains unique afflictions to that end. He explained to Rev. Whitford, "He appoints his ministers to be sorely exercised, both from without and from within, that they may sympathize with their flock."[99] Just as the Lord Jesus took on a human nature and was "tempted in all things as we are" such that He could sympathize with Christians in their weaknesses, Newton believed that God designs a similar program for His undershepherds who minister in His name.

Fourth, as ministers of the gospel experience trials and thus become more sympathetic toward others in afflictions, they develop competence in caring for them. Following his principle of "experimental knowledge," Newton believed that pastors would only be effective pastoral counselors insofar as they had experienced the promises and graces of God personally, sustaining them through their own afflictions. He wrote:

> The doctrinal parts of our message are in some degree familiar to us, but that which gives a savour, fulness, energy, and variety to our ministries is the result of many painful conflicts and exercises which we pass through in our private walk, combined with the proofs we receive, as we go along, of the Lord's compassion and mercies under all the perverseness and folly we are conscious of in ourselves. It is only in this school of experience that we can acquire the tongue of the learned, and know how to speak a word in season to those that are weary.[100]

For Newton, the "school of experience" was imperative for effective ministry, as it forces the application of biblical theology to life.[101] He believed

---

97. Newton, *Works* (1985), 6:264.
98. Newton, *One Hundred and Twenty Nine Letters*, 276.
99. Newton, *Letters*, 45.
100. Newton, *Letters*, 416.
101. Following his Puritan influence, Newton used the term "experimental

that ministers should be familiar with many forms of suffering since the difficulties of their parishioners will likewise be varied. Writing to Captain Scott, Newton explains: "Innumerable are the trials, fears, complaints, and temptation which the Lord's people are beset with; some in one way, and some in another; the minister must, as it were, have a taste of all, or it might happen a case might come before him to which he had nothing to say."[102] While doctrinally sound pastors may know *what* to speak to suffering believers, only those who have experienced God's grace in their own afflictions will know *how* to speak effectively to suffering believers.

Fifth, not only did Newton believe that afflictions were necessary to help a minister develop the skills of pastoral care, but he also believed that a pastor should be an example to the flock. In other words, the preacher should practice what he preaches. He wrote to Rev. Coffin, "I have often told my friends and hearers, when in affliction, that the post of *trial—is* the post of honor. *He now appoints me to practice my own lessons.*"[103] When the minister lives by his own counsel, it amplifies his influence and brings credibility to his care. He wrote to Rev. Whitford:

> Take care that you do not catch an angry spirit yourself, while you aim to suppress it in others: this will spoil all, and you will exhort, advise, and weep in vain. May you rather be an example and pattern to the flock; and in this view, be not surprised if you yourself meet some hard usage; rather rejoice, that you will thereby have an opportunity to exemplify your own rules, and to convince your people, that what you recommend to them you do not speak by *rote*, but from the experience of your heart.[104]

Ministers of the gospel must remember that their trials may not be for their sake alone but may be appointed by God to enhance their ministries to hurting people.[105] A robust, biblical theology of suffering, embraced and

---

knowledge" to reference spiritual truth that was embraced and believed in the affections. He believed that the "school of experience," the challenges of life where one must "work out" or apply one's theology in the midst of trials, was God's chief instrument to produce experimental knowledge. Newton believed that ministers would be more effective in pastoral care when they possessed experimental knowledge that was gained through the school of experience.

102. Newton, *Letters*, 145.
103. Newton, *Letters of John Newton*, 90. Emphasis original.
104. Newton, *Letters*, 45.
105. Newton wrote to John Ryland, "Your trials are not for your own sake alone. I am persuaded, they must have a good effect upon your ministry; to make your discourses

John Newton's Theology of Suffering and Its Application to Pastoral Care

lived out in an "experimental" way, is God's appointed grace to create humble, sympathetic, effective pastoral counselors who will be a blessing and help to suffering Christians.

Personal Dynamics in Pastoral Care

According to Richard Cecil, one of Newton's closest friends, it was not Newton's giftedness that made him a most effective pastor. Instead, his character, specifically his affection for his people and his sympathetic ability to enter into their trials, made him influential.[106] Newton also spoke often of his own struggles and difficulties as he endeavored to care for others. This section will address three personal characteristics of Newton, which were directly linked to his theology of suffering, that made him a particularly effective pastoral counselor.

Newton's Character in Pastoral Care

Those who knew John Newton consistently praised his character.[107] The Rev. William Jay called him "the most perfect instance of the spirit and temper of Christianity I ever knew."[108] Richard Cecil explained that "Mr. N could *live* no longer than he could *love*."[109] Likewise, his biographer Josiah Bull wrote:

> It was his *goodness* rather than his *greatness* that rendered him so especially attractive—the abundance of the grace of God that was in him. Some men excel in one virtue more than another; but Mr Newton's character was beautiful in its entireness. It rested on a solid foundation, the initial Christian grace of *humility*, and of this grace he was a most striking example.[110]

---

more varied, experimental and consolatory to your people, and to qualify you with wisdom, tenderness, sympathy and promptitude, in speaking a word in season to them that are weary." Gordon, *Wise Counsel*, 200.

106. Cecil, *Life of John Newton*, 193.

107. Several of Newton's biographers make this point. See Aitken, *John Newton*, 24, 348; Newton, *Letters*, 314; Cecil, *Life of John Newton*, 196; Jay, *Autobiography*, 322; Murray, *Beyond Amazing Grace*, 22–23.

108. Jay, *Autobiography*, 322.

109. Cecil, *Life of John Newton*, 196.

110. Newton, *Letters*, 314.

Newton's Pastoral Care

What created this grace of humility in the life of Newton? Bull asserted, "Mr Newton never for a moment forgot that by the grace of God he was what he was. Hence the frequent allusion to his former miserable and guilty state, in his diary, in his letters, his converse, his preaching. No day passed without the mingled feelings of self-abasement and gratitude which his circumstances awakened."[111] In other words, Newton's humility derived from his own theology of suffering, which convinced him of God's sovereign goodness in preserving and saving him. It persuaded him of his own vileness and insufficiency and demonstrated God's astounding grace in redeeming his suffering for good. He wrote:

> Yes, I have gained, that which I once would rather have been without, such accumulated proofs of the deceitfulness and desperate wickedness of my heart, as I hope, by the Lord's blessing, has, in some measure, taught me to know what I mean, when I say, Behold I am vile! And, in connection with this, I have gained such experience of the wisdom, power, and compassion of my Redeemer, the need, the worth, of his blood, righteousness, attention, and intercession, the glory that he displays in pardoning iniquity and sin and passing by the transgression of the remnant of his heritage, that my soul cannot but cry out, Who is a God like unto thee![112]

Newton believed that humility was one of the chief marks of the mature believer, and he made it the "chief thing" of his own spiritual pursuit.[113] He wrote:

> I hope the Lord will give me a humble sense of what I am, and that broken and contrite frame of heart in which He delights. This is to me the chief thing. I had rather have more of the mind that was in Christ, more of a meek, quiet, resigned, peaceful and loving disposition, than to enjoy the greatest measure of sensible comforts.[114]

The Lord saw fit to grant his request, as many of his contemporaries concluded that he exemplified a "humble gratitude" or a "thankful humility" that was the chief mark of his character.

Though Newton was gifted in pastoral care, his humble character made him an effective shepherd in public ministry and personal counseling.

---

111. Newton, *Letters*, 314.

112. Newton, *Works* (1985), 1:625.

113. In Newton's "three stages" of spiritual maturity, he wrote that "C" (the believer in the final stage of Christian maturity) is truly humbled. Newton, *Works* (1985), 1:212.

114. Newton, *Letters*, 76.

Though not exceptionally skilled in preaching, Cecil explained that "he possessed . . . so much affection for his people, and so much zeal for their best interests, that the defect of his manner was of little consideration with his constant hearers; at the same time, his capacity and habit of entering into their trials and experience, gave the highest interest to his ministry among them."[115] Newton wove a "parent-like tenderness and affection" into his preaching, which made others "prefer him to preachers, who, on other accounts, were much more generally popular."[116] Regarding his pastoral care, Cecil stated, "His ministerial visits were exemplary. I do not recollect one, though favoured with many, in which his general information and lively genius did not communicate instruction, and his affectionate and condescending sympathy did not leave comfort."[117] Grant Gordon attributes much of Newton's effectiveness as a "pastoral correspondent" to his "power of humiliation," writing that "his letters are from a humble heart."[118] J. I. Packer claims that Newton was "the friendliest, wisest, humblest, and least pushy of all the eighteenth-century evangelical leaders."[119] John Piper agrees and concludes that Newton's effectiveness was primarily due to his "winsome, humble, compelling tenderness."[120]

The effective pastoral counselor must not only possess the correct doctrine and skills, but he must also exemplify Christlike character. Newton himself believed that humility ought to be the great virtue of the minister. He prayed, "Give me a humbling sense of my sins, give me a humbling view of thy glory, give me a humbling taste of thy love, for surely nothing humbles like these."[121] Among his other graces, Newton's humility infused his counsel with winsomeness and powerful influence. But the key to developing this humility was God's sanctifying work through trials.[122]

---

115. Cecil, *Life of John Newton*, 193.

116. Cecil, *Life of John Newton*, 193.

117. Cecil, *Life of John Newton*, 195.

118. Gordon, "John Newton," 94.

119. As quoted in Reinke, *Newton*, 15.

120. Piper, "John Newton."

121. Newton, *Ministry on My Mind*, 25.

122. Newton is worth quoting at length on this point: "The Lord permits us to feel our weakness, that we may be sensible of it; for though we are ready in words to confess that we are weak, we do not so properly know it, till that secret, though unallowed, dependence we have upon some strength in ourselves is brought to the trial, and fails us. To be humble, and, like a little child, afraid of taking a step alone, and so conscious of snares and dangers around us, as to cry to him continually to hold us up that we may

Newton's Posture in Pastoral Care

Newton's humility directly affected how he approached pastoral care. His posture in ministerial care was not one of a cold professional or a disconnected academic but that of a sympathetic friend and fellow sufferer. E. Brooks Holifield documents a "shift" in the nineteenth century in pastoral care from a more "authoritative model" to one of an affectionate friend.[123] In this dynamic of ministerial counseling, Newton was apparently ahead of his time.

Writing to a suffering pastor, he related, "I feel for you a little in the same way as you feel for yourself. I bear a friendly sympathy in your late sharp and sudden trial. I mourn with that part of you which mourns; but at the same time I rejoice in the proof you have, and which you give, that the Lord is with you of a truth."[124] Newton's manner of relating to others as a sympathetic friend was his usual mode. He ministered this way to all types of people, including the poor of Olney, noblemen, members of parliament, family members, fellow pastors of various denominations, and even virtual strangers.[125] Aitken affirms that sympathy was a critical component of his ministerial care: "On his daily visits to the homes of his parishioners, especially to those with personal difficulties, he was a sensitive and sympathetic listener."[126]

What created his ministerial posture of a sympathetic fellow-sufferer in his pastoral care? Newton's letters demonstrate that his theology of suffering, worked out "experimentally" in his own life, led him to this approach.

---

be safe, is the sure, the infallible, the only secret of walking closely with Him. But how shall we attain this humble frame of spirit? It must be, as I said, from a real and sensible conviction of our weakness and vileness, which we cannot learn (at least I have not been able to learn it) merely from books or preachers. The providence of God concurs with his Holy Spirit in his merciful design of making us acquainted with ourselves. It is indeed a great mercy to be preserved from such declensions as might fall under the notice of our fellow-creatures; but when they can observe nothing of consequence to object to us, things may be far from right with us in the sight of Him who judges not only actions, but the thoughts and first motions of the heart. And indeed could we for a season so cleave to God as to find little or nothing in ourselves to be ashamed of, we are such poor creatures, that we should presently grow vain and self-sufficient, and expose ourselves to the greatest danger of falling." Newton, *Works* (1985), 1:693–94.

123. Holifield, *Pastoral Care*, 124.

124. Newton, *Works* (1985), 2:254.

125. For evidence of the variety of people whom Newton addressed in pastoral care, see the introductions of various recipients provided by Josiah Bull in Newton, *Letters*.

126. Aitken, *John Newton*, 197.

John Newton's Theology of Suffering and Its Application to Pastoral Care

When the wife of a fellow clergyman wrote to him about some distressing thoughts, Newton responded, "When you tell me what a sad heart you have, and what strange and evil thoughts pester your mind—you tell me nothing new. I also feel the same."[127] After his own wife endured a ten-week season of illness with "no prospect of her recovery," Newton wrote to a friend who was likewise enduring a trial:

> I sympathize for my friends, and I feel for myself. But, blessed be God, I do not mourn as those who have no hope. I know it is not an enemy hath done this. It is the Lord, who hath saved me out of all afflictions, he who gave me all my good things, he to whom I have surrendered myself and my all; he it is that hath laid this trial on me for my good. I believe it to be necessary, because he is pleased to appoint it; and, though at present it is not joyous, but grievous, I trust that in the end he will cause it to yield the peaceable fruits of righteousness. I desire to submit to his will in all things; and though I feel the depravity of my nature too often, yet, upon the whole, he enables me to trust to him, and leave all in his hands. I pray that her health may be restored when he sees best, but especially that her sickness may be sanctified to both our souls. In this we hope and desire the concurrence of your prayers.[128]

Newton's own experience of suffering kept him from counseling down to his parishioners and led him instead to minister alongside them and with them as a fellow sufferer.

Newton's example demonstrates that a pastor's theology of suffering ought to affect the manner of his counseling. God designs suffering to create humility, gratitude, dependence, and sympathy toward fellow sufferers. Newton regularly wrote of the gap that exists between "stated" theology and one's "practical theology," the actual belief system that emerges from a believer's behavior, especially in trials.[129] A pastor who is arrogant, indifferent, impatient, or lacks warmth and sympathy toward suffering believers

---

127. Newton, *Letters of John Newton*, 96.

128. Newton, *Works* (1985), 6:32.

129. For example, he challenged his fellow Calvinists who eagerly affirmed the doctrine of election but struggled with sovereignty in their own trials: "The doctrine of God's sovereignty ... is no less fully assented to by those who are called Calvinists. We zealously contend for this point in our debates with the Arminians; and are ready to wonder that any should be hardy enough to dispute the Creator's right to do what he will with his own.... But, alas! how often do we find ourselves utterly unable to apply [the doctrine of sovereignty], so as to reconcile our spirits to those afflictions which he is pleased to allot us!" Newton, *Works* (1985), 1:248.

actually denies the theology he professes and demeans the character of the Savior he is called to emulate. What pastors need, according to Newton, is the help of trials:

> Many of our graces likewise cannot thrive or shew themselves to advantage without trials; such as resignation, patience, meekness, long-suffering.... It is so in the Christian life: activity and strength of grace is not ordinarily acquired by those who sit still and live at ease, but by those who frequently meet with something which requires a full exertion of what power the Lord has given them. So again, it is by our own sufferings we learn to pity and sympathize with others in their sufferings: such a compassionate disposition, which excites our feelings for the afflicted, is an eminent branch of the mind which was in Christ. But these feelings would be very faint, if we did not in our experience know what sorrows and temptations mean.[130]

Newton's Disclosure in Pastoral Care

Newton's humility and ministerial posture as a fellow sufferer led him to be very open with others about his own trials and struggles. Gordon observes that he writes "with an amazing openness about his own weaknesses."[131] It is rare to read a pastoral letter from Newton that lacks reference to his own past or present-day struggle. For example, he is very open about his own heart-trials: "My chief and abiding trial lies within, but I hope the Lord will sanctify it, to make me by degrees little in my own eyes and to wean me from resting or trusting in any thing short of Himself."[132] Newton is also quick to admit his own sins: "The Lord forgive us if the comforts which we have acknowledged as our choicest earthly blessings have given occasion to manifest the most frequent and glaring proofs of the depravity and vile ingratitude of our hearts. It has certainly been thus with me."[133]

Since Newton focused chiefly on matters of the heart, he did not need to have experienced the identical circumstances of suffering to connect with a struggling person at the heart level. For example, when his friend's

---

130. Newton, *Works* (1985), 1:198.
131. Gordon, "John Newton," 94.
132. Gordon, *Wise Counsel*, 70.
133. Gordon, *Wise Counsel*, 214.

John Newton's Theology of Suffering and Its Application to Pastoral Care

wife approached death, Newton used his experience of his adopted daughter's death as an avenue to minister to him. He wrote:

> My dear Eliza was not indeed a wife, but she was very near my heart. A few weeks or days before her removal, had it been lawful and agreeable to the will of God, I think I would have redeemed her life at the price of a limb; yet when the stroke came very near, it was so circumstanced, so alleviated, so sweetened, that could the lifting up of my finger have detained her, and restored her to perfect health, I could not have lifted it up. Perhaps I never suffered more, perhaps I never suffered less, than when I saw her in the agonies of death. Then I found that the Lord was all-sufficient indeed; and I trust you will find him so.[134]

Notice Newton's pattern: he identifies a similar issue from his life, connects with the person regarding the common heart-level struggles in the difficulty, then uses his own experience (leaning on his theology of suffering) to minister hope and instruction to the person.

Newton's use of his own life and struggles strengthened his pastoral care in three ways. First, it gave credibility to his counsel. As Newton wrote to a fellow pastor, it demonstrates that "what you recommend to them you do not speak by *rote*, but from the experience of your heart."[135] Second, it gave his people hope. As the Lord had helped Newton, so it encouraged others that He would help them. This practice demonstrated Newton's "experimental" theology of suffering at work. As Newton encouraged Ryland, "Then I found that the Lord was all-sufficient indeed; and I trust you will find him so."[136] Finally, it formed a bond between the minister and parishioner. Gordon explains, "As a result of such openness, readers quickly realize that Newton struggles with many of the same things as they do. Hence, his self-disclosure forms a bond between himself and his correspondents. And it is encouraging to learn that one's struggles are common to others."[137] Thus, Newton's genuine openness and self-disclosure in pastoral care strengthened his effectiveness and enhanced his influence.

While the habit of openness in Newton's letters undoubtedly contributed to his popularity, some felt that it bordered on being inappropriate. For example, Cecil felt that Newton offered too many details about his love

---

134. Gordon, *Wise Counsel*, 186.
135. Newton, *Letters*, 45.
136. Gordon, *Wise Counsel*, 186.
137. Gordon, "John Newton," 95.

for his wife in his *Letters to a Wife*. Cairns describes Newton's memoir to his wife as "long and pathetic" and his annual journal entries on the anniversary of her death as "a series of pathetic little elegies."[138]

Though such openness in Newton's day about marital relations may have been somewhat taboo, the popularity and massive impact of Newton's pastoral letters demonstrate that a minister's self-disclosure brings credibility, authenticity, and influence to his pastoral care. But Newton's openness was not interpreted as self-focused or personally discouraging. Gordon explains, "Amazingly, Newton's letters are not depressing. This is because of his own strong faith in God's ability to keep him."[139] In addition, Newton's use of his own life and personal experiences always centered on Christ, not himself.

While effectiveness in ministerial counseling requires biblical knowledge and pastoral skills, Newton demonstrated that the pastor must also be transformed by his own theology. Shaped by his own experimental theology of suffering, Newton's pastoral care was marked by Christlike character, a sympathetic posture, and authentic self-disclosure. These personal qualities of the minister, developed through applying his theology to his own heart and life, produce unique dynamics in pastoral shepherding that lead to more effective care for others.

Keeping Christ Central in Pastoral Care

As noted in the previous chapter, the sufficiency of Christ was the central theme of Newton's theology of suffering and his main message and goal in pastoral care. It is remarkable that one can observe such consistency in his counsel in over one thousand letters of pastoral care covering a variety of subjects and topics. Tony Reinke concurs: "The core of his pastoral theology radiates the all-sufficiency of Christ. Christ is the comprehensive vision that unifies Newton's pastoral letters, his sermons, and the many hymns written out of his own spiritual experience and personal devotional life."[140] But the often unseen theological structure undergirding and upholding the centrality of Jesus in Newton's counsel is his theology of suffering. Newton's understanding of the Christian life, specifically how he understood God's sovereignty, Christ's work, the redemption of suffering for sanctification, his

---

138. Cecil, *Life of John Newton*, 195; Cairns, *Religion of Dr. Johnson*, 51–52.
139. Gordon, "John Newton," 95.
140. Reinke, *Newton*, 30.

perspective on trials, and the nature of temptation, is the key to understanding how and why Newton kept Christ central in his pastoral care to others.

Newton's theology of suffering undergirds the centrality of Christ in pastoral care in three ways. First, Christ must be central because He directs the highest desire of life, which ought to be the main goal in care. Newton wrote of his own heart, "I trust the great desire of my soul is that Christ may be all in all to me, that my whole dependence, love, and aim, may center in him alone."[141] His personal purpose was conformity to Christ, communion with Christ, and complete dependence on Christ. But he also believed this was the goal for all believers, and he made this end his chief aim in pastoral care. He encouraged a fellow believer:

> I trust you find the name and grace of Jesus more and more precious to you: his promises more sweet, and your hope in them more abiding; your sense of your own weakness and unworthiness daily increasing; your persuasion of his all-sufficiency to guide, support, and comfort you, more confirmed. You owe your growth in these respects, in a great measure, to his blessing upon those afflictions which he has prepared for you and sanctified to you. May you praise him for all that is past, and trust him for all that is to come.[142]

Not only does this quote illustrate Newton's intended purpose in pastoral care, it demonstrates his view that trials particularly promote this purpose in the believer's life: "You owe your growth in these respects, in a great measure, to his blessings upon those afflictions which he has prepared for you and sanctified you."[143]

In other words, God uses trials to magnify the person of Jesus and conform the believer ever more to His image. Wise pastors direct suffering Christians to see how their difficulties glorify Christ and draw them ever closer to Him. One of Newton's favorite verses was Phil 1:21: "For to me, to live is Christ, and to die is gain." Reinke summarizes Newton's viewpoint: "To live is Christ, and to live simply in Christ is the aim of the Christian life."[144] The centrality of Jesus in Newton's theology directed him to keep Christ as the focus in his pastoral care ministry.

---

141. Newton, *Twenty-Five Letters*, 57.
142. Newton, *Works* (1985), 2:220.
143. Newton, *Works* (1985), 2:220.
144. Reinke, *Newton*, 99–100.

Second, Christ must be central in counseling because He is the means by which Christians benefit from pastoral care. For Newton, every spiritual provision comes through the person of Jesus. Spiritual help in counseling is not achieved directly through the minister's efforts but through Christ Himself. But Newton also understood that God designed trials to enhance and magnify these spiritual provisions to the sufferer. Therefore, effective pastors direct suffering Christians to turn to Christ to see and experience these blessings in their own lives. Though Newton often used his own example, he always referred his people to Christ as their chief help. For example, Newton encourages believers to look to Christ since they "become by beholding" Him. He explained, "It is thus by looking to Jesus, that the believer is enlightened and strengthened, and grows in grace and sanctification. . . . By beholding we are gradually formed into the resemblance of Him whom we see, admire, and love."[145] For Newton, trials facilitate this process. He wrote, "By enduring temptation, you . . . have the honour of being conformed to your Head. He suffered, being tempted; and because he loves you, he calls you to a participation of his sufferings."[146] And through these temptations, "we are conformed to the life of Christ, so likewise, by the sanctifying power of grace, they are made subservient to advance our conformity to his image."[147] In other words, trials are the means by which God sanctifies believers as they look to and rely upon Christ.

The pastor also should direct believers to Christ to receive the mercy and grace they need to endure their trials (Heb 4:14–16). This process magnifies the work of Christ and makes believers more dependent upon Him. Newton illustrated this principle when he counsels a struggling Christian, "Above all, keep close to the Throne of Grace."[148] The maturing believer "is now taught to go to the Lord at once for 'grace to help in every time of need.' Thus he is strong, not in himself, but in the grace that is in Christ Jesus."[149] He should not "rest in grace received" but always "be pressing forward" to "grow in grace in the knowledge of Jesus."[150] Thus, Christ must be central in counseling because He is the means by which believers receive the help they need in their trials.

---

145. Newton, *Works* (1985), 2:487.
146. Newton, *Works* (1985), 1:230.
147. Newton, *Works* (1985), 1:231.
148. Newton, *Works* (1985), 2:147.
149. Newton, *Works* (1985), 1:211.
150. Newton, *Works* (1985), 6:73.

Third, Christ must be central in pastoral care because He alone is sufficient to help with counseling needs. Newton believed that God designed trials to demonstrate the all-sufficiency of Jesus as the sole hope for hurting people. Thus, the centrality of Jesus is upheld by and through suffering. Therefore, he affirmed that Christ's sufficiency was the only sure foundation of pastoral care, and the minister's role is to point strugglers to embrace this reality. Newton modeled this function when he wrote, "Here, indeed, we may expect some trials and difficulties, but His grace shall be sufficient to support and comfort, to sanctify and deliver."[151] Again, Newton explained, "It is by the experience of these evils within ourselves, and by feeling our utter insufficiency, either to perform duty, or to withstand our enemies, that the Lord takes occasion to show us the suitableness, the sufficiency, the freeness, the unchangeableness of his power and grace."[152] Thus, Christ must be central in pastoral care because Jesus alone is all-sufficient to bring hope and help to struggling believers.

Newton exemplified one central theme in his pastoral care: Jesus Christ. Jesus was the core of his theology, and his doctrine of suffering upheld Christ in a way that made the person and work of Jesus the primary focus of his counseling ministry. He believed that reliance upon Jesus was the goal of care, that the provisions of Jesus were the means of care, and that the sufficiency of Jesus was the basis of care. Further, he believed that the context of suffering is the training ground that God most often uses to uphold the centrality of Christ in the believer's life. These dynamics are illustrated well in Newton's counsel to a struggling Christian:

> How often have I longed to be an instrument of establishing you in the peace and hope of the Gospel! and I have but one way of attempting it, by telling you over and over of the power and grace of Jesus. You want nothing to make you happy, but to have the eyes of your understanding more fixed upon the Redeemer, and more enlightened by the Holy Spirit to behold his glory. Oh, he is a suitable Saviour! He has power, authority, and compassion to save to the uttermost. He has given his word of promise, to engage our confidence; and he is able and faithful to make good the expectations and desires he has raised in us. Put your trust in him.[153]

---

151. Newton, *Twenty-Five Letters*, 85.
152. Newton, *Letters*, 71.
153. Newton, *Works* (1985), 2:146.

Conclusion

The life and ministry of John Newton demonstrated that his theology was the central influence that shaped and directed his pastoral care. Specifically, Newton's theology of suffering formed a framework that guided his counseling ministry to struggling Christians. Newton's example illustrates that theology drives the content of counseling and that different doctrines can be utilized to facilitate particular ends in counseling, such as ministering hope or providing purpose. His theology also informed his expectations in pastoral care, such as growth benchmarks in sanctification and insight regarding the pace of Christian maturity. Newton's doctrine of suffering informed how he understood people, contributing to a framework that allowed him to better comprehend people and thus be more effective in caring for them. His understanding of trials helped him see the value of afflictions in the pastor's life, which brings credibility to a minister's pastoral care and produces sympathy in him toward strugglers. As Newton applied his theology of suffering in his own afflictions, it humbled him, causing him to relate to others as a fellow struggler and friend. Finally, Newton's theology of suffering was the foundation upon which he centralized the person and work of Christ in his pastoral care. Newton not only believed Jesus should be the focus of the Christian life, his theology of suffering provided the connection between the primacy of Christ and the various trials and struggles of his people. For Newton, making Christ the core of his ministerial care efforts was not artificial or contrived but was required by his own experimental theology. Like the apostle Paul, Newton found that he could not point sufferers to any other than "Christ, and Him crucified" (1 Cor 2:2).

These facets of Newton's theology, put into practice in both his own life and his pastoral care ministry, not only endeared him to his people but made him incredibly influential in his ministry to them. Newton believed that caring for God's people in the context of pastoral ministry was his highest privilege. He wrote to a friend, "To administer any comfort to his children is the greatest honour and pleasure I can receive in this life."[154] The next chapter will explore Newton's pastoral care to his two closest friends: his wife, Mary, and William Cowper.

---

154. Newton, *Works* (1985), 1:682.

4

Case Studies in Newton's Pastoral Care

While John Newton offered pastoral care to dozens of individuals during his ministerial career, he walked with two of his closest friends through severe, lifelong trials. Newton's wife, Mary (he referred to her as "Polly"), was his most intimate and best friend. Polly experienced thirty-six years of chronic health issues, which often left her confined to her room and in excruciating pain for weeks at a time. Newton was not only her loving husband; throughout her chronic illness, he was her caretaker, pastor, counselor, and best friend. Thus, the pastoral care relationship between Newton and his wife is both unique and long-standing.

Newton's second-closest companion was the poet William Cowper. Newton and Cowper's friendship extended over three decades and included a season of ministry together in the town of Olney. However, Cowper experienced five significant bouts of severe depression and attempted suicide on multiple occasions, leading to an ongoing season of melancholy and withdrawal from Christianity. Newton faithfully walked with him throughout his struggle in the darkness of despair and ministered to him. His ministry to Cowper is worthy of investigation since it highlights how Newton provided care in a particularly challenging situation over several decades and demonstrates that his theology of suffering formed the structure of his ministry to Cowper.

Case Studies in Newton's Pastoral Care

This chapter explores Newton's pastoral care ministry to Polly and Cowper as two case studies of his counsel. Newton's care for these two individuals demonstrates how his theology of suffering directed his ministry to his two closest friends over extended seasons of affliction.

Mrs. Mary Catlett Newton

John Newton first met Mary "Polly" Catlett on December 12, 1742. Polly's mother and Newton's mother were cousins, and Newton had been invited to visit his relative's home while traveling in the area. In his autobiography, Newton described meeting Polly for the first time: "Almost at the first sight of this girl . . . I was impressed with an affection for her, which never abated."[1] Over the next several years, Newton's love for Polly led to a series of irresponsible decisions but also provided him with a hope to persevere through dark and difficult times.[2] They maintained contact over seven years and married in February 1750. After three voyages to Africa, Newton's seagoing career suddenly came to an end when he experienced a seizure in the fall of 1754. He fully recovered and never experienced any similar incidents for the rest of his life. In contrast, Newton's seizure sent Polly into a yearlong "severe illness" that doctors were unable to explain.[3] While she eventually recovered, Polly would experience chronic ill health for the next three and a half decades. Roughly every ten years, she experienced a particularly debilitating season of affliction. Adding up all her months of misery, Newton estimated that she was significantly ill or in pain for ten of their forty years of marriage.[4]

Following her initial illness in 1754, Polly began a second season of suffering in August of 1763. Writing to his friend, Thomas Haweis, Newton mentioned Polly's "poor state of health" and that he "cannot leave her for long."[5] For two to three weeks, Polly's pain was so significant that she

---

1. Newton, *Narrative*, in *Works* (2015), 1:16.

2. For example, Newton intentionally arrived late for a lucrative job opportunity arranged by his father, which compromised the deal. He also deserted his naval post, resulting in a public flogging and demotion. In both cases, he made these irresponsible choices in order to be with Polly. See Aitken, *John Newton*, chapters 3–7, and Newton's autobiography, *Authentic Narrative*.

3. Newton, *Works* (1985), 5:487.

4. Newton, *Works* (1985), 5:613.

5. Newton, "Letters to Thomas Haweis," 37.

believed she would die.[6] For the next eight months, she remained confined to her chambers.[7] Finally, Newton spoke of her recovery in April of 1764: "I desire to praise God for the progress of your recovery; and begin now to think seriously of our removal."[8] Yet, Newton later lamented of Polly's "headache" and "frequent indispositions" that returned later that fall.[9]

In November 1775, Polly experienced a third and more severe season of illness. Over the next year, Newton mentioned in his diary several seasons of afflictions that she endured, leading up to a bout with shingles in September and seizures in November.[10] He wrote, "Last night my dear when going to bed was suddenly seized with an alarming, terrifying affliction in her head as if her senses must have immediately gone. O my poor heart. How ready to think, anything but this."[11]

While Polly recovered, she continued to experience various afflictions, culminating in October 1788 when she was diagnosed with breast cancer.[12] Her tumor was about the size of "half a melon" and was inoperable. For about six months, Polly was in significant pain.[13] However, in April 1789, her pain largely subsided, and she enjoyed more or less a pain-free existence until the fall of 1790, except for "three or four short intervals."[14] But by October, her pain returned, and Satan was allowed to "take advantage of her bodily weakness" such that she "lost all hold of the truth itself," including her belief in the Bible. She also spoke to Newton with "indifference." Newton described this event as the "high-water mark of my trial."[15] About two weeks later, "the Lord restored peace to her soul."[16] But her body continued to decline. By November, she was "severely disabled in

---

6. Newton, "Letters to Thomas Haweis," 23.
7. Newton, "Letters to Thomas Haweis," 43–62.
8. Newton, *Works* (1985), 5:538.
9. Newton, *Works* (1985), 5:546.
10. Entries from September 24 and 26, 1776 in Newton, "Diaries 1751–1807." See also Aitken, *John Newton*, 257–58.
11. Entry from November 19, 1776 in Newton, "Diaries 1751–1807." See also Aitken, *John Newton*, 258.
12. Newton writes about this incident in his memoir about his wife's last illness and death. See Newton, *Works* (1985), 5:614.
13. Aitken, *John Newton*, 329.
14. Newton, *Works* (1985), 5:616.
15. Newton, *Works* (1985), 5:617.
16. Newton, *Works* (1985), 5:617.

both body and mind."[17] She lost consciousness on Sunday, December 12, and died the following Wednesday.

Newton preached three times the day she died, believing it was his duty to minister to his people even in his own grief.[18] He also preached her funeral sermon. For several years following, Newton would honor his wife with unique essays, poems, and diary entries that he made on the anniversary of her homegoing.[19] In 1793, he published a selection of his correspondence with Polly entitled *Letters to a Wife*. These documents, his diary entries, and letters to others provide a clear picture of Newton's relationship with Polly and his care for her throughout her illnesses.[20]

Newton's Care and Ministry to Polly

Newton's care for Polly is a unique and significant case study of his pastoral care for three reasons. First, she was his wife and his dearest friend.[21] Observing Newton's care for his spouse demonstrates his most authentic convictions about suffering and care. This relationship also highlights how Newton himself was processing and dealing with Polly's grief, adding another dimension of insight into his thinking. Second, Newton's relationship with Polly was one of his most prolonged "pastoral care" relationships. There is significant literature available regarding Newton's relationship with Polly, providing comprehensive data for investigation. Third, Newton's care of his wife highlights ministry to an individual with a chronic, decades-long affliction. While he cared for many individuals in seasons of acute distress, his relationship with his wife marked a ministry in ongoing suffering.

---

17. Aitken, *John Newton*, 330.

18. Newton, *Works* (1985), 5:623. Newton seemed to follow God's counsel to the prophet Ezekiel in regard to the death of his wife: "Behold, I take away from thee the desire of thine eyes, with a stroke; yet neither shalt thou mourn nor weep, neither shall thy tears run down" (Ezek 24:16). See Newton, *Works* (1985), 5:489.

19. Newton, *Works* (1985), 5:631–43.

20. In addition, there are fifty-three letters from Polly to Newton in the Church Missionary Society Archive housed at Cadbury Research Library, University of Birmingham.

21. "Newton's closest friend and confidant was his wife." Aitken, *John Newton*, 195.

John Newton's Theology of Suffering and Its Application to Pastoral Care

Newton's Theology of Suffering Formed a Foundation of Friendship

Newton's Christian faith, including his theology of suffering, developed at the same time as his relationship with Polly. Thus, the progression of both his doctrine and his friendship with his wife is an interwoven story. Referencing his letters to his new bride, Newton wrote: "My Letters, which at first were trifling, soon became more serious: and, as I was led into farther views of the principles and privileges of the Gospel, I endeavoured to communicate to my dear correspondent what I had received."[22] John and Polly were married less than two years after the "storm" of 1748 that initiated Newton's conversion.[23] His early letters to Polly thus provide documentation of his progress in the Christian faith, including the development of his theology of suffering. As Newton progressed in faith, the letters came to focus on the same themes that form the foundation of his biblical understanding of affliction: the sovereignty of God, the sufficiency of Christ, the redemption of suffering, and biblical perspectives on trials.[24] Newton mentioned these four topics in the letters he wrote to Polly in their first year of marriage. Since John and Polly were separated from one another in the earliest years of their marriage, "trials" shaped the early context of their relationship development.[25] In other words, the Newtons were forced to

---

22. Newton, *Works* (1985), 5:311.

23. The exact time of Newton's conversion is disputed and is difficult to determine. While some biographers believe the storm event of March 1748 to be the occasion of his conversion, Newton's autobiography seems to contradict this understanding. Instead, Newton claims he was only confident that he was "enabled to hope and believe in a crucified Saviour" and was "delivered from the power and dominion of sin" a couple years later (1754) following a fever during his African voyage to Sierra Leone. See Newton, *Works* (2015), 1:59. A third option is that Newton was converted shortly after meeting Alexander Clunie in St. Kitts in 1754. Newton writes in his diary at the time, "I now see that I had not that perfect dependence on Jesus my Saviour and him only for justification and acceptance as I thought I had." As quoted in Cecil, *Life of John Newton*, 79. Newton stated he was not able to assign the time of his conversion "with exactness." See Letter 8 in Newton, "Letters to Benjamin Fawcett."

24. These four themes form the bulk of the foundation of Newton's theology of suffering. A fifth theme, his understanding of temptation and Satan, seemed to develop a bit later. See chapter 2 for more information on his theology of suffering.

25. The trials experienced through their early years of separation were not just emotional; seafaring was an exceedingly dangerous vocation in the 1700s. The likelihood that Polly would lose her new husband at sea was a realistic possibility. Both Newton's autobiography and his *Letters to a Wife* document some of these dangers.

work out their understanding of these critical doctrines through this early season of mild suffering.

God's providence was one of the first doctrines to develop in Newton's mind. His autobiography traces the development of this theme through various experiences and influences.[26] The emphasis on God's sovereignty was likewise a common topic in his early letters to Polly: "I am sensible that, in the most remote inhospitable clime, a protecting Providence will surround me, and is no less to be depended on in the most apparent dangers, than in the greatest seeming security."[27] Likewise, John encouraged Polly to look to Christ in her trials, to "endeavor to cast all your care upon him who has promised to care for us, if we will but put our trust in him."[28] Further, Newton communicated how God redeemed his suffering to preserve him from greater wickedness: "Providence was mercifully intent to make my situation completely miserable for a time, in order to preserve me from that utter ruin, into which my folly and wickedness might otherwise have plunged me."[29] Finally, he began to communicate to Polly unique biblical perspectives concerning trials. For example, following a perilous time at sea, Newton wrote to her: "I readily inform you of the danger we have been in, now it is happily over; and hope you will not be alarmed because I am still liable to the like; but rather be comforted with the thought, that in the greatest difficulties the same great Deliverer is always present. The winds and the seas obey him."[30]

These seeds of Newton's theology of suffering are reflected in the first years of marriage, demonstrating that such doctrinal distinctives influenced the foundation of John and Polly's relationship. Yet, these affirmations of sound principles lacked depth and development. In addition, Polly and John were likely not yet true believers at this stage of life.[31] In the preface of his *Letters to a Wife*, Newton writes that at the time of their marriage, they "knew not" the Lord God. He explained, "If I had any spiritual light, it was

---

26. See chapter 1 for more information.
27. Newton, *Works* (1985), 5:327.
28. Newton, *Works* (1985), 5:326.
29. Newton, *Works* (1985), 5:335.
30. Newton, *Works* (1985), 5:329.
31. As John and Polly were yet not Christians, it would take true conversion and time for Newton's theology of suffering to develop. But his early letters to Polly indicate that he had already acquired many biblical perspectives regarding trials.

but as the first faint streaks of the early dawn; and I believe it was not yet daybreak with my dear wife."[32]

Over time, however, these seeds began to sprout in evidence of true conversion and depth of theological understanding. Aitken argues that Newton's religious zeal was revived as he was forced to part with her for Africa.[33] The time away from Polly allowed him to focus on his walk with God. It gave him ample discretionary time, which he used to immerse himself in daily Bible reading, prayer, worship, and the study of Latin authors.[34] Over time, a notable shift occurred in Newton's letters to Polly away from superficial topics toward a more serious depth of spiritual truths.[35] But it was the onset of Polly's illness in 1754 that significantly developed his faith and eventually hers.[36]

Newton's Theology of Suffering Directed the Content of His Care

Since Newton had adopted many biblical principles regarding suffering prior to his seizure, the onset of Polly's illness was not so much an occasion to discover new biblical answers but a season in which to grow and apply them in an ongoing trial. The five themes that undergirded Newton's theology of suffering and formed the framework of his pastoral care likewise created the structure of his care for Polly. This section will develop his doctrines of affliction as they pertained to his wife's chronic suffering.

---

32. Newton, *Works* (1985), 5:306–7.
33. Aitken, *John Newton*, 106.
34. Aitken, *John Newton*, 107.
35. The beginning of this shift can especially be observed in late 1752 during Newton's second African voyage. The letters during his third voyage particularly contrast with those of the previous two, and his subsequent letters to Polly from Liverpool (following his seizure and the start of her illness) demonstrate a clear, maturing faith. One clear evidence of this transition is Newton's emphasis on Jesus Christ in his latter letters. Though he writes often of God's mercy and providence, the name of Jesus does not occur in his letters to Polly until April 18, 1754, on the occasion of his fever. This reality also gives credibility to the theory that this fever was the occasion of Newton's actual conversion, though Newton stated that he did not know the exact date. See Letter 8 in Newton, "Letters to Benjamin Fawcett."
36. It is unclear exactly when Newton became a Christian. However, there is good evidence that he was truly converted following his meeting with Alexander Clunie in May of 1754 (see chapter 1 for more information about Clunie's influence in his life). However, it is more difficult to determine the timing of Polly's conversion. This topic will be discussed later in this chapter.

Case Studies in Newton's Pastoral Care

Sovereignty and Chronic Illness

A frequent theme of Newton's earlier letters to Polly, God's sovereign goodness remained the backbone of his theological understanding of suffering. Writing to his wife in her affliction, Newton encouraged her to remember that both blessings and sufferings come from God's hand: "Your frequent indispositions are not pleasant; but I trust they are mercies, for which we have reason to be thankful. Our comforts and crosses are all from the same hand. We have chastisement, only because we need it. I aim to leave you in the Lord's hands."[37] Here, Newton wove together several perspectives regarding suffering that are rooted in the sovereignty and character of God. First, unpleasant "indispositions" are disguised mercies, though they do not seem like it. Second, since difficulties are gifts of grace, believers should learn to practice thankfulness toward them. Third, both comforts and crosses (afflictions) come from God's hand. Fourth, chastisement is necessary "because we need it" to accomplish God's good purposes. Thus, Newton concludes that he should entrust Polly into the Lord's hand.

Writing to another sufferer, Newton noted the necessity of remembering that it is God's hand that afflicts and that this perspective is a key to endurance: "Though he put forth his hand, and seem to threaten our dearest comforts, yet when we remember that it is his hand, when we consider that it is his design, his love, his wisdom, and his power, we cannot refuse to trust him."[38] On a different occasion, Newton directed Polly to focus on God's character as the primary cause in difficulties, though He works through "second causes" (such as illness). This practice helps believers to "see" His hand more clearly. He explained:

> I thank God I can now look through instruments and second causes, and see his wisdom and goodness immediately concerned in fixing my lot. He knows our wants and our infirmities. He knows what indulgencies [sic] may, by his blessing, promote our real good, and excite us to praise his name; and what those are which might be snares and temptations to us, and prove hurtful. And He knows how to bestow the one, and to withhold the other. He does all things well![39]

---

37. Newton, *Works* (1985), 5:546.
38. Newton, *Works* (1985), 6:33.
39. Newton, *Works* (1985), 5:500.

John Newton's Theology of Suffering and Its Application to Pastoral Care

Because God is full of wisdom and goodness, and He is fully knowledgeable of believers concerning what will help and hurt, He constantly works to accomplish the best good. Newton helped Polly meditate on God's character in affliction, remembering that He "does all things well," even in chronic illness.[40]

Christ's Sufficiency and Chronic Illness

As Newton's faith developed, Christ became a more central and deeper focus of his life and ministry. Regarding Polly's illness, he encouraged her by reminding her that Jesus is a sympathetic High Priest who has also suffered affliction. He wrote:

> This Jesus whom you seek, was in all points tempted and afflicted (sin excepted) like unto us. He has tasted suffering and anguish of mind, as well as death, for all his followers. Therefore He is a high priest who can have compassion upon our infirmities, and is able to succour them that are tempted, and knows what temptations mean. Go on, my dearest; I trust you are in the right way; wait patiently upon the Lord.[41]

While Newton could not personally relate to the chronic sufferings of his wife, he pointed her to Christ as one who could relate and provide sufficient strength to avoid surrendering to temptation.[42]

Many years later, as Polly approached the end of her life, Newton directed her to the centrality of Christ and His sufficiency in their relationship through many seasons of suffering. He wrote:

> The Lord Jesus is our best Friend: his character is supremely excellent, our obligations to him are inexpressible, our dependence upon him is absolute, and our happiness, in every sense, is in his hands. May our love therefore be fixed upon him, and we shall do

---

40. Newton, *Works* (1985), 5:500.

41. Newton, *Works* (1985), 5:498.

42. Both secular psychology and Christian pastoral care have been impacted by so-called "empathy" models of care, which ground success in counseling in the counselor's skill in empathizing with the client. In contrast, Newton pointed people to Jesus as a sympathetic High Priest, a focus that he likely learned from biblical texts like Heb 2:17 and 4:14–16, as well as from Puritans like John Flavel. For a brief introduction to John Flavel's pastoral care which emphasized Christ in contrast to the "empathy" model, see Elliott, "None So Tender-Hearted," 202–19.

well. He will guide us with his eye, guard us by his power, and his fulness and bounty will supply all our wants.[43]

Later, in the same letter, he connected this point to suffering: "He can support us, and sanctify the painful dispensation to us both. I pray to be enabled to intrust and resign every thing to him. This is not an easy lesson to flesh and blood; but grace can make it practicable."[44] Remembering Christ and His sufficiency enables the believer to entrust and resign all to Him. These thoughtful comments toward the conclusion of their marriage make it clear that the centrality of Christ and complete dependence upon Him was a theme of John's counsel and a key to Polly's encouragement and endurance through her trials.

God's Redemption of Chronic Illness

One way that John and Polly kept Christ central as they looked for His sovereign hand in her ongoing affliction was to recognize how He was redeeming her suffering for good. Chapter 2 catalogs several of these "redemptive" perspectives of suffering as themes Newton would often employ in counseling struggling believers. His consistency in sharing these same truths with Polly demonstrates authenticity in his doctrine and practice. In his letters, he focused on four ways that God worked to redeem Polly's afflictions for good.

First, the Newtons often discussed how Polly's affliction caused them to be weaned from the world and all its attachments, including their attachment to one another:

> Thus, at one time or another, every family and every person finds vanity entwined with their choicest comforts. It is best for us that it is so; for, poor and vain as this life is, we are sufficiently attached to it. How strong then would our attachment be, if we met with no rubs or thorns by the way? Is not the history of every day a comment upon those words, "This is not your rest?"[45]

---

43. Newton, *Works* (1985), 5:610.

44. Newton, *Works* (1985), 5:611. In context, Newton's immediate application is to an illness of their adopted daughter, Eliza Cunningham, though he would relate the same application to Polly in her afflictions.

45. Newton, *Works* (1985), 5:587.

In another letter, Newton reminded her that "sickness and pain, and a near prospect of death, force upon the mind a conviction of the littleness and vanity of a worldly life."[46]

On many occasions, John referenced his temptation to make Polly an idolatrous attachment.[47] He consistently affirmed that her chronic ill health was an intentional redemptive work of God to keep him from an inordinate attachment to her.[48] He wrote to her: "Let us watch and pray against setting up our rest here, and misplacing that regard upon each other, which is due only to him."[49] Similarly, he encouraged Polly by emphasizing that God designed her illnesses to prepare them for their future separation by death. He wrote, "I cannot feel how much I miss you, when you are from me but a few weeks, without thinking what support I should need if I was wholly deprived of you."[50] Newton added by way of conclusion:

> May the Lord impress the event of this unknown hour upon our minds; not to distress us, but to keep alive in us a sense of the insignificancy of every thing here, compared with the one thing needful! May He cause our faith to grow and take deep root, and fix in us such a persuasion of his all-sufficiency and grace, and of our interest in his promises, that we may trust and not be afraid, but cheerfully commit all that is before us to his care.[51]

---

46. Newton, *Works* (1985), 5:547.

47. For example, Newton, *Works* (1985), 5:556, 564, 608. See also Aitken, *John Newton*, 105, 195–96.

48. Newton reflected on this reality after Polly's death, looking back to her final decline. As she lost mobility and, eventually, consciousness, Newton made this observation: "All this was necessary on my account. The rod had a voice; and it was the voice of the Lord. I understood the meaning no less plainly than if He had spoken audibly from heaven, and said, 'Now contemplate your idol: now see what she is, whom you once presumed to prefer to Me!'" Newton, *Works* (1985), 5:619. Polly also understood Newton's perspective and claimed that she too struggled to avoid an idolatrous attachment to him. She wrote, "I am as easy as I can be in Your absence. I miss You and wish for You every moment. The Lord pardon my Idolatry and make me to love Him more and serve Him better than I have ever done" (Newton, "Letter to John Newton").

49. Newton, *Works* (1985), 5:513.

50. Newton, *Works* (1985), 5:593.

51. Newton, *Works* (1985), 5:593. Elsewhere, he writes: "We likewise have been long preserved, and often restored to each other. But a time will come when every gourd will wither, every cistern be broken. Let us pray for a waiting, resigned, and dependent frame of spirit; for ability to commit ourselves, and our all, into the merciful hands of Him who careth for us; and that, while we are spared, we may walk together, as help-meets and fellow-heirs of eternal life." Newton, *Works* (1985), 5:554–55.

Case Studies in Newton's Pastoral Care

In other words, Polly's illness was a powerful reminder of how much Christ's support will be needed on the day of their final separation, thus bolstering their perceived need for Christ's sufficient grace.

Second, Newton encouraged Polly to remember God's past deliverances and redemptive graces to endure her present suffering. He counseled her:

> How often has he made himself known as your Deliverer and Physician, in raising you up from the gates of the grave! May we always remember his goodness in your last affliction! How did he sweeten the bitter cup; strengthen you with strength in your soul; enable you to pray for yourself; engage the hearts of many in prayer for you, and then speedily answer our prayers! Let us then excite each other to praise him![52]

These recollections, according to Newton, were designed to help them see the sufficiency of Christ upholding her so that they would grow in both confidence in and devotion to Him. He wrote:

> I often think, and hope, you do not forget how graciously he supported and answered you in your late distress. There was a something that could, and did, bear you up under pain and anguish, and refresh your spirit when your bodily strength was almost worn out. This is an instance of what he can do; and should be a bond of gratitude upon both our souls. Your health is restored, and mine is preserved. May we devote our whole selves to him.[53]

Third, Newton helped Polly see that her illnesses are redeemed in how they caused them to lean more on Christ and His sufficiency. He often emphasized what he called "experimental knowledge," the reality that doctrine must be embraced in the affections, not just understood in the mind.[54] Newton believed that Christians often acquire experimental knowledge when known doctrines are worked out in application to life, particularly in trials.[55] He related the reality of this dynamic to Polly through her suffering:

> I often speak much, in public, of his all-sufficiency to uphold under every trial. I have seldom had a more remarkable proof of it, than in the course of this late affliction. May he enable you to

---

52. Newton, *Works* (1985), 5:548.
53. Newton, *Works* (1985), 5:549.
54. Newton likely inherited this view of experimental knowledge from the Puritans. For more information, see chapter 3.
55. Newton, *Works* (1985), 2:20–23, 2:174–76, 3:102, 6:142.

improve this instance of his goodness, as an argument against that vain reasoning of unbelief which has so often discouraged you."[56]

Polly's chronic suffering forced them both to lean more on Christ as a kind means of redeeming affliction: "We may praise God for that pain or sickness, however severe, which teaches us, in good earnest, to call upon Him. You have been in trouble, you called upon him, and he has delivered you according to his word."[57] In other words, her struggles created an occasion to lean on Christ more and observe His faithfulness in answering and sustaining her through it.

Finally, God redeemed Polly's suffering by using it as the vehicle to bring her to salvation. Newton wrote, "Next to the salvation of my own soul, I have had no desire so often in my heart, so often in my lips, as to see you wholly given up to him. . . . What a bauble, in my eye, would the possession of the whole earth be, in comparison with our being fellow-heirs of the hope of eternal life!"[58] Following Polly's recovery from a season of illness in 1766, he wrote to her regarding (what he seemed to conclude was) her conversion: "But with nothing has my heart been more affected, than with his goodness in and since your late illness. I am persuaded something passed then, that has left a relish and effect upon your mind ever since. Is it not so? Are you not determined to be his?"[59]

Newton's emphasis on the redemption of suffering permeated his interactions with Polly, consistent with his manner in other care relationships. He credited God's work in her grief as both a divine restraint from excessive love for each other and as the instrument of salvation in her life.

Divine Perspectives on Chronic Illness

The next theme of Newton's theology of suffering was his unique system of interpreting afflictions through a biblical framework. In his dialogue with Polly, he utilized many of the same perspectives covered in chapter 3. Three of these dynamics merit particular attention.

First, John encouraged Polly to utilize appropriate means to bring relief and restore her health: "Make use of means prescribed for the restoring

---

56. Newton, *Works* (1985), 5:584.
57. Newton, *Works* (1985), 5:497.
58. Newton, *Works* (1985), 5:551.
59. Newton, *Works* (1985), 5:550–51.

Case Studies in Newton's Pastoral Care

of your health."[60] In other words, the goal of "resignation to Christ" does not mean that Christians should avoid the pursuit of relief when it is possible. Polly followed John's advice, seeking help from physicians, medicine, and exercise.[61] However, Newton cautioned her: "Make use of means prescribed for the restoring of your health, but do not rest in them. The blessing must be from the Great Physician. To him let us apply for it; and ascribe to him all the praise if we obtain relief."[62] Maintaining his distinction between primary and secondary causes, he reminded her that hope and trust must be in God Himself, though He may utilize secondary causes as means of relief.[63] This outlook also means that God is ultimately to be praised when medicine or other means provide improvement to her condition.

Second, John helped Polly keep relief in perspective by reminding her that improvement is always temporary. He wrote, "If your health is fully restored, let us remember it is but a reprieve."[64] In other words, future trials will always come, including the "final" trial, which Newton often discussed: their separation from one another at death. These realties filtered into his counsel:

> When it shall please God to bring us together again, I hope we shall strengthen each other's hands. Let us pray for this, while we are yet separated, that we may not be left any more to live to ourselves, but to him; and may look upwards and forwards, to be prepared for the next trial; for sooner or later more will come.[65]

Newton always focused on Christ and His sufficiency, "to live . . . to him" and not for self. Resigning all to Christ, living for Christ, and seeing more of His sufficiency were the goals of his counsel.

60. Newton, *Works* (1985), 5:496.

61. Following her cancer diagnosis, she was prescribed laudanum to control the pain; however, she had an "aversion" to the drug and did not take it, leaving her in extreme pain for the next six months. See Aitken, *John Newton*, 329.

62. Newton, *Works* (1985), 5:496.

63. Newton helped suffering believers to remember that God's kind providence was the primary cause of their affliction, though He uses secondary causes to bring the difficulty (such as illness, the death of a friend, etc.). Newton wrote that "we are prone to fix our attention upon the second causes and immediate instruments of events," and thus forget that God's wise, sovereign hand is really behind the suffering. He goes on to write that a fixation on secondary causes usually leads to sinful responses in trials, whereas a focus on God as the primary cause lends itself to godly responses. Newton, *Works* (1985), 1:455. See also his discussion on providence and secondary causes in Newton, *Letters*, 360–61.

64. Newton, *Works* (1985), 5:495.

65. Newton, *Works* (1985), 5:502.

Finally, John helped Polly see that God sprinkled many mercies in with her difficulties as tokens of His love and care. He wrote:

> How great are our obligations for uniting us at first; for restoring us so often; or raising you up from so many illnesses; for preserving our affection; for overruling our concerns; for providing us friends; and, especially, for directing our hearts to seek his face. And still he is loading us with his benefits. Though we have not been without our trials, yet, all things considered, who has passed more gently through life thus far? And with whom, upon the face of the earth, could we be now content to change?[66]

Likewise, it is essential to remember that the believer is afflicted much less than his sins deserve. Therefore, he can "sanctify" the affliction and look for God's kind purpose in it: "While the rod is upon us, inquire into the meaning of it, and hear his voice by it. . . . He afflicts us far less than our iniquities deserve."[67]

It must have been challenging for the Newtons to apply these truths through thirty-six years of chronic, debilitating, and sometimes excruciating pain. Yet, their theology, worked out experientially, produced what it promised: sanctifying endurance that demonstrated the sufficiency and power of Christ in weakness and a joyful, contented resignation to His will.

Satan's Devices in Chronic Illness

As with others who received his pastoral care, Newton does not often reference the work of Satan in his counsel to Polly. However, on one occasion when she temporarily "lost" her faith and hope in the gospel during a particularly difficult season in her final days, Newton attributed this event to Satan's influence through her bodily weakness:

> But in October the enemy was permitted, for a while, to take advantage of her bodily weakness, to disturb the peace and serenity of her mind. Her thoughts became clouded and confused; and she gradually lost, not only the comfortable evidence of her own interest in the precious truths of the Bible, but she lost all hold of the truth itself. She doubted the truth of the Bible, or whether truth existed.[68]

66. Newton, *Works* (1985), 5:550.
67. Newton, *Works* (1985), 5:491–92.
68. Newton, *Works* (1985), 5:617–18.

Newton's explanation of Polly's situation is consistent with his perspective on Satan's influence in other cases of "bodily weakness," including that of William Cowper and his adopted daughter, Eliza Catlett.[69] He believed that Satan could take advantage of the imaginations of believers through bodily weakness.[70]

Likewise, he observed that "temptations follow tempers, and Satan is always subtle and busy in his attempts to break our peace, and divert our thoughts from the main object."[71] Recognizing that Polly was prone to making herself "uneasy about things which neither of us can help or alter," he encouraged her to guard her heart against temptation in this area.[72] Indeed, her chronic illness (which baffled doctors and lacked both diagnosis and cure) was an occasion in which peace could undoubtedly be broken, but Christ was a sufficient Savior to rescue and help.

Newton's care for Polly demonstrates how his theology of suffering was the essential structure of his doctrine of sanctification that guided the content of his pastoral care endeavors. His counsel to Polly through her poor health, which afflicted her for most of their forty years of marriage, proves that he consistently practiced the same doctrine at home that he taught to his parishioners.

Newton's Theology of Suffering Influenced the Manner of His Ministry

Newton's doctrine of affliction shaped both the topics that he focused on in ministering to Polly and the manner in which he went about caring for her. His ministry to his wife was marked by the same pastoral features observed in his ministry to others and articulated in chapter 3. Yet, there is a particular tenderness in Newton's methodology, fueled not just by his love for his wife but by his theology, which produced humility.[73] Specifically, his doctrine of affliction shaped his ministry to Polly in three ways.

First, Newton's theology directed him to balance encouragement and exhortation, resulting in a skill for making gracious yet instructive appeals. For example, he wove together gospel encouragements with gentle

---

69. Newton, *Letters of John Newton*, 89.
70. Newton, *Letters of John Newton*, 43.
71. Newton, *Works* (1985), 5:583.
72. Newton, *Works* (1985), 5:583.
73. See chapter 3 regarding how Newton's theology shaped his character, particularly his humility.

exhortations for Polly to practice spiritual disciplines while guarding her mind against fruitless musings:

> The blessings of the Gospel are open to you. Could you steadily strive against the hindrances and discouragements thrown in your way, and simply and patiently abide in the use of the means of grace, without giving way to vain reasonings, you would soon experience a growth in peace and comfort. To patient faith the prize is sure. May the Lord help you thus to wait; and may he give us more freedom to converse for our mutual encouragement.[74]

Newton asked God to help both of them to discuss these matters in a way that might lead to mutual encouragement. Though he sometimes found it challenging to discuss spiritual issues with her, he was humble enough to admit it, and appealed to her that they might both pray for growth in this area.[75]

Caring for chronic sufferers requires gospel-centered encouragements that bring comfort as well as biblically informed admonitions about one's thinking or perspective that may be misguided or unhelpful. Following his theology, Newton developed the competence to speak the truth in love, which produced both encouragement and correction.

Second, Newton's doctrine taught him how to show theologically directed sympathy. His understanding of Christology emphasized the high priestly role of Jesus, who sympathizes with believers in weakness.[76] Newton desired to emulate Christ's example in the sympathy he showed his wife. On the occasion of the passing of Polly's sister, Newton encouraged her:

> I *sympathize* with you; I already feel the concern that you will shortly feel, when you say farewell to your sister and your family. Methinks, if I could prevent it, you should not have a moment's uneasiness, pain, or trial, from the beginning to the end of the year. But how could you then be a partaker of that good which the Lord bestows upon his people through the medium of afflictions? I hope he will give you an entire resignation to his will; and that the grief you and your sister will feel at parting, will be compensated

---

74. Newton, *Works* (1985), 5:569.

75. "Next to the salvation of my own soul, there is nothing lies so near my heart as your spiritual welfare; and yet I am often tongue-tied, and can speak more readily to any body than to you. Let us mutually endeavour to break through every restraint, that we may be helpmates in the best sense of the word." Newton, *Works* (1985), 5:569–70.

76. See chapter 2 regarding Newton's understanding of Christology.

Case Studies in Newton's Pastoral Care

by a cheerful hope of meeting again, perhaps more than once, in this life; but, if not here, in a better world.[77]

While Newton felt for his wife in her grief and expresses his desire that he might prevent her every affliction, he also directed her to see God's good redemptive purposes that such sorrow produces. This perspective encourages him to pursue an entire resignation to God's will while reminding her of future hope. Newton's example demonstrates that biblical sympathy feels for the concerns and cares of others while also pointing them to see God's purpose in their pain and the biblical perspectives that produce hope and encouragement.

Third, Newton's perspective on trials assisted him in adopting a winsome manner in calling for repentance. His letters are full of admonishments, exhortations, appeals, corrections, and rebukes, yet grace and humility still characterized Newton's approach. The recipients of his admonishments usually felt helped rather than hurt. On one occasion, he corrected Polly for her unbelief while pointing her to God's many mercies:

> But you deprive yourself of comfort by listening to the voice of unbelief, which weakens your hands and prevents your progress. How often are you distressed, as though you were only to see the goodness of the Lord to others, and not to taste of it yourself! Yet the path of few people through life has been more marked with peculiar mercies than your's. How differently has he led us from the way we should have chosen for ourselves! We have had remarkable turns in our affairs; but every change has been for the better, and in every trouble (for we have had our troubles) he has given us effectual help. Shall we not then believe that he will perfect that which concerns us?[78]

Interestingly, Newton began his exhortation by addressing Polly, but he quickly changes to the first person plural pronoun. He did not stand over Polly in judgment but walked beside her as they pursued the Lord together.

---

77. Newton, *Works* (1985), 5:571–72. Emphasis original. He makes a similar appeal in a different letter: "I *feel* for you every day while you are at Chatham; but I hope and pray the Lord will sanctify all to your profit. If it depended upon me, you should have nothing to grieve you for a moment; but I am glad our concerns are in his wise and gracious hands, who appoints us a mixture of afflictions and trials, not because he takes pleasure in giving us pain, (our many comforts afford sufficient proofs of his goodness,) but because he sees that troubles are often better for us, than the continual enjoyment of our own wishes." Newton, *Works* (1985), 5:577. Emphasis original.

78. Newton, *Works* (1985), 5:588–89.

Newton often employed what might be called "reciprocal" instruction; he regularly admitted that he needed the same spiritual medicine for the same maladies as he dispensed to others. After correcting Polly for her "sinful distrust of the Lord" and her "over-much dependence" upon Newton himself, he concluded his exhortation with this request: "Keep this [letter] to read to me, when it may come to my turn to be pinched with unbelief. Perhaps you will soon have occasion to say, Physician, heal thyself."[79]

Newton's perspective on suffering was so significant in his thinking that it shaped his theology of marriage and his role toward Polly throughout her affliction. His letters demonstrate that he walked faithfully with her through every season of illness until her death in 1790. He remained tender, affectionate, encouraging, and engaging. During a diverse and demanding ministry, he spent countless hours with her, communicated with her, prayed with her, and regularly wrote to her when they were apart. By all accounts, Polly adored her husband, struggled significantly when he was away, and rejoiced when he returned. Yet he consistently pointed her to Christ (rather than himself) as the sole foundation of her hope and wellbeing. In one of his most direct, yet Christ-centered, exhortations to her, he made this very point:

> Do not you consider, that you yourself expose me to the greatest danger, by your sinful distrust of the Lord, and your over-much dependence upon a poor creature, who loves you, it is true, even as his own soul; but who, with the warmest desires of your happiness, is, in himself, quite unable to promote it; unable to procure you the smallest good, or to shield you from the greatest trouble. May it please God so to impress and fill your heart, that your supreme and undivided regard may be fixed upon Him who alone is worthy. Then we shall be happy in each other indeed, when all our thoughts and aims are properly subordinate to what we owe to Him.[80]

Newton's perspective is instructive: While marriage ought to include deep affection between husband and wife, afflictive providences direct them to look to Christ's sufficiency, which both demonstrates His sufficiency and produces proper marital happiness.

---

79. Newton, *Works* (1985), 5:578.
80. Newton, *Works* (1985), 5:577–78.

Case Studies in Newton's Pastoral Care

Newton's Theology of Suffering Ministered to His Own Heart in Grief

The apostle Paul declared that God "comforts us in all our affliction so that we will be able to comfort those who are in any affliction with the comfort with which we ourselves are comforted by God" (2 Cor 1:4). The fact that God comforts people in their affliction so they might be able to comfort others may have been the real secret to Newton's effectiveness in caring for his wife.[81] Though he often downplayed his own experience, his life before marriage included seasons of intense suffering.[82] Newton also observed that suffering is often more intense as one watches a loved one suffer. This reality was especially active as he observed his wife's chronic suffering. Writing to William Wilberforce, he noted, "We are liable to suffer, not only in ourselves, but perhaps more keenly in the persons of those whom we love."[83] He wrote to Polly, "Yet, at intervals, our trials have been very sharp. Mine are always so when I feel for you; though few things, with which your peace or comfort are not connected, give me much trouble. I pay, at some seasons, a heavy tax for loving you."[84]

As he watched Polly suffer, the evidence of Newton's life suggests that the application of his theology to his own grief enabled him to be particularly effective in caring for her. As he worked out his own sanctification in his sorrow for Polly, God equipped him to minister effectively to her for thirty-six years. There are two specific points about Newton's example that are instructive regarding personal grief and the care of loved ones who suffer.

First, Newton intentionally worked to practice the same instruction which he offered to others. In his wife's memoir, he stated that this was a conscious decision throughout his wife's illness: "It had been ... my frequent daily prayer [that I might confirm] by my own practice, the doctrine which I had preached to others."[85] He summarized some of the specifics in a letter to a friend shortly after Polly's significant illness on February 24, 1766.[86] He quoted Nah 1:7, affirming God's goodness and that He is a stronghold

---

81. On the first year of the anniversary of Polly's death, Newton wrote a poem reflecting on his marriage. He heads the poem by citing 2 Cor 1:3-4. Newton, *Works* (1985), 5:631. The poem also appears in his letters to the Taylor family in Newton, *Aged Pilgrim's Triumph*, 75-77.

82. See chapter 1, which overviews Newton's life, including his enslavement in Africa.

83. Wilberforce, *Correspondence*, 136.

84. Newton, *Works* (1985), 5:591.

85. Newton, *Works* (1985), 5:622.

86. Newton, *Works* (1985), 6:61-63.

and a refuge. He also alluded to the fiery furnace of Daniel and the burning bush in Exodus, noting that "he has put us in the fire, but, blessed be his name, we are not burnt."[87] Further, he mentioned many perspectives and redemptive uses of suffering that bring encouragement and endurance: God's supporting strength ("strength equal to our day"); the support and prayers of many affectionate people ("what a privilege it is to be interested in the prayers of those who fear the Lord!"); the reality that a final separation with his wife is coming, but eternity is secure ("if Jesus is our beloved, and heaven our home; we may be cast down for a little season, but we cannot be destroyed"); the truth that God redeems all things for His purposes ("whatever sufferings are appointed for us, they shall work together for our good"); and a reminder that afflictions are small in comparison with eternal reward ("they are but light and momentary in comparison of that exceeding and eternal weight of glory to which we are drawing nearer every hour").[88] With eternity in focus, Newton concluded, "Then [in heaven] shall we remember the way by which the Lord led us through this dark wilderness; and shall see that all our afflictions, our heaviest afflictions, were tender mercies, no less than our most pleasing comforts. What we shall then see, it is now our privilege and duty to believe."[89]

In another letter, written a few months before Polly's death, Newton shared his "walk of faith" through her decline with some friends. He mentioned the need to "submit to his will" given "his wisdom and goodness," that afflictions "spring not out of the ground" but always have a "need-be," and that they are "tokens of favour," not wrath, and are designed to bring the "blessings of sanctifying" after they have been "daily exercised by" their afflictions.[90] As demonstrated in chapter 3, Newton is voicing in these letters the same perspectives and doctrines that he espoused to others in their grief.

Newton practiced what he preached, but he also illustrated a related principle he often shared with fellow ministers: namely, that the pastor's afflictions qualify him to serve suffering people better. Trials squelch pride and promote humility, inhibit spiritual backsliding, create sympathy toward others who suffer, and produce competence as biblical principles are worked out in "experimental knowledge." As Newton reminded his friend, Rev. Coffin, the place of trial is a place of privilege: "I have often told my

---

87. Newton, *Works* (1985), 6:61–63.
88. Newton, *Works* (1985), 6:61–63.
89. Newton, *Works* (1985), 6:61–63.
90. Newton, *Aged Pilgrim's Triumph*, 63.

Case Studies in Newton's Pastoral Care

friends and hearers, when in affliction, that the post of *trial—is* the post of honor. *He now appoints me to practice my own lessons.*"[91] While Newton often admitted he was a "poor student" in Christ's school, he genuinely lived out in dependent faith the principles of his theology applied to the trial of Polly's chronic suffering.

Second, in Polly's chronic suffering, Newton's self-counsel demonstrated the absolute need to actively seek and draw strength from Christ Himself as one's sole hope in grief and sorrow. Writing to a friend, he shared this perspective as he contemplated the overwhelming thought of losing Polly: "But when my foreboding mind has anticipated the possibility of surviving my dear Mary, the question, How I could bear it? How I could ever expect to see another cheerful hour? [I was] involved [in] a difficulty which could only be solved by referring it to the mighty power of God—of Him that raised the dead."[92] Just a few months before Polly's death, Newton shared how he came to this conclusion:

> I believe it was about two or three months before her death, when I was walking up and down the room, offering disjointed prayers from a heart torn with distress, that a thought suddenly struck me, with unusual force, to this effect:—"The promises of God must be true; surely the Lord will help me, if I am willing to be helped!" It occurred to me, that we are often led, from a vain complacence in what we call our sensibility, to indulge that unprofitable grief which both our duty and our peace require us to resist to the utmost of our power. I instantly said aloud, "Lord, I am helpless indeed, in myself, but I hope I am willing, without reserve, that thou shouldest help me."[93]

In other words, with his heart full of distress and his will tempted to give in to "unprofitable grief," he saw his need to be helped, and he cried out to the Lord, who he knew would help.[94] He thus walked in this perspective through Polly's last days. Writing to a close friend, Newton described God's faithfulness to strengthen him through these final months:

---

91. Newton, *Letters of John Newton*, 90. Emphasis original.
92. Newton, *One Hundred and Twenty Nine Letters*, 258.
93. Newton, *Works* (1985), 5:621–22.
94. Newton was so convinced of his own inability and his utter dependence on God for help, he wrote: "I strongly felt that, unless He was pleased to give me this submission [to the will of the Lord], I was more likely to toss like a wild bull." Newton, *Works* (1985), 5:615.

> At length, the trial which I most dreaded came upon me. Suspense was long; sensations were keen. My right hand [a favorite way of referring to Polly] was not chopped off at a stroke (I would be thankful, however, that it was not). It was sawn off by slow degrees; it was an operation of weeks and months; almost every following week more painful than the preceding. But did I sink? Did I despond? Did refuse my food? Did sleep forsake my eyes? Was I so troubled in mind or weakened in body that I could not speak? Far, far from it. The Lord strengthened me, and I was strong.[95]

In other words, God was faithful to strengthen him in the dreaded season just as Newton had concluded was consistent with God's promises in His word.

Following her death, Newton shared that he was sustained in his grief, "not . . . by lively sensible consolations, but by being enabled to realize to my mind some great and leading truths of the word of God. I saw, what indeed I knew before, but never till then so strongly and so clearly perceived."[96] As Newton had often counseled others, known promises from God's word take on new life and significance through the "experimental" dynamic of application in difficulty, which demonstrates the mighty strength and sufficiency of Jesus. The power, sufficiency, and grace of Christ was Newton's central theme in his counsel, and it was the sustaining reality in his own experience. Reflecting on Polly's death, he concluded: "[Her death] set me free from a weight of painful feelings and anxieties, under which nothing short of a divine power could have so long supported me."[97]

Newton's example throughout Polly's suffering and eventual death demonstrates his often-cited point that believers are happiest when they resign all to Christ: "How happy are they who can resign all to him, see his hand in every dispensation, and believe that he chooses better for them than they possibly could for themselves!"[98] This resignation allowed him to "moderate" his grief and live contentedly before the Lord through and following her homegoing.[99] While his care for and counsel to Polly through the thirty-six years of her chronic ailments was exemplary, Newton's life

---

95. Newton, *One Hundred and Twenty Nine Letters*, 258.

96. Newton, *Works* (1985), 5:623. In this same paragraph, he shares some of the "scriptural truths" that were helpful to him, which follow a similar pattern as his counsel to others.

97. Newton, *Works* (1985), 5:621.

98. Newton, *Works* (1985), 1:456.

99. Newton, *Works* (1985), 2:25.

Case Studies in Newton's Pastoral Care

demonstrated that the sufficiency of Christ and a resignation to His good and wise will were the real spiritual energies behind his pursuits.

Conclusion: John and Polly Newton

John and Polly Newton shared a close and unique relationship in marriage and ministry for over forty years. John's care for her through decades of her ongoing ailments, illnesses, and pains provides a unique case study into his doctrine of suffering and pastoral care. The hundreds of letters he wrote to Polly and his narratives to other friends demonstrate that Newton held the same theology at home as he did in his church. The chronic nature of Polly's suffering and the deep affection she and John had for one another reveal an uncommon depth in his doctrine lived out in the context of a most personal and intimate relationship. While the example of Newton's care for Polly shows authenticity in both his life and doctrine, he also becomes a kind of case study himself for his doctrinal points, as his life exemplified the sufficiency of Jesus as he resigned all, even his precious wife, to Him.

Mr. William Cowper

William Cowper was an eminent English poet and hymn-writer of the eighteenth century. Trained as a lawyer and a member of the Inner Temple Society, Cowper is most famous for his hymns, such as "God Moves in a Mysterious Way," and his poetry, such as "The Task." He is also known for his translations of Homer's *Iliad* and *Odyssey*. He met John Newton in 1767 shortly after the tragic death of Rev. Morley Unwin, whose family had taken Cowper in following his release from a mental asylum.[100] Cowper had previously suffered two significant bouts of depression and multiple suicide attempts. Following his most recent attempt, his family moved him to a Christian asylum, where he was converted to Christ in 1764 under the ministry of Dr. Nathaniel Cotton. Upon his release, he moved in with the Unwin family, becoming an "adopted son."[101] Newton's arrival in 1767 initiated a friendship that led Cowper and Mrs. Unwin to move to Olney

---

100. A thorough biography of William Cowper is beyond this scope of this chapter. There are dozens of biographies of Cowper available. Some of the more important works include Thomas, *William Cowper*; Ella, *William Cowper*; King, *William Cowper*; Cecil, *Stricken Deer*.

101. Aitken, *John Newton*, 206.

to be next-door neighbors to the Newtons.[102] The four quickly formed a friendship that would last a lifetime. According to Newton, Cowper was his closest friend, next to his wife.[103] For the next six years, Newton and Cowper were seldom apart. Cowper eventually became Newton's "lay curate," assisting him in pastoral work in Olney. They also found a mutual joy in spiritual conversation and the composing of hymns, which resulted in the publication of *The Olney Hymns* in 1779.

While both friendship and ministry were flourishing in the early 1770s, a tragedy occurred in the early hours of January 2, 1773, when Cowper's depression returned, and he attempted suicide.[104] This incident was the third of five bouts of severe, acute depression. The first occurred in 1753 when he was twenty-one years old.[105] The second, precipitated by an interview before the House of Lords in 1763, led to multiple suicide attempts.[106] Though he was converted to Christianity in 1764, a series of tragic events in 1772 likely stirred up old temptations with depression, and he succumbed to the darkness on January 2, 1773. Amid nightmares and hallucinations, Cowper again attempted to take his own life.[107] Mrs. Unwin and John Newton intervened, likely saving his life. Cowper continued to struggle for the next several weeks. In late February, he experienced another dream in which he concluded that God had condemned him eternally.[108] In the wake of his instability, he and Mrs. Unwin moved in with the Newtons to better

---

102. William Cowper and Mary Unwin moved to a home called Orchard Side in the marketplace of Olney. Behind the house, separated by a garden, was Newton's vicarage.

103. Aitken notes that they were "kindred spirits" (210). In Cowper's funeral sermon, Newton stated, "The Lord has given me many friends but with none have I had so great an intimacy, as with my friend Mr. Cowper." Jowett, "Mr. Newton's Account."

104. For more details, see Aitken, *John Newton*, 218–22.

105. Cowper, *Letters and Prose Writings*, 1:xix. Other sources list the date as 1752.

106. Cowper writes about these attempts in his spiritual autobiography, *Adelphi*. See Cowper, *Letters and Prose Writings*, 1:23–25.

107. Cowper somehow came to the conclusion that God was commanding him to slay himself as an offering to God as Abraham offered his son Isaac. For more details on the events leading up to the tragedy of 1773, see Aitken, *John Newton*, 218–19. See also Jowett, "Mr. Newton's Account."

108. "He dreamed that God appeared at his bedside to pronounce his death sentence with the words, 'Actum est de te periisti,' which Cowper translated as, 'It is all over with thee, thou hast perished.'" Aitken, *John Newton*, 219. Over a decade later, Cowper wrote to Newton in reference to this dream: "I had a dream twelve years ago, before the recollection of which, all consolation vanishes, and, as it seems to me, must always vanish." Cowper, *Letters and Prose Writings*, 2:385.

care for Cowper. He resided in the vicarage for over a year. Following this third bout of depression, Cowper never returned to church.[109]

In subsequent months and years, Cowper enjoyed seasons of mental stability, though he largely kept himself isolated from society. He wrote poetry and translated two significant works of Homer into English. However, he experienced two additional assaults of severe depression, the first in 1786 and the second in 1794. Cowper never fully recovered following the latter incident. He died on April 25, 1800.

Newton's Care and Ministry to Cowper

Newton and Cowper remained friends from their earliest days in 1767 until Cowper's death in 1800. Though the Newtons moved to London in 1780, Newton and Cowper corresponded with each other until Cowper became too weak to write.[110] The last known letter written by Cowper was to Newton in 1799.[111] In the wake of Cowper's depressive episode in 1773, Newton's relationship with him shifted from a ministerial partnership to pastoral care. However, Newton always treated him as an equal and close friend. Reflecting on their twelve years together in Olney, Newton wrote, "The first six I passed in daily admiring and trying to imitate him; during the second six I walked pensively with him in the valley of the shadow of death."[112] Newton's friendship and pastoral care to Cowper were exemplary, though some biographers have accused Newton of being an agent of Cowper's depression. These unwarranted attacks have been convincingly shown to be false.[113] Cowper's personal testimony speaks to this conclusion: "A sincerer or more affectionate friend no man ever had."[114] While many as-

---

109. Jowett, "Mr. Newton's Account."

110. Oddly, the vast majority of known letters from Cowper to Newton have been published, while only a fraction of the letters from Newton to Cowper that likely existed have been discovered, and less than ten have been published.

111. Cowper, *Letters*, 4:466.

112. Bull, *Life of John Newton*, 135.

113. Several scholars, both early and late, have shown these charges against Newton to be misguided, ill-informed, and erroneous. For example, see Aitken, *John Newton*, 219–21; Thomas, *William Cowper*, 129; Bull, *Life of John Newton*, 160–61; Ella, "John Newton's Friendship," 10–19; Cairns, "John Newton: A Vindication," in *Religion of Dr. Johnson*; Cecil, *John Newton*; Cromarty, "Grace in Affliction," 73–74; Cecil, *Memoirs*, in *Works* (1985), 1:60.

114. Piper, *Hidden Smile*, 95.

pects of Newton's relationship with Cowper could be explored, this section will demonstrate that Newton's theology of suffering informed and directed his understanding of Cowper's depression and his approach to care for him.

Newton's Theology of Suffering Informed the Diagnosis of Cowper's Depression

The nature and cause of Cowper's depression are somewhat mysterious and the focus of significant disagreement among scholars.[115] A complete analysis of Cowper's depression is beyond the scope of this work. However, his self-assessment of his condition is relatively straightforward. Bull summarizes Cowper's perspective as follows:

> The malady of Mr. Cowper . . . was a temptation to commit self-destruction. And thenceforth to the end of his days, while perfectly sane in all other respects, he labored under the most extraordinary and terrible hallucination that he had received a command from Heaven to execute this deed, and that his disobedience to that command had for ever shut him out from the hope of mercy. He thought that there was salvation for every man who would accept it but himself, and that consequently it was a sin for him to engage in any religious act.[116]

Strange as it may seem, Cowper's conclusion explains why he immediately stopped attending church, ceased praying, and in all other ways wholly disconnected from Christian practice. He believed so strongly in the validity of these experiences that to make any religious effort would be, in his mind, to go against the will of God.[117]

---

115. Several authors have put forth their theories. See Piper, *Hidden Smile*, 104–19, along with most biographies of Cowper, including Ella, Thomas, King, and Cecil.

116. Bull, *Life of John Newton*, 159. See also Bull, *Memorials*, 112; Cowper, *Letters*, 2:82–84. Apparently, the dream, vision, or hallucination he experienced in the early morning hours of January 2, 1773, communicated the "command from heaven" that he ought to offer his own life (by taking it via suicide) as Abraham offered Isaac. Cowper attempted but failed. Later in February, he experienced a second dream where he supposedly received the verdict of eternal condemnation: "It is all over with thee, thou hast perished." This conclusion was supposedly the response of God for failing to successfully offer up his life to God.

117. In his funeral sermon for Cowper, Newton stated, "[Cowper] said he knew the Lord was a Sovereign and had a right to do with and lay upon him what he pleased and if he [it?] was that by holding out a finger he could remove what he then felt, he would not do it unless he knew it were the will of God. He has often said he thought the Lord had

Case Studies in Newton's Pastoral Care

Newton and many of Cowper's other friends strongly disagreed with Cowper's conclusion that God had rejected him forever.[118] Since Newton's theology of suffering is the essential structure that informed his pastoral care and counseling, it influenced how he interpreted Cowper's situation.[119] Specifically, Newton's theology of suffering directed him to three factors that influenced Cowper's struggle with depression.

Physical Factors

Both Newton and Cowper believed that Cowper suffered from a physical illness or malady, which was called a "nervous disorder" in the eighteenth century.[120] Cowper drew a connection between his "nervous fevers" and the onset of melancholy.[121] In his funeral sermon for Cowper, Newton stated, "Mr. Cowper was afflicted with what is called a nervous complaint to such a degree as might justly be called insanity."[122] Other friends who knew Cowper well confirmed this point. Richard Cecil, Newton's friend and biographer, regarded Mr. Cowper's affliction as a "constitutional malady."[123] At the

---

not a child who loved him with a more simple heart than he did." Jowett, "Mr. Newton's Account."

118. For example, this was the view of Mrs. Unwin, Mrs. Newton, William Bull, and Richard Cecil. See Cowper, *Letters*, 1:260, 2:83. Even Cowper himself agreed that this was the case (2:200).

119. For development, see chapters 2 and 3.

120. At this time in history, "nervous disorders" referenced three main maladies: hypochondria (which could result in melancholia), hysteria, and dyspepsia. Both in the eighteenth century and today, these types of disorders manifest themselves in bodily symptoms that lack any clear origin in local disease or body pathology. However, in Newton's day, there was a general consensus that they had a physical component. In the twenty-first century, "nervous disorders" are understood as psychological disorders that lack a clear, medical pathology. See Hare, "'Nervous Disorders,'" 37–45.

121. "Melancholy" was the term used in the eighteenth century for feelings of depression. For Cowper's connection between his fevers and his melancholy, see Cowper, *Letters*, 3:449–50.

122. Jowett, "Mr. Newton's Account."

123. Bull, *Life of John Newton*, 163. Cecil also quotes William Jay, who wrote that Newton "always regarded his friend's depression and despondency as a physical effect, for the removal of which he prayed, but never reasoned or argued with him concerning it"; as quoted in Cecil, *Life of John Newton*, 282. But Jay is only half correct. Newton did consistently regard Cowper's condition as involving a physical malady and he did pray for its removal, but he also regularly reminded Cowper of the truth of the gospel and the evidences of faith (see below for examples). Newton knew that reason alone would not convince Cowper, but God through His word would do the work.

request of Cowper's aunt, Newton sought medical treatment for Cowper from Dr. Cotton.[124]

Newton's conclusion that a physical disorder partly influenced Cowper's condition led him to view his friend's situation as one that involved genuine suffering. As with Polly's chronic affliction, Newton was open to medical interventions that might bring some relief, but this was not the primary source to which he directed Cowper for hope and encouragement.[125]

The Influence of Satan

Newton believed that Satan often played a role in a believer's suffering, particularly related to the temptations that Christians experience.[126] He theorized that Satan had special access to the imaginations of believers afflicted with various disorders, especially "nervous" disorders.[127] Newton demonstrated the application of his theological understanding to the case of William Cowper in a letter to Rev. Samuel Greatheed:

> While dear Mr. Cowper was in his right mind he was as far from resting his hope upon his feelings as I could be. I have had much to do with those whom we call nervous people. And I believe that when the nervous system is greatly disordered, it opens a door to the enemy of our peace, to pour in his black temptations, and to fasten upon the imagination, with a violence which can only be

---

124. At first, the medicines seemed to help. But over time, they worsened Cowper's condition and so he ceased taking them. Bull, *Life of John Newton*, 159. Later in life, Cowper mentions the use of laudanum in conjunction with his "nervous fevers." See his letter to Newton in Cowper, *Letters*, 4:216.

125. Newton, *Works* (1985), 5:496.

126. Newton's two most significant works on this subject are his letters "On Temptation" in his *Omicron and Vigil* series and his twenty-third letter to Lord Dartmouth ("Letters to a Nobleman") in *Cardiphonia*. See Newton, *Works* (1985), 1:226–35 and 1:525–33.

127. See Newton, *Works* (1985), 1:529–30; Newton, *Letters of John Newton*, 42–43, 89. Newton believed that the imagination was the "medium of the soul's perceptions during this present state of union with the body . . . [related to] that mysterious connection between soul and body." Newton, *Works* (1985), 1:529. Newton's view of the imagination, Satan, and melancholy is similar to that of the English Puritans, who greatly influenced his understanding of theology in his formative years (see chapter 1). As just one example, compare Newton's view with William Perkins in "The First Book of Cases of Conscience" in *Works of William Perkins*, 8:213–18. Perkins held a similar view in that persons afflicted with the physical disorder called "melancholy," where the "imagination is disturbed," were particularly prone to Satan's "strange conceits." Perkins includes some examples of this situation that coincide with symptoms that Cowper experienced.

restrained by the power of God, so that the grossest absurdities, are received as no less certain than a mathematical demonstration, and our reasonings against them are as ineffectual, as to talk to the east wind—though in the common affairs of life, a man may still have the use of his rational faculties, I think there is an invisible agency in such cases. I believe our friend's derangement, was attended by a real *possession*.[128]

Newton then related Cowper's condition to that of Job in Scripture, who was assaulted with "dreams" and "visions" and became suicidal, having concluded that God had handed him over to the Wicked One (Job 7:14–15; 16:11–14):

> But when the Lord's permission to Satan ran thus, "Behold he is in thine hand, only save his life," then Job was scared with dreams and terrified with visions. Like Mr. Cowper he chose strangling rather than life, and complained, that God had turned him over into the hands of the Wicked One, who had taken him by the neck, shook him to pieces, and set him up for his mark and run upon him like a giant.[129]

Newton held to the same explanation when his adopted daughter, Eliza Catlett, went through a season of dark depression. He explained, "The disorder has had an awful effect upon her nervous system . . . and, by the Lord's permission, has given Satan an open door to fill her imagination with horrible thoughts concerning God and his word."[130] While Newton was open to utilizing medical interventions, he was clear that only God could ultimately bring about restoration. As he contemplated sending Eliza to Mr. Ring, a "medical man," he wrote: "I am willing to use the means [of medical care]; but I believe only the help of him who made heaven and earth, and who raises the dead, can effectually relieve us."[131]

---

128. Newton, "Letter to Rev. Samuel Greatheed," 1.
129. Newton, "Letter to Rev. Samuel Greatheed," 1.
130. Newton, *Letters of John Newton*, 89.
131. Newton, *Letters of John Newton*, 89–90. Newton writes similarly about Eliza to John Ryland: "But her case is in the Lord's hand, and I believe He only by his voice which raises the dead, can effectually relieve her." Gordon, *Wise Counsel*, 389.

John Newton's Theology of Suffering and Its Application to Pastoral Care

SPIRITUAL DYNAMICS

While Newton embraced a view of Cowper's depression that allowed for physical and diabolical factors, he ultimately believed that it was a spiritual trial that required spiritual intervention. Newton is clear and consistent with his advice and perspective that God must (and, as he believed, would) ultimately work to bring relief. He wrote to Cowper:

> I hope to continue sympathizing with you, sorrowing for you, not as without hope, but confident that the hour of your deliverance approaches, when the Lord, your Lord & Beloved, will make that pastoral song your own, Cant. 2.10–13. Then he will take off your sackcloth & gird you with gladness, & comfort you perpetually to the time & the degree in which you have been afflicted, & as I have felt for your distress, I shall be a partaker in your joy.[132]

With these three factors in mind, Newton cared for his friend for the next twenty-seven years. His theology of suffering shaped the content and manner of his ministry to Cowper.

Newton's Theology of Suffering Directed the Content of His Care

Newton's doctrinal viewpoint on trials and afflictions guided the counsel and encouragement that he offered to Cowper, which followed the same five themes as observed in his other letters: the good, wise providence of God; active, central Christology; redemption of the suffering; biblical perspectives on trials; and the nature of Satan's temptations. However, Newton ministered in some unique ways to Cowper compared with others.

GOD'S FAITHFUL, WISE PROVIDENCE IN DEPRESSION

Newton's chief encouragement to Cowper throughout his afflictive depression was that God is faithful and does not abandon His children. When Cowper and Mrs. Unwin moved away from their house at Orchard Side in Olney, they later returned to find the place abandoned. In his poetic way, Cowper related the scene of the "woeful spectacle, deserted of its inhabitants" to himself as to the soul "that God has forsaken."[133] Newton replied:

---

132. Newton, "Letter to William Cowper, May 20, 1780," in Letters, Princeton University Library Collection of William Cowper Materials, Princeton University.

133. Cowper, *Letters*, 2:618. "Once, since we left Olney, I had occasion to call at our

Case Studies in Newton's Pastoral Care

> You have forsaken Orchard Side, with a fixed purpose to return & dwell in it no more forever. But the Lord does not so withdraw from the soul in which he has once dwelt. He says, I will see you again & your heart shall rejoyce. For a small moment have I forsaken thee, but with great mercies will I gather thee. Sing & rejoyce, for lo, I come again, & I will dwell with thee, saith the Lord. For the Lord will not cast off his people, but tho' he cause grief, he will have compassion because he delighteth in mercy. These & such as these, are the sure words of God, & tho Heaven & Earth pass away, yet not one jot or tittle of what he hath spoken shall fail.[134]

Newton's assurances of God's presence and His future deliverance were the regular means of supporting his friend. He offered these reminders as simple statements of fact but also presented them in biblical argument: "How strange that a person who considers the earth, the planets, and the sun itself as mere baubles, compared with the friendship and favour of God their Maker, should think the God who inspired him with such an idea, could ever forsake and cast off the soul which he has taught to love him!"[135] In another letter, he wrote, "We have in time past experienced his supporting, delivering power, and we shall again, for he is unchangeably the same, a God hearing prayer, a Saviour in time of trouble."[136]

While Cowper was convinced of divine providence over his affliction, he misapplied the doctrine in that he believed that it was aimed at his destruction.[137] Newton sought to correct this error by assuring him of God's good purpose and Cowper's final deliverance. He wrote, "All things are in the Lord's hands, all agents, Angels, Devils, & Men are under his control. The conduct of instruments may be wrong, but his overruling management of their conduct in subservience to his own purposes and plan, is holy, wise & good."[138] Likewise, Newton's common refrain to Cowper was his confi-

---

old dwelling; and never did I see so forlorn and woeful a spectacle. Deserted of its inhabitants, it seemed as if it could never be dwelt in for ever. The coldness of it, the dreariness, and the dirt, made me think it no inapt resemblance of a soul that God has forsaken." Cowper, *Letters*, 2:618.

134. Newton, "Letter to William Cowper December 19, 1786," in Letters, Charles Ryskmap Collection of William Cowper, Princeton University.

135. Newton, *Works* (1985), 6:162.

136. Newton, "Letter to William Cowper March 10, 1780," in Letters, Princeton University Library Collection of William Cowper Materials, Princeton University.

137. Cowper, *Letters*, 2:200.

138. John Newton, "Letter to William Cowper December 16, 1780," in Letters, Princeton University Library Collection of William Cowper Materials, Princeton University.

dence that God would deliver him: "Yes, my friend, when the Lord shall break the fetters which have so long entangled your spirit (& of this happy event you have yourself conceived & expressed a hope), you will rejoice, & I shall rejoice with you, whatever reception our books may meet with."[139]

CHRIST'S WORK IN DEPRESSION

Newton's Christology also guided him to minister to Cowper. Two facets of Newton's view directed his care.[140] First, he rehearsed the gospel to him:

> These things I am sure of, that the proper wages of sin is death; that I and all mankind have sinned against the great God; that the most perfect character is unable to stand the trial of his holy law. When I saw things in this light, I saw the necessity of a Mediator. And in the account the Scripture gave me of Christ, his adorable person, his offices, his matchless love, humiliation, obedience, and death, I saw a provision answerable to my need. His blood is declared to be a complete atonement for sin; his righteousness, a plea provided for the guilty; his power and compassion are both infinite; and the promise of pardon, peace, and eternal life, is made to them who believe in his name.[141]

The work of Christ was central to Newton's theology. His ministry to Cowper maintains and exemplifies this key focus of his doctrine.

---

139. John Newton, "Letter to William Cowper March 11–13, 1786," in Letters, Charles Ryskmap Collection of William Cowper, Princeton University. Cowper struggled with the thought of God's deliverance, sometimes hopeful of it but often believing it would never come. "Oh for the day when your expectations of my complete deliverance shall be verified! At present it seems very remote: so distant indeed that hardly the faintest streak of it is visible in my horizon." Cowper, *Letters*, 4:234.

140. However, there is a glaring difference to observe. Newton's letters to Cowper sometimes lack an emphasis on Christ's sufficiency that so many of his other letters demonstrate. This observation is limited by the fact that only a fraction of the total letters from Newton to Cowper are available for study.

141. Newton, *Works* (1985), 6:152. Newton also reminded him in the same letter, "I have been led into some reflections on the admirable suitableness of the gospel-way of salvation by Jesus Christ, to all the possible varieties of a sinner's condition. When once he knows himself, and is acquainted with the holiness, justice, and majesty of the God with whom he has to do, no other expedient can ever satisfy him, or give peace to his conscience. And when once he knows Christ as the way, and receives faith in his name, he is provided with an answer to every discouragement and fear that can arise." Newton, *Works* (1985), 6:152.

Case Studies in Newton's Pastoral Care

Second, Newton sought to emulate the sympathy of Jesus toward Cowper. Shortly after the Newtons left Olney, they received a letter describing Cowper's continued struggle. They responded in Christlike compassion, weaving in themes of His wise providence and the expectation of Cowper's relief:

> [Your letter] drew tears from our eyes, but there is a pleasure in the tears of friendship especially when we sorrow not as those without hope, and can perceive not only the dark cloud, but the hand that guides it, and which will in due time remove it. I have an assured hope of a bright hour which will make you abundant amends for all that you have suffered, though you have suffered very much, and I who have sympathised with your grief shall be a sharer in your joy.[142]

The Christlike sympathy that both the Newtons demonstrated to Cowper is a consistent theme in their letters to him.

Redemption in Depression

Newton maintained that God had redemptive purposes in Cowper's chronic trial. First, he reminded Cowper that God designed his suffering to keep him from greater sins. Several letters between Newton and Cowper reference Cowper's cousin, chaplain Martin Madan. In a misguided effort to deal with the problem of prostitution, Madan wrote a book advocating polygamy. Understandably, it had a negative impact on the church.[143] Newton theorized that Cowper's depression was designed to keep him from greater sins, such as his cousin's publication. He writes:

> You have suffered much, and I can truly say, I have suffered with you. But oh how much more I should have felt, than I ever did in the times of your greatest distress, if you like him had been permitted to deviate from the good way. If you instead of him had written a book to grieve the children of God and to open the

---

142. Newton, "Letter March 10, 1780," in Letters, Princeton University Library Collection of William Cowper Materials, Princeton University. Newton wrote on a different occasion to Cowper, "The subject [of his suffering] engages my sympathy and revived painful feeling—yet there is a sort of pleasure in feeling pain for a beloved friend; besides that I accept all you say on that head as a proof of your friendship." Newton, "Letter to William Cowper October 21, 1780 (unpublished letter, transcribed by the John Newton Project).

143. Madan's work was called *Thelyphthora*.

mouths of his enemies! . . . Oh how much better to be distressed and tossed with tempests even for years, to experience all the trials and calamities to which human nature is liable, than to be led by Satan like Samson in chains and with shorn locks to make sport for the Philistines.[144]

Second, Newton assisted Cowper in seeing how his affliction revealed more of his heart depravity. Cowper himself made this observation in response to one of Newton's letters to him. He wrote, "Could I assuredly hope that God would at last deliver me, I should have reason to thank him for all that I have suffered, were it only for the sake of this single fruit of my affliction,—that it has taught me how much more contemptible I am in myself than I ever before suspected."[145] While Cowper was still uncertain that God would deliver him, he saw some evidence of redemptive grace in his heart.

Third, Newton often employed the same redemptive themes with Cowper as he used with other sufferers. He wove together several perspectives regarding Cowper's suffering in his last letter to the aging poet. He wrote that God redeems suffering such that it teaches humility and dependence upon God, keeps one from overrating gifts or necessary usefulness, and displays the power and faithfulness of God ultimately for His glory and the instruction and benefit of the person.[146] These familiar themes in Newton's letters to suffering people model his consistent theology of suffering.

---

144. Newton, "Letter to William Cowper." In another letter, Newton shares, "Dearly as I love you, yea because I dearly love, I think your long dark state of trial much preferable to the case of my poor friend the author of that book with the hard name, which in defiance of many petitions and remonstrances that have been presented against it, will shortly make its appearance." Newton, "Letter March 10, 1780," in Letters, Princeton University Library Collection of William Cowper Materials, Princeton University.

145. Cowper, *Letters and Prose Writings*, 2:368. Echoing Newton's counsel to Mrs. Wilberforce, Cowper reflected: "But the heart is a nest of serpents, and will be such while it continues to beat. If God cover the mouth of that nest with his hand, they are hush and snug; but if he withdraw his hand, the whole family lift up their heads and hiss, and are as active and venomous as ever. This I always professed to believe from the time that I had embraced the truth, but never knew it as I know it now. To what end I have been made to know it as I do, whether for the benefit of others or for my own, or for both, or for neither, will appear hereafter." Cowper, *Letters and Prose Writings*, 2:368. Cf. Newton, *Works* (1985), 2:199.

146. "But the Final causes of your sufferings are the Glory of God, & one's instruction & benefit. We admire the Power & Faithfulness of the Lord, when we see you, like the bush which Moses saw in the wilderness, in the midst of the fire for so long a [page torn] yet not consumed. And when we think of a person whose gifts & talents [page torn] beyond the common standard, & by him simply devoted & employed to [page torn] [the] service of God & his fellow creatures, & yet so long & so totally laid [page torn]

Case Studies in Newton's Pastoral Care

PERSPECTIVES ON SUFFERING IN DEPRESSION

Newton regularly ministered to suffering people by highlighting biblical perspectives on trials that brought encouragement and hope. He employed this same strategy to care for his discouraged friend.[147] Newton used three main views to assist Cowper in finding biblical hope in his affliction.

First, Newton helped him remember that the weight of glory in eternity will be sufficient to "make up for" the heavy (but, by comparison, light) afflictions he was experiencing. Newton wrote, "And as to you, He is rich enough, & Eternity is long enough, to make you [full] amends for all that his wise plan requires you to suffer here."[148] Second, Newton employed the biblical image of the burning bush to illustrate the sustaining power of God in affliction in Cowper's life. He wrote to him, "We admire the Power & Faithfulness of the Lord, when we see you, like the bush which Moses saw in the wilderness, in the midst of the fire for so long a [page torn] yet not consumed."[149] Third, Newton encouraged Cowper that God's timetable is not our timetable. In a compassionate and winsome way, he shared this perspective:

> Thus if I had a dear friend secluded from year to year from society, to which he would otherwise be a blessing & an ornament, tho' my feelings for him, for myself & for many would prompt me to pray for his enlargement & tho' the answer should be long, long delayed; yet in such a case my principle could I apply it would bear me out,

---

it inculcates upon us a lesson of humility & dependence, that we [page torn] not overate our abilities or services, nor think ourselves necessary. He can carry on his designs, without the help of the most promising instruments, & he can work effectually by the meanest. And as to you, He is rich enough, & Eternity is long enough, to make you [full] amends for all that his wise plan requires you to suffer here." Newton, "Letter to William Cowper August 11, 1798," in Letters, Kenneth Povey Collection of William Cowper, Princeton University.

147. For several examples of this strategy to a variety of different people, see chapter 2.

148. Newton, "Letter August 11, 1798," n Letters, Princeton University Library Collection of William Cowper Materials, Princeton University. Newton spoke with similar terms at Cowper's funeral: "He suffered much here for twenty-seven years, but eternity is long enough to make amends for all." Jowett, "Mr. Newton's Account." Shortly after the funeral, he wrote to Hannah More, "But we are sure that He is rich enough, and that eternity is long enough to make them abundant amends for whatever his infinite wisdom may see meet to call them to." Roberts, *Memoirs*, 2:60.

149. Newton, "Letter August 11, 1798," n Letters, Princeton University Library Collection of William Cowper Materials, Princeton University. Newton also used this illustration at Cowper's funeral (Exod 3:2–3 was his text) and with Hannah More and other friends with whom he corresponded regarding Cowper.

& keep me both from impatience & despondence. I might say to myself, This delay is only an indication that the Lord's hour is not yet come, tho it tarry wait for it, for come it surely will, & when it comes you will see & say, It was the best time possible. Especially you would say so, were you acquainted with the whole train of dependencies & consequences connected with every part of the dispensation & with every hour of what you call a delay. What other events have been prevented by it, & what other events may be produced by it. And even this comprehensive view you may be favoured with hereafter. Then at least you will praise—praise him for all, but most for the severe.[150]

Fourth, Newton consistently assured Cowper that his strong impressions of divine rejection did not invalidate the evidence of regenerative grace that Cowper previously demonstrated. Instead, his trials were designed to bolster and prove the reality of his faith by magnifying the sufficiency of Christ. The letters shared between Newton and Cowper reveal a friendly "disagreement" regarding Cowper's spiritual condition. Repeatedly, Newton wrote:

> Though your comforts have been so long suspended, I know not that I ever saw you for a single day since your calamity came upon you, in which I could not perceive as clear and satisfactory evidence, that the grace of God was with you, as I could in your brighter and happier times. In the midst of all the little amusements, which you call trifling, and which I would be very thankful you can attend to, in your present circumstances, it is as easy to see who has your heart, and which way your desires tend, as to see your shadow when you stand in the sun.[151]

Again, he shared:

> If we were to write queries upon your case, we should still differ about it. You think you are right, I am sure to the contrary, but we shall agree by & by. Till then I hope to continue sympathizing with

---

150. Newton, "Letter December 16, 1780," in Letters, Princeton University Library Collection of William Cowper Materials, Princeton University. Newton makes the same point in a more direct fashion in a different letter: "How secret, patient, slow & yet sure are the methods of Divine Providence! He has a time to let all know that he governs the Earth. But as a day & a thousand years are the same in his sight, he often has things take so long a course." Newton, "Letter to William Cowper September 2, 1780," in Letters, Princeton University Library Collection of William Cowper Materials, Princeton University.

151. Newton, *Works* (1985), 6:161.

you, sorrowing for you, not as without hope, but confident that the hour of your deliverance approaches, when the Lord, your Lord & Beloved, will make that pastoral song your own, Cant. 2.10–13.[152]

Patiently, kindly, yet persistently, Newton reminded his friend of the clear evidence of grace that Cowper displayed before the return of his depression in 1773. He also communicated the hope that Cowper would one day agree with Newton's assessment and Cowper would regain his confidence in the Lord.

These perspectives were undoubtedly familiar to Cowper as they both ministered the same truths to the afflicted of Olney.[153] But Newton wisely wove these perspectives into his regular correspondence with him as his main means of encouraging and caring for his friend.

Satan and Temptation in Depression

As mentioned earlier, Newton believed that Cowper was afflicted with a "constitutional malady" that made him particularly prone to Satan's lies and temptations. Though he held this view, Newton did not believe that medical interventions were the ultimate solution, nor did he think that Cowper was a passive victim of spiritual forces. While acknowledging the probability of physical factors and satanic influence, Newton instructed his friend to see God's glory and his own good as the primary causes of his suffering. He writes:

> The proximate cause of your distress is a Constitutional Malady of that peculiar kind, which gives Satan advantage & access to harass your imagination. But the Final causes of your sufferings are the Glory of God, & one's instruction & benefit. We admire the Power & Faithfulness of the Lord, when we see you, like the bush which

---

152. Newton, "Letter May 20, 1780," in Letters, Princeton University Library Collection of William Cowper Materials, Princeton University.

153. Newton published his first set of letters between the years 1771 and 1774, which means several of these letters were likely written during the season when Cowper served as Newton's lay curate in Olney. Many of these early letters, such as "Of the Practical Influence of Faith," "The Full Corn in the Ear," and "On Temptation," contain the same perspectives on suffering that Newton would later share with Cowper in his affliction. Likewise, several of the hymns that Cowper and Newton wrote together reveal Newton's theology of afflictions. For example, see hymn CXXXV, "Love Tokens," in Newton, *Works* (1985), 3:456–57, and "Prayers Answered by Crosses" in *Works*, 3:607–8. These facts substantiate the likelihood that Cowper was already familiar with Newton's perspective.

> Moses saw in the wilderness, in the midst of the fire for so long a [page torn] yet not consumed. And when we think of a person whose gifts & talents [page torn] beyond the common standard, & by him simply devoted & employed to [page torn] [the] service of God & his fellow creatures, & yet so long & so totally laid [page torn] it inculcates upon us a lesson of humility & dependence, that we [page torn] not overate our abilities or services, nor think ourselves necessary. He can carry on his designs, without the help of the most promising instruments, & he can work effectually by the meanest. And as to you, He is rich enough, & Eternity is long enough, to make you [full] amends for all that his wise plan requires you to suffer here.[154]

Here, Newton brings together several of his redemptive purposes and biblical perspectives on Cowper's trial, highlighting God's sustaining power and faithfulness. Thus, while Satan's influence was a likely reality, the Lord's work is to bring help, hope, and ultimate deliverance.

The content of Newton's counsel to Cowper is not new or unique but reflects his theology of suffering as observed in other letters. Newton displays a remarkable consistency in the content of his counseling, demonstrating that his doctrine of trials formed a crucial structure in both his theory and practice. His example with Cowper also reveals that Newton did not abandon, add to, or restructure his theology for more complex situations.

Newton's Theology of Suffering Influenced the Manner of His Care

While Cowper was consistently thankful for Newton's faithful friendship and remained affectionate with him concerning his efforts to care well for him, he was primarily unreceptive to his counsel.[155] As with others, Newton's theology shaped the dynamics of care that he employed in his ministry to Cowper. As demonstrated in chapter 3, Newton had realistic expectations about the pace of counseling with Cowper. He utilized his understanding of people to better minister to him. He demonstrated genuine

---

154. Newton, "Letter August 11, 1798," in Letters, Princeton University Library Collection of William Cowper Materials, Princeton University.

155. Cowper's letters to Newton substantiate this sad reality. There was a moment in July 1792 when Cowper seemed to heed some of Newton's encouragement. Following a visit that Newton made to Cowper, Cowper wrote a letter in which he expressed gratitude for his visit and voiced some encouragement and hope for the resolution for his condition. However, this optimism quickly abated, and he returned to his hopeless condition. This letter can be found in Cowper, *Letters*, 4:162.

Case Studies in Newton's Pastoral Care

love and humility, coupled with a posture of sympathy toward him. Beyond these facets of pastoral care, Newton's example toward Cowper highlights three dynamics that further reveal his theology.

First, Newton faithfully reminded Cowper of the gospel. Though he said of Cowper, "I don't know a person upon earth I consult upon a text of Scripture or any point of conscience so much to my satisfaction as Mr. Cowper,"[156] Newton consistently shared gospel truths with him. As John Piper writes, "Never cease to sing the gospel to the deaf."[157] Newton believed that exposure to the gospel—even when one, like Cowper, rejected its application to himself—would still manifest the mighty work of God (Rom 1:16; 2 Cor 4:3–6). While he did not harass Cowper with the gospel, he did share it with him and make regular efforts to sprinkle aspects of it into his correspondence with him.

Second, Newton maintained a consistent, warm, and affectionate friendship with Cowper for over thirty-three years. For twenty-seven of those years, Cowper walked in darkness. Though Newton and Cowper disagreed about the reality of the most critical truth in life, Cowper's salvation, this did not inhibit or extinguish their friendship. Many of Newton's letters to Cowper make no mention of his depression. Newton was not overbearing in his conversation about the topic. Instead, their letters contain news about friends, writing projects, theological controversies, and world events. He strengthened his friendship with Cowper by intentionally building other common topics into their relationship beyond their glaring area of disagreement. While Newton did not shy away from or avoid the essential matter, he wisely moderated the frequency and manner he discussed it with him. Newton's warmth is especially exemplary, as Cowper's depression created a coldness toward Newton in his final years.[158]

Third, Newton did not let the reality of Cowper's depression keep him from challenging his faulty thinking and erroneous conclusions. In light of the depth and longevity of Cowper's darkness, one might be tempted to treat such a person with a delicacy that would avoid any uncomfortable topic or area of disagreement. But Newton believed, because of his

---

156. Jowett, "Mr. Newton's Account."

157. Piper, *Hidden Smile*, 117.

158. For thirty-one years, Newton and Cowper would always address each other in correspondence as "my dear friend." But in Cowper's last two known letters to Newton, he shockingly addresses his closest friend simply as "sir." His last letter is particularly troubling. Cowper concludes, "Adieu Dear Sir, whom in those days I call'd Dear friend, with feelings that justified the appellation." Cowper, *Letters*, 4:466.

John Newton's Theology of Suffering and Its Application to Pastoral Care

theology, that Cowper needed both compassion and correction. Newton was an exceptionally skilled pastoral counselor in this regard. While Cowper thought that the conclusions of his hallucinations and dreams trumped the clear teaching of Scripture regarding his eternal state, Newton affirmed that the biblical evidence of grace proved the validity of his salvation. He attempted to correct Cowper creatively and indirectly in this way:

> How strange that your judgment should be clouded in one point only, and that a point so obvious and strikingly clear to every body who knows you! How strange that a person who considers the earth, the planets, and the sun itself as mere baubles, compared with the friendship and favour of God their Maker, should think the God who inspired him with such an idea, could ever forsake and cast off the soul which he has taught to love him! How strange is it, I say, that you should hold tenaciously both parts of a contradiction![159]

Instead of challenging him directly, Newton frames the obvious incongruities in Cowper's judgment in softer language: "How strange." He also employs undeniable examples from creation to illustrate truths about God's character, which were in question.

Other times, Newton did correct Cowper more directly, yet still in a gracious manner:

> My distress would be very great indeed, had I met a conviction equal to that which I have of my own existence, that in all you say about yourself & your state, you are entirely mistaken. In the course of your very long & sore affliction, a thousand things have occurred in which you & I have differed as much in opinion, as we now do about one. And when we have so differed, you have lived to see that I was right, & you were imposed on. So it is still.[160]

True to his style, he immediately followed his rebuke with a word of encouragement:

> You are cast down but not forsaken, tempted but not destroyed. If I cannot take upon me to say that the dark cloud which hangs over your mind, will be soon, yet I am confident it will be certainly dispelled. I am sure that this long night will at length issue in a

---

159. Newton, *Works* (1985), 6:161–62. His letter on Dec. 16, 1780 manifests a similar creative exhortation.

160. Newton, "Letter to William Cowper November 20, 1779," in Letters, Princeton University Library Collection of William Cowper Materials, Princeton University.

bright & glorious day. I am sure that you are as safe in the arms of Everlasting love, & as dear to him.[161]

In his last known letter to Cowper, Newton likewise challenged him regarding his spiritual condition. It had been four years since Cowper had written to him. After expressing joy in the "long and painful interval of silence," Newton wrote:

> I am aware that you think yourself the best judge in your own case, & that the terrible suggestions which trouble you, are forced upon you with a seeming evidence almost equal to Mathematical Demonstration, and therefore it gives you pain if you are contradicted upon this point. I must dissent from you, but I would do it as gently as possible.[162]

Newton recognized that challenging him regarding his own experience could bring real "pain." Cowper described this same reality: "It is better on every account that they who interest themselves so deeply in that event should believe its certainty than that they should not."[163] Yet, Newton believed that the possibility of creating pain by challenging Cowper was worth it to bring lasting relief through repentance and acceptance of the truth.

Cowper's conclusion about his eternal condemnation rested upon two fallacies. First, Cowper clung to the authenticity of two dreams that supposedly revealed God's will, though both messages contradicted the Scriptures. Second, he relied solely upon himself as the determiner of truth regarding these experiences.[164] Newton attempted to help Cowper see the error of his conclusions. Cowper stated, "God gave [comforts] to me in derision and took them away in vengeance. Such however is, and has been my persuasion many a long day, and when I shall think on that subject, more comfortably, or as you will be inclined to tell me, more rationally and Scripturally, I know not."[165] Newton's efforts to help his friend think more "rationally and Scripturally" failed because Cowper wrongly believed that only a similar event, such as he experienced in the two dreams he had in 1773,

---

161. Newton, "Letter to William Cowper November 20, 1779," in Letters, Princeton University Library Collection of William Cowper Materials, Princeton University.

162. Newton, "Letter August 11, 1798," in Letters, Princeton University Library Collection of William Cowper Materials, Princeton University.

163. Cowper, *Letters*, 1:424. See also 4:254.

164. Cowper, *Letters*, 1:424. Cowper also told Newton that he was unable to communicate his reasons to others because they were based upon his own experience.

165. Cowper, *Letters*, 2:581.

could change his mind. Cowper was fully conscious of this conclusion. He wrote, "But distresses of mind, that are occasioned by distemper, are the most difficult of all to deal with. They refuse all consolation; they will hear no reason. God only, by His own immediate impressions, can remove them; as, after an experience of thirteen years' misery, I can abundantly testify."[166] Newton agreed that ultimately, only the work of God could change Cowper's mind, but not through delusional impressions as he had previously experienced.[167] Instead, the Lord works through His providence and the ordinary means of grace to produce such change.

Newton also used wisdom regarding both the strength and frequency of his challenges to Cowper. For example, Newton disputed with him about the certainty of his future relief: "If I cannot take upon me to say that the dark cloud which hangs over your mind, will be soon, yet I am confident it will be certainly dispelled. I am sure that this long night will at length issue in a bright & glorious day."[168] Then, Newton pulled back in moderation: "Excuse this, which your letter [extracted] from me. I will however press you no farther at present."[169] In his dealings with Cowper, Newton exemplified a wise, pastoral balance of compassion and biblical exhortations.

Questions Regarding Newton's Ministry to Cowper

While Newton's care for Cowper was exemplary and modeled many biblical principles and Christian graces in pastoral ministry, three questions arise. First, did Newton ever challenge Cowper concerning the delusional nature of his dreams of 1773? Cowper's entire outlook and his hopeless conclusion about his eternal condition rested solely upon the ultimate authority

---

166. Cowper, *Letters*, 3:11.

167. He writes to Cowper, "I hope to continue sympathizing with you, sorrowing for you, not as without hope, but confident that the hour of your deliverance approaches, when the Lord, your Lord & Beloved, will make that pastoral song your own, Cant. 2.10–13. Then he will take off your sackcloth & gird you with gladness, & comfort you perpetually to the time & the degree in which you have been afflicted, & as I have felt for your distress, I shall be a partaker in your joy." Newton, "Letter May 20, 1780," in Letters, Princeton University Library Collection of William Cowper Materials, Princeton University.

168. Newton, "Letter November 20, 1779," in Letters, Princeton University Library Collection of William Cowper Materials, Princeton University.

169. Newton, "Letter November 20, 1779," in Letters, Princeton University Library Collection of William Cowper Materials, Princeton University.

Case Studies in Newton's Pastoral Care

of his dreams. He wrote to Newton: "I had a dream twelve years ago, before the recollection of which all consolation vanishes, and as it seems to me, must always vanish."[170] Newton's primary ministry strategy to Cowper was to assure him that his previous evidence of true conversion validated his Christian position, but his efforts failed to convince him. Would it have been a wiser strategy to challenge the validity of Cowper's dream to represent God's true will? Though Cowper seemed fully closed to reconsider his position, Newton could have questioned the authenticity of the dream in light of clear Scriptures to the contrary.[171] Because of the relatively small number of available letters from Newton to Cowper, it remains uncertain whether or not Newton ever challenged him along these lines.[172]

Second, was Newton overly confident that God would remove Cowper's affliction in this life? When Cowper's affliction reappeared in 1773, Newton's consistent hope from that moment until Cowper's death was that God would remove his darkness and restore him to his former condition.[173] When Cowper finally died without such relief, Newton surmised:

> I have had hopes the Lord would remove his malady a little time before his death but it continued. The last twelve hours of his life he did not speak nor seem to take notice of anything but lay in a state of apparent insensibility. But I seem to think that while the curtains were taken down in the tabernacle removing, glory broke in upon his soul.[174]

Shortly following his funeral, Newton concluded:

---

170. Cowper, *Letters*, 2:385.

171. For example, 2 Cor 11 teaches that Satan disguises himself as an "angel of light." Romans 8 reveals that there is no condemnation for those who are in Christ Jesus, and that nothing can separate the believer from the love of God in Christ.

172. Cowper's *Letters* reveals a much larger number of letters from Cowper to Newton than the number currently available between Newton and Cowper. In other words, we know that many more letters existed between Newton and Cowper. Sadly, only some of those are available today.

173. For example, "If I cannot take upon me to say that the dark cloud which hangs over your mind, will be soon, yet I am confident it will be certainly dispelled." November 20, 1779. See also his letters to Cowper from March 10, 1780; May 20, 1780; July 29, 1780; August 19, 1780; October 21, 1780; December 16, 1780; March 11–13, 1786; August 11, 1790, in Letters, Princeton University Library Collection of William Cowper Materials, Princeton University. Cowper's letters to Newton also reflect the fact that Newton anticipated his deliverance. For example, see Cowper, *Letters*, 4:234.

174. Jowett, "Mr. Newton's Account."

> The last twelve hours of his life he lay still, and took no notice—but so long as he could speak, there was no proof that his derangement was either removed or abated. He was, however, free from his great terrors. There was no sign either of joy or sorrow when near his departure. What a glorious surprise must it be to find himself released from all his chains in a moment, and in the presence of the Lord.[175]

Over time, Newton observed that a wise providence overruled the manner and timing in which Cowper's relief arrived. He expected Cowper's relief soon and in this life, whereas God's providence brought about his freedom after thirty-three long years at his death. Why was Newton so confident that his dear friend would indeed find relief in life?

Newton admitted that his favorite pastoral subject was *anatomy*, the "study of the human heart."[176] While in Olney, he had the opportunity to study many people who displayed various "nervous disorders" to the degree that he thought of himself as a kind of "doctor to persons troubled in mind."[177] As he related to Cowper, in every other case he had observed of melancholy, the person was restored in time.[178] The fact that Cowper did not recover provides a needed caution about pastoral observations. Newton modeled the need for and skill of acquiring an understanding of people for pastoral ministry. In this regard, Newton was unmatched in his craft. But Cowper's example ought to remind pastors that human observations must always be held subservient to the Scriptures and submissive to God's wise providence.

Third, did Newton ever address Cowper's pride concerning his erroneous spiritual conclusions? Strange as it seems, a key feature of Cowper's melancholy is underlying pride, which rendered him the sole interpreter of his experiences and determiner of his spiritual condition. This practice left

---

175. Roberts, *Memoirs*, 2:60.

176. Newton, *Works* (1985), 1:478. In regard to studying human nature as it relates to practical theology, Newton is considered highly skilled. "He was, and remains, one of the church's most perceptive and practical theologians on the Christian Life." Reinke, *Newton*, 27.

177. Newton, *Letters of John Newton*, 42–43.

178. "During the first seven years of your disconsolate state, I walked with you alone. And in that space I acquired more knowledge of the nature & effects of Nervous disorders than I could have learned from many books & much study. Since my removal to London, I have met with several instances not very different from yours, but not of so long continuance." Newton then relates one particular example of a woman and her eventual restoration. Newton, "Letter August 11, 1798," in Letters, Princeton University Library Collection of William Cowper Materials, Princeton University.

Case Studies in Newton's Pastoral Care

him unwilling to consider contrary opinions from his closest friends or the Scriptures themselves. Further, he continued to embrace Christian doctrine and the power of the gospel of Jesus to save people, but he believed that he alone was the sole exception.[179] In a sense, Cowper had painted himself into an unreachable corner, where no one, other than his own fallen perceptions, was allowed to go. He wrote:

> It is a long time for a man, whose eyes were once opened, to spend in darkness; long enough to make despair an inveterate habit; and such it is in me. My friends, I know, expect that I shall see yet again. They think it necessary to the existence of divine truth, that he who once had possession of it should never finally lose it. I admit the solidity of this reasoning in every case but my own. And why not in my own? For causes which to them it appears madness to allege, but which rest upon my mind with a weight of immovable conviction.[180]

In another case, Cowper reflected on Newton's memoir of his teenage niece, who died of tuberculosis.[181] The account extolled Christ's sufficiency and goodness to sustain her as she approached death. But Cowper's self-focus led him to respond to the memoir with bitterness and self-pity.[182]

A more overt example of Cowper's pride is revealed in one of his exchanges with William Bull:

> Prove to me that I have a right to pray, and I will pray without ceasing; yes, and praise too, even in the belly of this hell, compared with which Jonah's was a palace, a temple of the living God. But let me add, there is no encouragement in the Scriptures so comprehensive as to include my case, nor any consolation so effectual as to reach it.[183]

179. Cowper, *Letters*, 2:83.

180. Cowper, *Letters*, 2:200.

181. Newton, *Works* (1985), 5:105–26.

182. "I do not know that I am singularly selfish; but one of the first thoughts that your account of Miss Cunningham's dying moments and departure suggested to me, had self for its object. It struck me that she was not born when I sank into darkness, and that she is gone to heaven before I have emerged again. What a lot, said I to myself, is mine!" Cowper, *Letters*, 2:385.

183. Cowper, *Letters and Prose Writings*, 2:83. In Bull's letter to Cowper, he apparently pointed him to gospel truths. Cowper responded, "Both your advice and your manner of giving it are gentle and friendly, and like yourself. I thank you for them, and do not refuse your counsel because it is not good, or because I dislike it, but because it is not for me; there is not a man upon earth that might not be the better for it, myself only

So, the question arises: did Newton challenge his friend's pride and self-focus?[184] Again, Newton's limited number of letters to Cowper renders a firm answer impossible. Based on the available material, it does not appear that Newton addressed this issue directly with him, at least in written correspondence. Perhaps Newton did challenge him on some occasions in person. On the other hand, maybe he believed that Cowper's constitutional disorder, coupled with the influence of Satan, rendered any such reasonings fruitless. Instead, he opted to assure his friend of his security in Christ based on convincing evidence from Cowper's past while encouraging him that God would lift his burden one day and allow him to see with gospel eyes again.

Conclusion: John Newton and William Cowper

Newton's relationship with William Cowper provides a unique case study in pastoral care. Newton was a faithful friend who loved him for over thirty years in both word and deed. In both his content and methodology, Newton's manner of counsel reflects his theology of suffering that formed a key structure in his overall Christian understanding. His relationship with Cowper reveals that Newton did not abandon or weaken his theology in a "difficult case." Instead, the wisdom, longevity, and strategy of his care toward Cowper display the depth and breadth of his doctrine of trials applied in the most challenging of circumstances to his closest friend.

Conclusion

John Newton's theology of suffering formed a crucial structure in his overall doctrinal understanding and constituted the primary influence in his pastoral care and counseling approach. His personal and pastoral relationships with his wife, Polly, and his closest male friend, William Cowper, yield the

---

excepted." Cowper, *Letters and Prose Writings*, 2:83.

184. It is interesting to compare Newton's approach with that of William Perkins, the "father" of Puritanism. Newton was influenced by the Puritans of the previous generation, but he seems to depart a bit from his Puritan heritage in the manner of his response to Cowper. For example, Perkins recommends that depressed persons cease trusting themselves and instead be "advised and ruled by the judgment of others." Further, he states that they must be exhorted to "rest" upon the promises of God, and "at no time to admit any imagination or thought that may cross the said promises." Perkins, *Works*, 8:217.

most significant examples of his pastoral practice at work in challenging and long-standing trials. These two case studies affirm three truths: First, Newton consistently applied the same doctrinal distinctives in his most personal and grievous situations as in his other pastoral care relationships. Second, he applied his theology to his own heart for his own encouragement and to better qualify himself to care for Polly and William. Third, Newton's theology of suffering indeed formed an essential structure in his view of the Christian life that upheld his life personally and directed his ministry to others.

5

Conclusion

JOHN NEWTON, BEST KNOWN as the author of the hymn "Amazing Grace," was better known in his day for his pastoral care through written correspondence. His "frequent and favourite" subject was the topic of trials since he often ministered to suffering people. Newton's pastoral care is infused with his theology of suffering, since this doctrine greatly influenced him as he aimed to bring Christ-centered encouragement in the midst of life challenges.

Summary of the Study

This work argues that Newton's theology of suffering formed an essential structure that shaped, informed, and directed his model of pastoral care and counseling. The Introduction surveyed the relevant literature on Newton and demonstrated that his pastoral care is a worthy subject for research, since he was the "leading evangelical commentator on religious subjects in Britain" and wrote over a thousand letters of pastoral counsel to various people. Yet, this aspect of his ministry has been largely ignored in the field of pastoral care.

Chapter 1 traced the historical background of John Newton, including his upbringing by a Christian mother, his sinful lifestyle in his young adult years at sea, his conversion to Christianity, and his work as a minister in the Church of England. Next, events and experiences were discussed that helped shape his theology and his pastoral care model. First, influential relationships with certain individuals were explored, such as George Whitefield and Alexander Clunie. Second, the impact of critical authors was examined, such as Isaac Watts, John Owen, and John Bunyan. Finally, books that were vital to Newton's development were identified, such as *Some Remarkable Passages in the Life of Colonel James Gardiner* by Philip Doddridge and *The Life of God in the Soul of Man* by Henry Scougal. The chapter demonstrated how these influences developed Newton's theology of affliction and his pastoral care practice.

Chapter 2 unpacked Newton's theology of suffering, demonstrating what he believed about the nature and purposes of trials in the Christian life. Five key components form the basic structure of Newton's understanding of affliction: the sovereignty of God in suffering, how Christ helps believers in trials, the redemption of suffering for good purposes, biblical perspectives on affliction, and the role of temptation and Satan in suffering. The chapter showed how these vital doctrines form a central structure that undergirds his pastoral care model.

Chapter 3 identified the connections between Newton's theology of suffering and his practice of pastoral care. First, an overview of Newton's pastoral care was presented. Second, connections were established between Newton's five doctrinal distinctives of suffering and his methodology in pastoral care. Third, connections were made between Newton's theology of suffering and key components of pastoral care: expectations for care, studying people, the value of suffering, personal dynamics, and the centrality of Christ. These associations show the crucial junction between Newton's theology of trials and his approach to ministerial care.

Chapter 4 presented case studies that explore Newton's pastoral care for two different individuals: his wife, Polly, and his friend, William Cowper. These close-up examinations of Newton's care show the consistency of his doctrine of trials in long-standing and complex cases of pastoral care. These examples affirm Newton's viewpoint on affliction and validate the link between his theology and his ministerial care methodology.

Contribution of the Study

This work aims to contribute to the field of pastoral care and counseling. Historic models of pastoral care are valuable as they move beyond the realm of theoretical study to demonstrate actual examples of biblical doctrine applied in ministerial care to real people. This study has demonstrated that John Newton is a worthy model of ministerial care for three reasons.

First, he demonstrated that theology is really the foundation of pastoral care. Newton's ministry, whether to a virtually unknown correspondent or to his own wife, was driven by his doctrine. He trusted in the sufficiency of Scripture for his counsel, believing the Bible alone is adequate for the care of souls. Even in difficult cases, Newton did not abandon this theology but clung ever more to it, trusting that God will work through His established means.

Second, Newton's example shows that a biblical understanding of suffering is a key structure for comprehending sanctification, the doctrine of spiritual growth. He believed that affliction, what he sometimes called the "school of the cross," was God's main vehicle to conform believers into the image of Christ. Pastoral care, while aiming to bring relief from suffering when possible, must primarily encourage afflicted believers to find encouragement and hope in the redemption of their trials for the purpose of their own sanctification and an ever-growing dependence upon Christ.

Third, Newton's life shows the necessity of experimental knowledge for effective pastoral care. It is not enough for a pastor to simply know biblical doctrine or how to apply it in care for others. "Notional" knowledge is not sufficient. Instead, the pastor must embrace biblical doctrine in his own heart (experimental knowledge) and be transformed by biblical doctrine as he applies it in his own life, particularly in his own seasons of suffering (sanctification). These dynamics change the man and equip him in unique ways to be a more effective pastoral counselor.

Suggestions for Further Research

While this study has endeavored primarily to establish the link between Newton's theology of suffering and his pastoral care, it has also uncovered additional topics that are worthy of future investigation. This project has revealed four main areas for further study.

First, it would be valuable to study Newton's model of sanctification beyond the essential structure of his doctrine of suffering. While Tony Reinke's book provides a helpful introduction of Newton's view of the Christian life, there would be great benefit in a more comprehensive look at his doctrine of sanctification as it pertains to pastoral care. It would be

Conclusion

particularly valuable to explore the reasons for Newton's more simplistic view of casuistry as compared to some of his influences who were much more exhaustive, such as Richard Baxter.

Second, Newton's pastoral care relationship with William Cowper is worthy of a more thorough treatment. As established in chapter 4, several important questions remain that need to be answered. Though limited by the relatively small number of letters from Newton to Cowper, other letters may contain further insights that will provide greater understanding of Newton's counsel. While other authors have written more generally on their friendship or their joint hymn-writing endeavors, no major work exists regarding the pastoral care relationship between Newton and Cowper.[1]

Third, Newton's view of Satan and his influence on people struggling with "nervous disorders" could be further studied. Newton seemed to follow the common Puritan view that Satan could influence the imagination of some persons afflicted with various physical maladies, but he appears to depart somewhat from the Puritans regarding how to best care for such individuals.[2] Newton was influenced by Richard Gilpin's massive volume *Daemonologia Sacra; or, A Treatise of Satan's Temptations*. It would be beneficial to study the impact of this work on Newton's theology and to further understand how his view of Satan impacted his pastoral care.

Finally, the breadth of Newton's ministry yields ample material to study additional topics in pastoral care. While "affliction" was his favorite topic, his letters discuss other life challenges, such as fear, anxiety, depression, loss, grief, marriage, parenting, and death. Any of these topics could be studied in detail to discover Newton's model for ministering to others struggling with life difficulties.

Conclusion of the Study

The ministry of John Newton is a largely untapped resource for pastoral care. His work demonstrates that theology is critical to counseling. Ministers of the gospel care for others in ways that are determined by their doctrine. Even then, it is a pastor's "experimental knowledge," or "heart theology," that really drives all aspects of his ministry to others. Similarly,

---

1. For example, Ella, "John Newton's Friendship"; Huntly, "Newton and Cowper," 29–33.

2. For example, compare Newton's view with the perspective of William Perkins. Perkins, *Works*, 8:213–18. See also chapter 4.

John Newton's Theology of Suffering and Its Application to Pastoral Care

Newton's example illustrates that pastoral care is really a function of practical theology, built upon the sufficiency of Scripture. Convinced by the Bible and confirmed by his own experience, he understood that sanctification is usually fueled by affliction governed by wise providence, which God uses to wean believers from self-sufficiency in order that they will lean "only and entirely upon [their] beloved."[3] This was Newton's aim in his pastoral care: that Christians would know and embrace the sufficiency of Jesus as their primary hope in the midst of trials. As believers look to Christ, they are transformed more into His image, from glory to glory (2 Cor 3:18).

---

3. Newton, *Letters*, 81.

Appendix

Scripture Verses Often Cited by Newton in His Theology of Suffering

Scripture Reference	Citation in Newton's Works[1]
Deut 33:25-27—"strength equal to days"	1:296, 393-94; 2:143, 178, 597-98; 5:269, 299-300, 574; 6:63, 215
Rev 21:4—"wipe away every tear"	1:250; 2:32, 36, 106, 200, 434, 475-76; 4:52, 239, 478; 5:177, 235, 543; 6:8, 28, 33, 63, 77, 347
Nah 1:7—"the Lord is good"	2:254; 6:62, 136, 176, 218
Matt 10:30—"hairs on head are numbered"	1:127, 243-44, 312, 443, 456, 613, 628; 2:21, 130, 228, 248, 317; 4:111, 432-33, 534; 5:269, 300, 518; 6:5, 87, 99, 345
Matt 13:46—"pearl of great price"	1:312, 585; 2:34-35, 159, 386, 471; 3:151, 404; 4:102; 5:222
Luke 22:42—"not my will but thine be done"	2:19-20; 5:590; 6:217, 270
Mark 7:37—"He has done all things well"	1:232, 459-60, 537, 620, 624, 629, 643; 2:200, 248, 254, 316, 362, 436-37; 3:452; 4:367, 410; 5:107, 500, 588; 6:33, 48, 78, 88, 136, 143, 146-47, 191, 204, 216

1. These references reflect the volume and page number from the 1985 edition of Newton's *Works*, published by Banner of Truth.

Appendix

Rom 8:28—"working for good"	1:443, 448, 509, 619; 2:147–48, 178–79, 182; 5:383; 6:61, 68, 255, 359
2 Cor 3:18—"beholding . . . being transformed"	1:198, 212, 315, 348, 522, 562; 2:81, 99, 146, 193, 445, 487; 3:295–96, 454–55; 4:83; 6:73
2 Cor 4:17—"momentary, light affliction producing eternal weight of glory"	1:472; 2:189, 498; 4:11–12, 487; 5:445; 6:63, 379, 425
2 Cor 12—"weakness, power, sufficient grace"	1:621; 2:174–78, 316; 5:584; 6:52–53, 58, 145
Heb 12—"not joyous but grievous"	1:249–50, 297; 2:25, 33, 106, 197, 495; 4:465; 6:32, 35, 148, 216, 253–54
1 Pet 5:7—"casting cares"	1:169–70, 279, 301, 312, 325–26, 402, 441, 468; 2:226, 230, 431, 576, 597–98; 3:71, 450–51, 628; 4:110, 170; 6:123, 135, 196, 475

Bibliography

Adams, Jay. *Competent to Counsel*. Grand Rapids: Zondervan, 1970.
Aitken, Jonathan. *John Newton: From Disgrace to Amazing Grace*. Wheaton, IL: Crossway, 2013.
Ames, William. *The Marrow of Theology*. Translated by John Dykstra Eusden. Grand Rapids: Baker, 1968.
Babler, John, et al. *Counseling by the Book*. Maitland, FL: Xulon, 2007.
Barlass, William. *Sermons on Practical Subjects: With Correspondence Between the Author and the Rev. John Newton*. New York: J. Eastburn, 1818.
Baxter, Richard. *A Christian Directory*. In *The Practical Works of Richard Baxter*. 4 vols. Orlando, FL: Soli Deo Gloria, 2000.
———. *The Practical Works of Richard Baxter*. 4 vols. Orlando, FL: Soli Deo Gloria, 2000.
Bebbington, D. W. *Evangelicalism in Modern Britain: A History from the 1730s to the 1980s*. London: Unwin Hyman, 1989.
Beeke, Joel, and Mark Jones. *A Puritan Theology: Doctrine for Life*. Grand Rapids: Reformation Heritage, 2012.
Bernard, Martin. *John Newton: A Biography*. London: W. Heinemann, 1950.
Blanch, Allan M. "The Pastoral Wisdom of John Newton." *Banner of Truth* 658 (2018) 1–12.
Boston, Thomas. *The Crook in the Lot*. Fearn, Scotland: Christian Focus, 2012.
———. *Human Nature in Its Fourfold State*. London: Banner of Truth, 1964.
———. *The Whole Works of the Late Reverend Thomas Boston of Ettrick*. Edited by Samuel M'Millan. Aberdeen, Scotland: George and Robert King, 1848.
Bray, Gerald, ed. *Documents of the English Reformation*. Cambridge: James Clarke, 1994.
Brooks, Thomas. *The Complete Works of Thomas Brooks*. Edited by Alexander Balloch Grosart. Edinburgh: James Nichol, 1866.
Bucer, Martin. *Concerning the True Care of Souls*. Translated by Peter Beale. Carlisle, PA: Banner of Truth, 2009.
Buckland, A. R., ed. *Selected Sermons of George Whitefield*. Philadelphia: Union, 1904.
Bull, Josiah. *The Life of John Newton*. Carlisle, PA: Banner of Truth, 2007.
Bull, Josiah, ed. *Memorials of the Rev. William Bull, of Newport Pagnell. Compiled Chiefly from His Own Letters, and Those of His Friends, Newton, Cowper, and Thorton, 1738–1814*. London: James Nisbet, 1864.

Bibliography

Bull, William, ed. *One Hundred Twenty Nine Letters from the Rev. John Newton to the Rev. William Bull of Newport Pagnell: Written During a Period of Thirty-Two Years, from 1773–1805.* London: Hamilton Adams, 1847.

Bunyan, John. *The Pilgrim's Progress.* Minneapolis: Desiring God, 2014.

Burnett, Gilbert. *The Life and Death of Sir Matthew Hale.* London: William Shrowsbery, 1682.

Cairns, William Thomas. *The Religion of Dr. Johnson and Other Essays.* Freeport, NY: Books for Libraries, 1969.

Campbell, John, ed. *Letters and Conversational Remarks by the Late Rev. John Newton, Rector of St. Mary Woolnoth, Lombard-Street, London.* New York: S. Whiting, 1811.

Carson, D. A. *How Long, O Lord?* 2nd ed. Grand Rapids: Baker Academic, 2006.

Cecil, David. *The Stricken Deer: Or the Life of Cowper.* London: Constable, 1929.

Cecil, Richard. *The Life of John Newton.* Edited by Marylynn Rouse. Fearn, Scotland: Christian Focus, 2000.

Champion, L. G. "The Letters of John Newton to John Ryland." *Baptist Quarterly* 27 (1977) 157–63.

Cieglo, Sarah. "The Problem of Pastoral Care in the Thought of Anglican, Presbyterian, and Congregationalist Ministers in England, c. 1689–c. 1730." PhD diss., Yale University, 2013.

Coffey, John. "Puritanism, Evangelicalism and the Evangelical Protestant Tradition." In *The Advent of Evangelicalism: Exploring Historical Continuities,* edited by Michael Haykin and Kenneth Stewart. Nashville: B & H Academic, 2008.

Cowper, William. Letters. Charles Ryskamp Collection of William Cowper. Princeton University, Princeton, NJ.

———. *Letters and Prose Writings of William Cowper.* 5 vols. Edited by James King and Charles Ryskamp. Oxford: Clarendon, 1979.

———. *Letters of William Cowper.* Edited by J. S. Memes. Glasgow, Scotland: W. R. M'Phun, 1861.

———. *Memoir of the Most Remarkable and Interesting Parts of the Life of William Cowper, Esq. of the Inner Temple.* London: E. Cox and Son, 1816.

———. *Memoir of William Cowper.* Edited by Maurice J. Quinlan. *Proceedings of the American Philosophical Society* 97.4 (1953) 359–82.

Cromarty, John. "Grace in Affliction: William Cowper, Poet of Olney (Part 1)." *The Reformed Theological Review* 58.3 (1999) 65–82.

———. "Grace in Affliction: William Cowper, Poet of Olney (Part 2)." *The Reformed Theological Review* 58.3 (1999) 135–50.

Cosby, Brian. *Suffering and Sovereignty: John Flavel and the Puritans on Afflictive Providence.* Grand Rapids: Reformation Heritage, 2022.

Davidson, Noel. *How Sweet the Sound: The Story of John Newton and William Cowper.* Belfast, Ireland: Ambassador, 1997.

Deckard, Mark. *Helpful Truth in Past Places: The Puritan Practice of Biblical Counseling.* Ross-Shire, Scotland: Mentor, 2010.

Demaray, Donald. *The Innovation of John Newton (1725–1807): A Synergism of Word and Music in Eighteenth Century Evangelism.* Lewiston, NY: Mellen, 1988.

Doddridge, Philip. *Some Remarkable Passages in the Life of Colonel James Gardiner.* Boston: Thomas and Andrews, 1792.

Dolezal, James. *All That Is in God: Evangelical Theology and the Challenge of Classical Christian Theism.* Grand Rapids: Reformation Heritage, 2017.

Bibliography

Edwards, Brian. *Through Many Dangers: The Story of John Newton*. Durham, UK: Evangelical, 2005.

Ella, George. "John Newton's Friendship with William Cowper." *Banner of Truth* 269 (1986) 10–19.

———. *William Cowper: The Man of God's Stamp*. Dundas, Canada: Joshua, 2000.

Elliott, Matthew. "None So Tender-Hearted: The Christological Pattern of Compassion in the Pastoral Care of John Flavel." PhD diss., The Southern Baptist Theological Seminary, 2022.

Flavel, John. *Keeping the Heart*. Ross-Shire, Scotland: Christian Focus, 1999.

———. *The Works of John Flavel*. Carlisle, PA: Banner of Truth, 1968.

Gertz, Steven. "Pastor to the Nation." *Christian History and Biography* 81 (2004) 37–45.

Gilbert, Thomas. *William Cowper and the Eighteenth Century*. London: Allen and Unwin, 1948.

Gilpin, Richard. *Daemonologia Sacra; Or, a Treatise of Satan's Temptations, in Three Parts*. Edited by Alexander Balloch Grosart. Edinburgh: James Nichol, 1867.

Goodwin, Thomas. *The Heart of Christ in Heaven Toward Sinners on Earth*. Carlisle, PA: Banner of Truth, 2011.

Gordon, Grant A. "John Newton: A Study of a Pastoral Correspondent." ThM thesis, Princeton Theological Seminary, 1987.

Gordon, Grant A., ed. *Wise Counsel: John Newton's Letters to John Ryland Jr*. Carlisle, PA: Banner of Truth, 2009.

Gordon, James. *Evangelical Spirituality from the Wesleys to John Stott*. London: SPCK, 1991.

Greatheed, Samuel. *Memoirs of the Life and Writings of William Cowper, Esq*. Rev. ed. London: Whittingham and Arliss, 1814.

Greggo, Stephen, and Timothy Sisemore, eds. *Counseling and Christianity: Five Approaches*. Downers Grove, IL: IVP Academic, 2012.

Hare, Edward. "The History of 'Nervous Disorders' from 1600 to 1840, and a Comparison with Modern Views." *British Journal of Psychiatry* 159 (1991) 37–45.

Harris, John. "The Preaching of John Newton." In *The Truth Shall Make You Free: Papers Read at the 2007 Westminster Conference*. Mirfield: The Westminster Conference, 2007.

Haykin, Michael A. G. "The Life of John Newton, with Particular Reference to His Hymns and Letters." *Sovereign Grace Fellowship Pastoral Studies* 35.3 (2007) 1–24.

———. "'With Ev'ry Fleeting Breath': John Newton and the Olney Hymns." *The Banner of Truth* (2007) 30–39.

Hayley, William. *The Works of William Cowper: His Life and Letters*. 8 vols. Edited by T. S. Grimshawe. London: Saunders and Otley, 1835.

Hervey, James. *Meditations Among the Tombs in a Letter to a Lady*. London: J. and J. Rivington, 1746.

Hindmarsh, Douglas Bruce. "'I Am a Sort of Middle Man': John Newton and the English Evangelical Tradition Between the Conversions of Wesley and Wilberforce." PhD diss., University of Oxford, 1993.

———. "'I Am a Sort of Middle-Man': The Politically Correct Evangelicalism of John Newton." In *Amazing Grace: Evangelicalism in Australia, Britain, Canada, and the United States*. Edited by George Rawlyk and Mark Noll. Grand Rapids: Baker, 1993.

———. *John Newton and the English Evangelical Tradition: Between the Conversions of Wesley and Wilberforce*. Oxford: Oxford University Press, 1996.

Bibliography

———. *The Life and Spirituality of John Newton.* Vancouver, BC: Regent College Publishing, 2003.

———. "The Olney Autobiographers: English Conversion Narrative in the Mid-Eighteenth Century." *Journal of Ecclesiastical History* 49.1 (1998) 61–84.

Holifield, E. Brooks. *A History of Pastoral Care in America: From Salvation to Self-Actualization.* Nashville: Abingdon, 1983.

Huntly, Dana. "Newton and Cowper: The Olney Hymns." *British Heritage* (2005) 29–33.

Jay, William. *The Autobiography of the Rev. William Jay, with Reminiscences of Some Distinguished Contemporaries, Selections from His Correspondence, and Literary Remains.* Edited by George Redford and John Angell James. New York: Robert Carter, 1855.

Jenkins, Bruce. "The Wisdom of John Newton." In *Triumph Through Tribulation: Papers Read at the 1998 Westminster Conference.* England: Westminster Conference, 1998.

Johnson, T. Dale Jr. *The Professionalization of Pastoral Care.* Eugene, OR: Wipf & Stock, 2020.

Jowett, Hannah. "Mr. Newton's Account of Mr. Cowper in a Funeral Sermon." Cowper and Newton Museum, Olney, Buckinghamshire.

Kaufmann, U. Milo. *The Pilgrim's Progress and Traditions in Puritan Meditation.* New Haven, CT: Yale University Press, 1966.

Keller, Timothy. "Puritan Resources for Biblical Counseling." *Journal of Pastoral Practice* 9.3 (1988) 11–44.

Kemp, Charles. *Physicians of the Soul: A History of Pastoral Counseling.* New York: Macmillan, 1947.

King, James. *William Cowper: A Biography.* Durham, NC: Duke University Press, 1986.

Knight, Elizabeth. *William Cowper's Olney.* Olney: C. J. Knight, 2000.

Kushner, Harold S. *When Bad Things Happen to Good People.* New York: Avon, 1983.

Law, William. *A Serious Call to a Devout and Holy Life.* Grand Rapids: Christian Classics Ethereal Library, 2010.

Lee, Mark. "'Divine Madness': Experiences of Religious Melancholy and Madness in Eighteenth Century England." *Crux* 51.2 (2015) 28–37.

Legge, William. *Historical Manuscripts Commission, Fifteenth Report, Appendix, Part 1.* Vol. 3 of *The Manuscripts of the Earl of Dartmouth.* London: Eyre and Spottiswoode, 1896.

Loane, Marcus. *Oxford and the Evangelical Succession.* Ross-shire, Scotland: Christian Focus, 2007.

Lonsdale, Kirkby. *The Life and Writings of Mrs. Dawson of Lancaster, with Nine Unpublished Letters from the Rev. John Newton and an Introductory Preface by the Rev. Wm. Carus Wilson.* London: Arthur Foster, 1828.

Martin, Bernard. *The Ancient Mariner and the Authentic Narrative.* London: Heinemann, 1949.

———. *John Newton: A Biography.* London: Heinemann, 1950.

Miller, Andrew. "Sick with Sin, Healed in Christ: Lessons from John Newton." *Midwestern Journal of Theology* 20.1 (2021) 72–85.

Murray, Iain. "John Newton: 'A Wonder to Myself.'" *The Banner of Truth* (2007) 3–25.

———. "William Cowper and His Affliction." *The Banner of Truth* 96 (1971) 12–32.

Murray, J. Todd, ed. *Beyond Amazing Grace: Timeless Pastoral Wisdom from the Letters, Hymns, and Sermons of John Newton.* Great Writing, 2016.

Bibliography

Newton, John. *The Aged Pilgrim's Triumph over Sin and the Grave; Illustrated in a Series of Letters by the Rev. John Newton, Written, During the Decline of Life, to Some of His Most Intimate Friends.* New York: Wilder and Campbell, 1825.

———. *An Authentic Narrative of Some Remarkable and Interesting Particulars in the Life of Mr. Newton: Communicated in a Series of Letters to the Rev. Mr. Haweis, Rector of Aldwinckle, Northamptonshire, and by Him, at the Request of Friends, Now Made Public.* Philadelphia: W. Young, 1795.

———. *Cardiphonia: Or the Utterance of the Heart: In the Course of Real Correspondence.* London: Morgan and Scott, 1911.

———. *The Christian Correspondent: Or a Series of Letters, Written by the Rev. John Newton, (Author of Omicron, Cardiphonia, &c.) to Captain Alexr. Clunie, From the Year 1761, to the Death of the Latter in 1770. Never Before Published.* England: George Prince, 1790.

———. *The Correspondence of the Late Rev. John Newton with a Dissenting Minister on Various Subjects and Occasions.* London: Maxwell and Wilson, 1809.

———. "Diaries 1751–1807." 2 vols. Unpublished. Princeton, NJ: Princeton University.

———. "Diary." Unpublished. Manhattan, NY: The Morgan Library and Museum.

———. *John Newton's Diary: 1764.* Edited by Marylynn Rouse. Northamptonshire: The John Newton Project, n.d.

———. *John Newton's Diary: 1765.* Edited by Marylynn Rouse. Northamptonshire: The John Newton Project, n.d.

———. "Letters to Benjamin Fawcett." Unpublished. Manhattan, NY: The Morgan Library and Museum.

———. "Letters to David Jennings." The John Newton Project, n.d.

———. "Letter to Rev. Samuel Greatheed on September 18, 1800." The John Newton Project, n.d.

———. "Letter to William Cowper, December 8, 1780." The John Newton Project, n.d.

———. "Letter to William Wilberforce, March 6, 1786." The John Newton Project, n.d.

———. *Letters of John Newton.* Edited by Josiah Bull. Carlisle, PA: Banner of Truth, 2007.

———. "Letters to Thomas Haweis." Unpublished transcript. The John Newton Project, n.d.

———. Letters. Kenneth Povey Collection of William Cowper. Princeton, NJ: Princeton University.

———. Letters. Nielson Campbell Hannay Collection of William Cowper 1711–1965. Princeton, NJ: Princeton University.

———. Letters. Princeton University Library Collection of William Cowper Materials. Princeton, NJ: Princeton University.

———. *Letters to a Wife.* London: J. Johnson, 1793.

———. *Memoirs of the Life of the Late Rev. William Grimshaw, with Occasional Reflections, by John Newton, in Six Letters to the Rev. Henry Foster.* London: W. Baynes and Son, 1825.

———. "Memoirs of William Cowper." Unpublished manuscript. Ontario: McMaster University.

———. *Ministry on My Mind: John Newton on Entering Pastoral Ministry.* Edited by Marylynn Rouse. Stratford-upon-Avon: The John Newton Project, 2008.

———. "Mr. Newton's Account of Mr. Cowper in a Funeral Sermon Preached in St. Mary Woolnoth, Lombard Street May 1800." Unpublished. John Newton Project, n.d.

Bibliography

———. *One Hundred and Twenty Nine Letters from the Rev. John Newton to the Rev. William Bull of Newport Pagnell. Written During a Period of Thirty-Two Years, from 1773–1805*. London: Hamilton Adams, 1847.

———. *Letters of John Newton to James Coffin and His Family*. The John Newton Project, n.d.

———. *Twenty-Five Letters Hitherto Unpublished of the Rev. John Newton, Rector of Olney and St. Mary, Woolnoth, London From the Years 1757–1779*. Edinburgh: J. Johnstone, Hunter Square, 1840.

———. *Twenty-One Letters Written to a Near Relative at School. By the Rev. John Newton, Late Rector of St. Mary Woolnoth, London; Extracted from His Posthumous Works, to Which are Annexed, a Few Pieces of Poetry, by the Same Author*. London: J. Johnson, 1809.

———. *The Works of John Newton*. 6 vols. Carlisle, PA: Banner of Truth, 1985.

———. *The Works of the Rev. John Newton*. 6 vols. New York: Williams and Whiting, 1810.

———. *The Works of John Newton*. 4 vols. Carlisle, PA: Banner of Truth, 2015.

Newton, Mary. "Letter to John Newton." The John Newton Project, n.d.

Noll, Mark. *The Rise of Evangelicalism*. Downers Grove, IL: InterVarsity, 2018.

Oden, Thomas C. *Becoming a Minister*. Vol. 1 of *Classical Pastoral Care*. Grand Rapids: Baker, 1987.

———. *Care of Souls in the Classic Tradition*. Philadelphia: Fortress, 1984.

Owen, John. *The Works of John Owen*. Edited by William H. Goold. Carlisle, PA: Banner of Truth, 1965.

Parker, Barbara. "Hope and Despair in the Writings of William Cowper." *Social Research* 66.2 (1999) 545–64.

Perkins, William. *The Works of William Perkins*. 10 vols. Edited by Joel Beeke and Derek Thomas. Grand Rapids: Reformation Heritage, 2020.

Piper, John. *The Hidden Smile of God*. Wheaton, IL: Crossway, 2001.

———. "John Newton: The Tough Roots of His Habitual Tenderness." *Desiring God*, January 30, 2001. https://www.desiringgod.org/messages/john-newton-the-tough-roots-of-his-habitual-tenderness.

———. *The Roots of Endurance*. Wheaton, IL: Crossway, 2002.

Pollock, John. *Abolition!: Newton, the Ex-Slave Trader, and Wilberforce, the Little Liberator*. Leominster: Day One, 2007.

Powlison, David. "Biblical Counseling in the Twentieth Century." In *Introduction to Biblical Counseling*, edited by John MacArthur and Wayne Mack, 56–59. Dallas, TX: Word, 1994.

———. *The Biblical Counseling Movement*. Greensboro, NC: New Growth, 2010.

Pratt, Josiah, ed. *Eclectic Notes: Or Notes of Discussions on Religious Topics at the Meetings of the Eclectic Society, London, During the Years 1798–1814*. Carlisle, PA: Banner of Truth, 1978.

Purves, Andrew. *Pastoral Theology in the Classical Tradition*. Louisville: Westminster John Knox, 2001.

Pytches, Peter Norman Lambert. "The Development of Anglican Evangelicalism in London 1736–1836 with Special Reference to the Revd. John Newton." MPhil thesis, The Open University, 2006.

Quinlan, Maurice J. "William Cowper and the Unpardonable Sin." *The Journal of Religion* 23.2 (1943) 110–16.

Bibliography

Reinke, Tony. *Newton on the Christian Life*. Wheaton, IL: Crossway, 2015.

Rinehart, John. *Gospel Patrons*. Minneapolis: Reclaimed, 2016.

Roberts, William, ed. *Memoirs of the Life and Correspondence of Mrs. Hannah More*. New York: Harper and Brothers, 1841.

Rouse, Marylynn. "A Double Portion of My Thoughts and Prayers: John Newton's Letters to William Wilberforce." *Midwestern Journal of Theology* 17.2 (2018) 15–41.

———. "Introduction to the Olney Hymns." *JohnNewton.org*. The John Newton Project, August 28, 2013. https://www.johnnewton.org/hymns.

———. *365 Days with Newton*. Leominster: Day One, 2005.

Ryskamp, Charles. *William Cowper of the Inner Temple, Esq.: A Study of His Life and Works to the Year 1768*. Cambridge: Cambridge University Press, 2011.

Sarles, Ken L. "The English Puritans: A Historical Paradigm of Biblical Counseling." In *Introduction to Biblical Counseling*, edited by John MacArthur and Wayne Mack. Dallas, TX: Word, 1994.

Schaefer, Gregory L. "'My Dear Friend . . .': Concepts on Mentoring a Hymn Writer Based on Selected Correspondence of Rev John Newton and William Cowper, 1767–1786." *The Hymn* 50 (1999) 34–37.

Scott, Stuart, and Heath Lambert, eds. *Counseling the Hard Cases*. Nashville: B & H Academic, 2012.

Scott, Thomas. *A Commentary on the Whole Bible, Containing the Old and New Testaments According to the Authorized Version: With Explanatory Notes, Practical Observations, and Copious Marginal References*. Philadelphia: W. S. & A. Martien, 1858.

———. *The Force of Truth: An Authentic Narrative by Rev. Thomas Scott, to Which Are Added Eight Letters to Dr. Scott by Rev. John Newton*. Philadelphia: Presbyterian Board of Publication, 1841.

Scougal, Henry. *The Life of God in the Soul of Man*. Ross-Shire, Scotland: Christian Focus, 1996.

Sibbes, Richard. *The Works of Richard Sibbes*. Carlisle, PA: Banner of Truth, 1973.

Sowder, Larry. "The Preaching of John Newton (1725–1807): A Gospel-Centric, Pastoral Homiletic of Biblical Exposition." PhD diss., The Southern Baptist Theological Seminary, 2006.

Thomas, Gilbert. *William Cowper and the Eighteenth Century*. London: George Allen and Unwin, 1946.

Tillman, Keith Alan. "'He Worked Out His Salvation with Fear and Trembling': The Spirituality of John Ryland, Jr." ThM thesis, The Southern Baptist Theological Seminary, 2014.

Trafton, Jennifer M. "The Captain and the Castaway: The 'Tempest-Tossed' Friendship of John Newton and William Cowper." *Christian History and Biography* 81 (2004) 34–36.

Watts, Isaac. *Divine and Moral Songs for the Use of Children*. London: Darton and Clark, ca. 1800.

Wilberforce, William. *The Correspondence of William Wilberforce*, edited by Robert Isaac and Samuel Wilberforce. Philadelphia: Henry Perkins, 1841.

Wood, David. "'We Are All Brother-Journeymen in One Shop': John Newton as Pastor." Unpublished paper, n.d.

Wood, A. Skevington. "The Influence of Thomas Haweis on John Newton." *Journal of Ecclesiastical History* 4.2 (1953) 187–202.

Bibliography

———. *The Inextinguishable Blaze: Spiritual Renewal and Advance in the Eighteenth Century.* Grand Rapids: Eerdmans, 1960.

Yrigoyen, Charles, and Susan Warrick. *Historical Dictionary of Methodism.* Lanham: Scarecrow, 2013.

www.ingramcontent.com/pod-product-compliance
Lightning Source LLC
Chambersburg PA
CBHW071450150426
43191CB00008B/1299